Eamonn Vincent was born in London in 1952. He is married and lives in Crouch End. He has three adult children and a female cat called Henry. He has been founder and Chief Technology Officer of a number of companies. Retirement does not currently seem to be on the agenda.

```
A R B
U   T H
N O T
```

This edition published by Arbuthnot Books 2018
ISBN 978-0-9927467-6-6

# Me Neither

## A Memoir

**Eamonn Vincent**

ARB
UTH
NOT

ARBUTHNOT BOOKS

# CONTENTS

# Introduction

**M**E NEITHER IS A memoir of the years 1974-88.It celebrates a haphazard approach to building a career in the wake of the turbulent economic circumstances generated by the oil crisis of 1973. It also documents what were in effect the first stirrings of the gig economy.

Despite the advantage of a privileged education the author's first job on graduating from Cambridge University is as a milkman, followed by stints as a bus conductor, stage hand and theatre box office assistant. After a sojourn in the Western Highlands writing a play, the author returns to London and talks his way into a number of jobs in marketing and magazine publishing. This phase is in turn superseded by a move into politics first as a local government officer at the GLC in the Ken Livingstone era and then as a magazine publisher for the Labour Party.

Along the way there are glimpses of Cambridge, London and Scotland in the 1970s and Germany and the USA at the start of the 1980s. There is an account of the difficulties of magazine publishing in the pre-digital age and about parliamentary pro-cedure in the House of Lords before it was reformed by Tony Blair's administration. There is inevitably some discussion of Labour politics. There are also plentiful references to the popu-lar music of the era, both live and recorded.

Memoir cannot help looking back and in the case of Me Neither with a certain amount of affection at a period whose stock is currently low. As the sorrows emanating from the Pandora's box of digital technology and a multi-polar world order become ever more apparent, the analog, bilateral world of the Cold War era is inevitably bathed in a nostalgic glow. If there is a nascent revisionism towards the 1970s, then this book is a part of that tendency.

# Brought to Book

S EVERAL YEARS AGO MY friend, Adam Mars-Jones, was compos-
ing a further volume in the John Cromer sequence of nov-
els. This particular volume, which at the time of writing
remains unpublished, is set in the 1970s. Adam remembered
that shortly after graduating I had had a job as a milkman in
Cambridge. He wondered whether I might be able to remember
a few details which he could use to touch in a character in the
new novel. I was happy to oblige and a little flattered to be im-
mortalised as a supporting character in the Mars-Jones oeuvre.
I started to jot down some thoughts and before I knew it I had
covered quite a few pages. Adam had not been expecting anything quite so extensive but he expressed his gratitude in his
customarily witty and charming way.

In due course I shared the piece with members of my family
and some close friends. It seemed to elicit a reasonably mirthful
response which I found gratifying. Undoubtedly I am an inveterate anecdotalist and I have bored many a guest at the supper
table with lurid accounts of the some of the jobs I have done.
My kids had heard the one about the milk round many times,
but perhaps conscious of my advancing years were pleased to
have it written down and requested that a few more of their
favourites might be similarly preserved. I was both flattered by
this request from my darlings and at the same time conscious
that the issue of my demise was already an agenda item. But I
was happy to accommodate this extension of Adam's original
request and without any thought of structure or tone I roughed
out a couple more episodes.

Then I made the mistake of announcing the fact to a slightly wider circle and found myself, no doubt after a glass or two of wine, speculating out loud that I could work the whole thing up into a book. Naturally enough I almost immediately regretted mentioning this possibility and did nothing further about it for some considerable time. But the idea continued to nag at me and from time to time I found that I had added a few more stones to the cairn. Even so these were fairly meagre scrapings, but then on a holiday in Greece in an attempt to stay out of the midday sun I found myself extending the material in unforeseen directions.

A critical point had now been reached. The material was not nugatory enough to ignore, but nor was it substantial enough to be considered anything more than a collection of jottings. On the other hand the project now had a definite shape in my mind even if I was a long way from realising that shape on the page. I had reached the fork in the road where one sign points in the direction of autobiography and the other points in the direction of memoir.

Whilst I was thinking about the choice that faced me I came across a piece by Ian Jack in *The Guardian* in which he makes the distinction between a biography or autobiography which tells the story 'of a life' and a memoir which tells a story 'from a life'. I realised that I was much happier with the narrower focus of the memoir this formulation implies. Autobiography seems to demand a much more comprehensive approach and is interested in antecedents, motivations and relationships. I had no desire to grapple with such subjects. I did not feel I had scores to settle or records to set straight. Nor did I want to expose details of personal relationships or offer a record of my emotional state. So far as I am concerned the fluctuations of the emotional life are just psychological weather and I am no psychic meteorologist. I certainly did not feel that I needed to justify myself. In fact I was not really writing about myself so much as the work situations I found myself in and some of the people that I encountered in those situations in the years 1974-88.

But even before I had begun writing, the issue of a suitable title arose. I began a cursory study of memoirs and was irritated to find that Gore Vidal had already bagged *Palimpsest*, a title I had been toying with. But as I grumpily leafed through the book I discovered that Vidal had had his own qualms about the genre. In fact he claims in the introduction that he had never previously entertained the idea of writing a memoir because he did not consider himself his own subject, but now he was not so sure.

'Me neither,' I thought as I read those lines. And as I did so I realised that a version of my rejoinder to Vidal in this imagined dialogue of the memoirists had been used in another context. There is a famous *Private Eye* pocket cartoon, written by Peter Cook and drawn by Barry Fantoni, in which one man (Dud?) in a bar says to another 'I'm writing a book', to which the other (Pete?) replies 'Neither am I'. I hope there will not be too much of an outcry if I consider 'Me neither' and 'Neither am I' to be equivalent. 'Neither' in the normal context of the phrase expresses agreement with a previous negative statement. The humour in the cartoon is generated by the fact that the syntax of the opening statement is positive but the rejoinder treats it semantically as a negative sentence. Furthermore shorn of its provoking statement 'Me neither' implies in the Vidalian sense some kind of cancellation of the first person personal pronoun, in other words a memoir in which the writer is not the subject. QED.

My inner Peter Cook has undoubtedly been in the ascendancy for forty years. But if one accepts the slightly tortured algebra above, then my inner Dud has finally triumphed in bringing to book a first person account which is not about me, or at least in which I am not the centre of attention. If this rationalisation seems a bit obtuse and full of high sentence, you will note that the bottoms of my trousers are rolled.

12

# Electricar Manoeuvres

I GRADUATED FROM MAGDALENE COLLEGE, Cambridge in June 1974. I had been living beyond my means and I was gently reminded by the college bursar just as I was sitting my finals that I would not be able to take my degree if my college bill remained unpaid by graduation day. It would appear that I owed the college £156.35 and one half new penny. It has been a matter of ribald comment amongst my friends ever since that this was because of the size of my bar and buttery bill but I see from the final statement of account that my buttery bill was 80p and my bar bill £6.52. Not particularly excessive it seems, even when you consider that a pint of bitter in 1974 was about 15p—that's just over 40 pints or 5 pints a week for an eight week term. Of course that does not include pints consumed in pubs, which is undoubtedly where the damage had been done to my bank account which at that point was under water as the expression has it but which might better be described as being under beer. If one does the opposite calculation and converts the debt into present day values via the cost of a 2017 pint of beer (£4), then the amount I needed to find in a matter of weeks was a little over £4,000, a daunting prospect.

Of course I could have asked my father for the money but that's not the way I liked to do things, so I decided to pull the money together myself. A little research revealed that the best money you could get for a casual job was doing a milk round. The pay was about £25 a week paid weekly in cash in a little brown envelope. That was a lot of money. A year or so later when I was working as a stage-hand at the Arts Theatre I earned about £15 a week. You were expected to work for six weeks without a day off and then had a full week off. So you worked for 42 days in every 49. No previous skill or experience was needed apart from an ability to get up early, a valid driving licence and the aerobic capacity of a cross-country runner. I just hoped that I was as good a runner as I had always claimed to be.

The job was with the Co-operative Dairy just off Sleaford Street. The site is now the Beehive Retail Park, the beehive being a well-known symbol of the Co-op. A day or two before my last exam I was invited for an interview which in fact turned out to be a driving test. The examiner nodded at a fairly big van—not an electric float and handed me the keys. He said we were going to go out for a short drive so that he could assess my driving. I can't remember the model of the van but it was certainly one I had never driven before. I was not totally inexperienced in driving commercial vehicles. I had driven dumper trucks and agricultural tractors on holiday jobs but had never had the pleasure of this particular model.

There was a notable absence of dials and switchgear in the cab and the gearstick was extremely loose. The examiner asked me if I was OK with a crash gear box. I had no idea what he meant and just nodded. I explored the pedals, revved the engine a bit and managed to free the calliper type handbrake and bang the gearstick into gear. We jerked off out of the gates of the dairy and into the side streets around Sleaford Street. This was nothing like a proper driving test. I wasn't asked any Highway Code questions, no emergency stops or three point turns. But he did ask me to park a few times and to reverse on one occasion. Eventually he indicated that we should return to the dairy and park up. We got out of the cab and he told me that my driving was awful, but seeing that I had been able to start off in second gear every time without stalling and had negotiated the gearbox without double-declutching, he was prepared to pass me. I hand't even realised that I was starting off in second gear or that I needed to double-declutch. Just as well really. I went back into the office to see the manager and he told me to be at the depot the following Monday at 5.30am for my induction week.

Bear in mind this was the period immediately after finals, indeed some unlucky souls like engineers and medics were probably still doing exams. Those who had completed their finals were punting, getting stoned and waiting for May Balls and graduation. I should have felt resentful but I don't remember that I did. Probably I had had my fill of punting and getting stoned when I should have been attending lectures or writing essays. For the academic year 1973-74 my friends and I had been sharing a house in Victoria Road on the far side of Cambridge from Sleaford Street. But for successive summers a subset of us had rented a tiny terrace house in Ainsworth from two postgraduates studying Chinese. So before the due date I transferred my few possessions to Ainsworth Street and attempted to get to bed by 10pm on the Sunday evening not an easy feat in a house full of spaced-out graduands.

One interesting feature of the English summer is that a lot of it happens before most people get up. A month before mid-summer sunrise is already 5am. The air is fresh, the light because it is slanting has a wonderful golden hue and there are few people or cars about. Nevertheless on that first morning I trudged uncertainly along to the dairy. My first impression as I entered the gates was of the unpleasant smell of stale milk, an odour I was to become familiar with over the next few months.

The term dairy is a complete misnomer. There was certainly no milking going on. Really this was a milk-transfer facility to coin a phrase in the mode of contemporary management discourse. Large milk tankers discharged their loads into reservoirs which fed the bottling machinery. The filled bottles were capped with aluminium foil and loaded into plastic crates which were then barrowed to the edge of a loading bay alongside which the milkmen parked their floats so that they could load up with the appropriate number of crates for their round. This was still the era of the skittle-shaped bottle before the introduction of the shorter, dumpier bottle. A glass bottle full of milk is quite heavy and a fully loaded crate is not a negligible weight.

I went to the foreman's office and was introduced to the man who was going to show me the ropes. I can't remember his name, so let's call him Ron, but I do recall that he smoked cigarillos, more likely Hamlet rather than Café Crème. I am no smoker so I found the smell of cigar tobacco smoke at this time of morning rather overpowering though on that particular occasion, it helpfully masked the smell of stale milk.

Ron was a taciturn man. I imagine that being a milk roundsman suits those who have little need for chit-chat. He also approached the job with extreme vigour. Naively I had supposed that the job might give scope to my contemplative tendencies. Not the way that Ron ran things unfortunately. He was constantly checking his watch, working out the best place to park in order to service the maximum number of houses per stop. And when he loaded his bottle carrier he then jogged between houses. It was as if he was participating in an obscure sport or a fiendishly extended version of *Jeux Sans Frontières*. What was particularly puzzling was that it had been made clear to me by the foreman that it wasn't of the utmost importance to deliver milk by a particular time as long as it was all done by 10:00 am. The way that Ron did it, we were finished by 8:30. It was only after a couple of days that I discovered that Ron needed to get finished by 8.30am because he had to clock on for another job. I was aghast with admiration and incomprehension. I never discovered whether he was obliged to do two jobs because he had many mouths to feed or because he had got himself into severe financial difficulties or whether he just liked working and being active. The plan was for me to take over Ron's round for six weeks. I don't think he was taking a holiday or sabbatical for that long, so I imagine he must have been covering some other round. Perhaps a more gruelling one?

The round I was learning in that first week was bounded by Mill Road between Devonshire Road and Mawson Road as far down as Harvey Road then Hills Road on both sides up to the railway bridge and then part of Brooklands Avenue including Clarendon Road and the Botanic Gardens. The Hills Road stretch included the blocks of flats between Coronation Street and Union Road and also Highsett on the other side of Hills Road which was a modern development of executive flats and townhouses set amid lawns and shrubbery. And the final leg was Station Road all the way up to the Station Hotel opposite the station.

I hated delivering to the block of flats off Union Road because it involved carting several crates into the flats and then running up and down flights of stairs. There was a lift but waiting for the lift prolonged by a considerable amount the time needed to finish the block. On the other hand I loved delivering to Highsett because at that time of morning the scent of honeysuckle was completely overpowering. I also enjoyed delivering to the Botanic Gardens because this was a brief detour into a less urban world. Clearly I hadn't yet abandoned my hippie *Weltanschauung*!

As that first week wore on I began to memorise the route and started to feel that I would be able to cope with the job. Then on Friday Ron announced that for the next two days we were going to collect payment as well, a little on the Friday and the majority on the Saturday. This added considerably to the routine. Instead of just dashing up to a front door and depositing one or several milk bottles and scooping up the empties, you had to knock on the door and wait for a minute or two to see if anyone would reply. A small percentage of customers were organised enough to know exactly what they had consumed and would leave the money in an envelope on the doorstep.

As in all businesses, collecting money was by far the hardest part of the operation. To begin with all the milk was delivered on credit so it was down to the roundsman to decide how far to extend the credit with the implied jeopardy that he was responsible for any bad debts. A student household at that time of the year might suddenly disappear leaving a largish unpaid bill. The other problem was record keeping. Some people had a regular order and so the bill each week was the same. Others had one of those milk bottle holders which had a dial on it which could be set to vary the number of bottles a day. Today two, the next day three. Fair enough. The thing was you had to remember to write it in your logbook when you got back to the float. And then of course even with the regular orders, occasionally there would be a note when you got to the doorstep saying no milk today. Once again it was easy to forget to cancel the order in the logbook. And even if the records were accurate, the customer would often forget that they had varied their order. I was soon to learn that collection day could involve numerous disagreements as to the amount owed, some of which might turn quite nasty.

Ron was more than equal to all these challenges. Apart from the endurance of a marathon runner and the ability to calculate the shortest route with some kind of instinctual GPS he also had a near perfect memory, at least for the vagaries of his customers's orders. He also managed to exude a vague kind of menace so that he seemed to get immediate compliance from difficult customers. I never learned how to develop a similar mien and I'm pretty sure I was seen as a soft touch. On the positive side I don't remember getting any grief from my governor on that score. I suppose he knew that Ron would sort things out when my assignment was over.

I never really got to know much about Ron in the week we spent together, although a couple of conversations remain with me. There seemed to be a mythology that milkmen were quite often fortunate enough to encounter housewives still in their nightclothes. Furthermore it was also well known that many of the roundsmen had houses where they might get a cup of tea or coffee with the lady of the house. And it would appear that some of them, got even more than that including, improbably as it seemed to me, Ron. I lived in a kind of queasy anticipation that I might soon be feebly fending off some Highsett Sophia Loren in a whirl of négligée. Alas I never got so much as a glimpse of winceyette pyjamas.

On another occasion a tipsy May Ball reveller festooned in crumpled splendour passed us on his way home from a night of excess. His long lank locks were topped off with a paisley bandana. 'Look at that nancy boy', opined Ron, 'What does he think he looks like?' and spat a shred of tobacco into the gutter. Severely brilliantined himself, Ron was clearly no fan of the contemporary feminised sartorial style for men. But as we drew level with the weary roisterer I realised with faint horror that he was an acquaintance of mine. I shrank down in the cab and made sure that when we stopped for the next delivery that I chose the other side of the road. Fortunately my friend was too woozy to pay much attention to a couple of guys on a milk float and perhaps would not even have recognised me lightly disguised as a milkman. As I crept back to the cab I wondered how Ron and I would have got on if he had encountered me a few weeks earlier before I had had my own lustrous barnet cropped.

I like to think that Ron wished me well when he finished the round on the Saturday and he handed me over the keys to his kingdom, although I think it is more likely that he said nothing at all. Absurdly I felt confident and also relieved to be out of the constant fug of Hamlet smoke. My confidence was, of course, short-lived. On my own everything seemed to take more than twice as long. To begin with I got into a terrible muddle loading the float. The different kinds of milk were indicated by aluminium foil bottle-tops—silver for whole milk, red for homogenised, red and silver for semi-skimmed (rare in those days) and green for unpasteurised. And a few people required sterilised milk which came in a different shaped bottle with a crown cap like a beer bottle. So it was important to get the right quantities on your float. Unfortunately I had forgotten to make this calculation before arriving at the depot, so I was trying to add up quantities from my log book whilst parked up at the loading-bay much to the annoyance of my colleagues.

Having made a late start I then realised that I hadn't committed to memory all Ron's stopping places. It soon became clear that one minute extra here, two minutes there added considerably to the time the round was going to take. The realisation induced a rising sense of panic. The accumulating time deficit meant that by the time I got to the Hills Road section of the round, the morning rush-hour was in full swing. I got stuck in the traffic, could find nowhere to park and lost even more time. I was reassured by the foreman's assertion on my first day that time was not of the essence and eventually I rolled back into the depot around midday. I think I was the last man in by a long way. After I had parked my float at the charging station the foreman came over to me and said that he had had several phone calls complaining of late delivery. When he had told me that I could be relaxed about the time I took to do the round, he hadn't expected me to be quite so late. The residents of Highsett were outraged. They had had to leave for work without milk for their cornflakes. Even worse the milk would curdle if left on the doorstep in the summer sun all day long. I had better improve my performance on the morrow.

I was absolutely shattered. I went back to the little house in Ainsworth Street and went straight to bed. I did not get up for many hours. On that first day on my own I had determined at several points to jack the job in. But after a good sleep, I decided to give it one more day. Somehow I got through the rest of the week. I was dog-tired most of the time and when I wasn't working, I kept to my bed. The life of an undergraduate had not prepared me for a job involving a considerable amount of physical activity. In fact it took a couple of weeks for my body to adjust to the new regime. As it did so I improved on the time it took me to complete the round. Soon I was getting finished by 9.30 to 10. And as a bonus my consumption of beer plummeted thus further improving my financial standing. Despite these improvements I never came anywhere near Ron's finishing time of 8.30 and my admiration for him went up considerably.

I can't actually remember when graduation day was, but I had accumulated enough money by then to settle my college account and attire myself correctly for the great day. My parents were able to enjoy the public recognition of my modest degree without concerning themselves with my lack of good husbandry. And I was able to proceed to the stage of financial independence without any career plans whatsoever. Bliss.

The six weeks sped by and I actually came to enjoy the routine of getting up early and getting my round done. Money collecting days were tedious but no more than that. And I was driving my float like a pro now. The vehicles we had were Morrisons. The top speed of an electric milk float is nothing to write home about although its acceleration from 0-15 mph or so is considerable. There was no gear stick, just a switch for forward and reverse, an accelerator pedal, a brake pedal and a hand brake. The cab had a windscreen and a roof but was open at the sides. One of the things I had admired about Ron was the way he drove standing up with the log book in front of him and a pencil behind his ear. And I concluded one of the reasons why he got around so quickly was the way he would jump in the cab and stamp down on the accelerator whilst checking on his next delivery. My attempts to emulate this advanced technique brought me to grief on two occasions.

On the first of these I was parked at the top of Station Road pointing towards the station. I had just delivered to the Station Hotel on the other side of the road. I crossed back to the float jumped in and without sitting down aimed the float at the mini roundabout in front of the station. As I went into the roundabout I realised that I was going a little fast to be going into a 180 degree turn. To make matters worse because I was standing up I was thrown off balance and my weight came down more forcibly on the accelerator. A milk float with its attendant batteries is too heavy to turn over but I had not been particularly meticulous in stacking and restacking the crates on the flatbed of the float and as I careened around the roundabout one of the crates toppled of the back of the float and crashed onto the road.

There was broken glass everywhere though fortunately not too much milk, the uppermost crates being for the empties. I brought the float to a halt and went back and surveyed the damage. I scooped up as much glass as I could without lacerating my hands and kicked the rest into the gutter and then I made off back down Station Road a little more sedately, vaguely aware of the stares of commuters heading for the London train. I lived in dread for the next couple of days that complaints would flood into the depot from taxi drivers and motorists about broken glass in Station Road causing punctures. Fortunately there were none as far as I was aware.

An even more embarrassing accident lay in wait for me a few weeks later. The last task of the working day before driving the float to the charging station was to offload the empties. Once again I was a little late in getting back and a large tanker was already parked at the loading bay. I pulled in front of it and then had to back up to it to get my crates off. Space was tight but I was only going to be a few minutes. So I got very close indeed to the tanker and then set about getting the crates off. Split splat. Done in no time at all. I jumped into the cab once again and in full emulation of Ron's technique stamped on the

21

accelerator and reversed rapidly into the tanker. Once again broken glass everywhere, this time the brake and the rear side lights of the float. I had had to switch to reverse to back up to the tanker but had forgotten to switch to forward before leaving the cab.

I was conscious of incredulous guffaws from around the depot. As I discovered then it is not a good idea to screw up in front of workplace colleagues. The event was almost immediately mythologised. Workmates I had never spoken to before came up to me over the next few days to congratulate me on a fine bit of driving. What they were implying of course was that they knew I was just another student tosser. In fact I never really lived the incident down. Crashes were not unknown. You could even display a bit of swagger about a public highway prang, whereas a smash in the depot was beneath contempt. I was also afraid that I would be sacked or that the cost of the repairs would be docked from my wages. The foreman had a fairly low opinion of my capabilities but on this occasion he just laughed wearily and told me to take the float over to the workshop. The tanker was unscathed.

I retain no memory of my week off, but in all probability I just slept until some unfeasibly late hour like 9.00am and luxuriated in the ability to stay in a pub until closing time. Soon enough the week was over and when I returned to the depot I was told that my route had been changed. For the next six weeks I was to supply the Cherry Hinton customers. Because I was now an experienced roundsman, no one showed me the round. I was given the log book and told to get on with it. I took a look at it to work out what I was going to need to load and was pleasantly surprised to see that there were many fewer customers than on my previous round. Thoughts of equalling Ron's 8.30 finish time began to fill my head.

I should have known better. What I hadn't taken into account was how far away Cherry Hinton was in a milk float. I had been to Cherry Hinton once in my student career but in general it was one of those mythical areas of Cambridge and environs to which undergraduates seldom penetrated. I knew roughly where Cherry Hinton was but the individual street names meant nothing to me. In the event they turned out to be the residential roads on either side of the High Street.

My first problem was what route to take. By now I knew every inch of Mill Road and Hills Road. But for all I knew beyond the end of Mill Road there be dragons. So I drove to the end of Mill Road and turned right onto Perne Road and carried on until I got to the Cherry Hinton Road where I turned left and trundled along until I got to Cherry Hinton High Street. That first journey seemed to last forever and I wasn't really sure whether I was going in the right direction or not. I didn't reach the first delivery address for more than half an hour. I realised subsequently that the route I took meant that the distance was probably 4 or 5 miles. With the anxiety induced by the first day on a new round the float seemed to go considerably slower than its notional 15 mph. I was beginning to seriously doubt whether I would actually get the round finished and be back at the depot before the evening.

My worry dissipated when I reached the High Street and I realised that most of my stops were close to each other on modern housing estates and that traffic was light. So the delivery didn't take as long as I feared. Nevertheless I was far from breaking Ron's record. For the return trip to civilisation I decided to try going back down Coldham's Lane. This was a strangely desolate road and for a while I thought I'd got lost but eventually I worked my way back to York St and Sleaford St.

In due course I came to enjoy those runs out and back. On this round I could actually let my thoughts drift and I no longer had to steel myself for the guerrilla warfare of city centre delivery. And though the Coldham's Lane route was undoubtedly shorter, for some reason I stuck to the route I had inadvertently devised on the first day—out on the Cherry Hinton Road and back via Coldham's Lane. This meant that each morning I drove by Cherry Hinton Hall. Since 1963 this had been the site of the Cambridge Folk Festival. The Hall was not actually part of my round but I was aware from the many posters that the festival would be taking place during my Cherry Hinton tour of duty. The line-up was right up my street—Arlo Guthrie, Loudon Wainwright III and Alan Stivell. I was starting to work out ways that I could do my round and still attend the festival. In the end common sense or apathy won out and I had to resign myself once again to observing gilded youth frolicking in a sylvan setting while I got my finances in order. At least I got to sleep in a comfortable bed.

The real problem with the milk round was the havoc that it played with my social life. I found that if I didn't get up at 4.30am the working day would lurch out of control, which meant I needed to be in bed by 9.30pm or so. This was not easy in a demob-happy household. My housemates always seemed to be sloping off to the pub just as I was having to go to bed. The last straw was the present I gave my father on his birthday. I had bought tickets for *Die Fledermaus*. We had a meal in Covent Garden and then had a lovely evening listening to Johann Strauss's sparkling music in the burnished comfort of the Coliseum, a far superior auditorium to the Royal Opera to my mind. After the show my parents headed back home in their car while I got the last train back to Cambridge from Liverpool Street. I eventually got back to Ainsworth Street in the small hours.

I was now in something of a quandry. I realised that if I went to bed at this late hour I might find it difficult to wake at 4:30. So I decided to sit up and get to the dairy as early as I possibly could. The hours between 2am and 4am were terrible because of course I had been up early the previous day for my round. I could hardly keep my eyes open. Towards 4am I doused my head under the cold tap and had a couple of cups of strong coffee and headed into the dairy. Even though I lived close by I had not been one of the earliest starters so there were a few quizzical looks in the dawn light. As I lugged the crates onto my float I realised that I had made a terrible mistake. My body was leaden, my brain, never too good in the morning, was stuck in neutral. I wasn't even sure that I had the energy to get through the next five or six hours. Somehow I managed to complete the round without crashing the float, went straight to bed when I got back to the house and slept right through to the next day.

# Setright Conundrums

I DECIDED THEN THAT IT was time to look for another job. After all, I had righted my wonky finances, paid my college bill and graduated. I started to think ahead to the colder, shorter days of autumn and winter. The open cab of a milk float was no place to be on a drear, dark, fenland day. And I needed a job that wouldn't make such inroads into my personal life whilst I pondered what I was meant to be doing with that life. So it is hard now to reconstruct the thought process which led me to apply for a job as a bus conductor on the Eastern Counties bus service. Bus services ran from early morning to late at night and therefore crews had to work shifts. One week early starts; the next late finishes. The bus service also ran seven days a week, so there was no improvement there either. In some ways the hours were even more unsocial as we now say. Clearly I had engaged Daniel Kahneman's System One mental process, intuitive, or in my case indolent, rather than logical. The bus garage was on Hills Road where it met Station Road and so it was on the route of my original milk round.

The interview this time involved doing some simple arithmetic. To check that one was capable of giving the correct change I suppose. The main focus of the rather abbreviated period of training thereafter was to learn how to use the Setright machine, the device that printed the tickets. The Setright was a marvellous steampunk contraption all dials and hieroglyphics with a name that seemed to be a triumph of branding. But I subsequently discovered that there had in fact been a Mr Setright who had invented the device and simply given his name to the company. This was no doubt one of the more obscure examples of nominative determinism, much more unlikely than Igor Judge eventually becoming Lord Chief Justice after passing through that phase of his professional life when he was Judge Judge.

The Setright had a series of dials set in concentric rings one above the other on the front of the machine, the topmost of which was for ticket prices with an inner ring for ten pence values and an outer ring for the units, and selector rings for the ticket type, fare stage and date below that. The range of fares and fare types was quite limited but we were told to be careful not to issue zero value tickets. Apparently it was a trick of some less ethical conductors to issue a zero value ticket and then pocket the fare. Few passengers actually studied the jumble of numbers and words on their tickets, which was a pity because they were actually rather beautiful with magenta ink for the company name and information about terms and conditions and purple ink for the details set by the concentric rings all printed on cream paper. (If that makes me sound a bit of an anorak, so be it.)

If an inspector came across a zero value ticket you'd be in serious trouble because the ticket also bore the unique serial number of the machine that had issued it. I seem to recall that there were legitimate reasons for issuing zero value tickets but I can't remember what they were now. As I went through the induction process I started to imagine scenarios where in the scramble to deal with a crowded bus I would issue a whole batch of zero tickets and be hauled before the Eastern Counties Inquisition. It was also possible to set the machine to other values that were inappropriate. If you set it to a value which was in excess of the fare you took, you were going to have to make up the difference out of your own pocket or appeal to the company's sense of leniency. If on the other hand you set the fare selector to a positive value but to less than the fare you took, you'd be in surplus at the end of your shift and could pocket the difference. This was a more subtle fraud and one that was harder for the inspectors to spot.

The bottom ring was for the date which only needed to be

set first thing each day, so that wasn't too much of a problem, although I am sure that on occasion even that was set erroneously. The next ring up was the ticket type. Potentially you could issue return tickets and child tickets and so on but for the most part one was dealing with single tickets so that didn't need to be fiddled with too much. Above that was the fare stage selector and that's where the problems began. As you passed each stop this dial had to be advanced one notch. This was fine so long as you had been able to collect fares from all the passengers who had got on at the previous stop. But on a full bus it was sometimes difficult to identify the new passengers. Indeed it was not unknown for some to deliberately avoid catching your eye. And of course it was made much more difficult by the fact that there were two decks. A passenger making a short journey could alight before you got around to collecting his fare. Even worse at busy times of day or on busy routes the weight of passengers getting on made it difficult to collect all the fares before the next fare stage was reached.

And of course most buses were open at the back. There were signs posted about the cabin as to the number of people allowed to stand on the bottom deck and standing on the top deck was completely prohibited. But people in a hurry to get the London train or to get to school on time were not inclined to worry about whether they were in breach of the rules on standing. So that meant that on these occasions you had to barge through the crowd to collect new fares and then rush back to the platform before you reached the next stop so as to prevent too many people getting on, a manoeuvre certain to enrage those whom you had blocked as well as those whom you had jostled in your anxiety to get back to the platform. In fact at busy times it was easier just to station oneself on the platform and collect fares as people got on and off.

Another complexity was that for some reason the bus company did not provide a float of change at the start of each shift. Bus fares were quite low value but not infrequently at 7.30 in the morning especially on the station run you would be proffered a pound note with your money satchel decidedly empty of coins. At that point you had three options. The first was to issue the ticket but decline the note and return to that person once you had collected enough change. This was almost always a bad idea. It was easy to forget to collect the original fare or to discover that the passenger had already hopped off. Then the cash in your satchel and the total for the day shown on the Setright would not agree and the shortfall would have to be made up out of your own pocket. The second approach was to take the note, issue the ticket and give what change you had promising to return to the short-changed passenger forthwith. Naturally this was not an option that most passengers would accept in advance. So it was necessary to perform a bit of a pantomime, discovering that, *mirabile dictu*, you were completely out of change and moving away fast from the complaints. The advantage of this approach was that the onus was on the passenger to collect the change that he or she was owed, but it involved many more negative interactions and emotionally was more of a strain. The neatest option it seemed to me was neither to take the note nor issue a ticket but to promise to return a little later with the correct spondulicks. OK, you might lose a few but your cash and your machine would balance and if an inspector came across the ticketless passenger the story had a degree of credibility.

Even that approach could backfire. On one particular occasion on the rush-hour station run a passenger proffered me a five pound note on the first leg of the morning. In present day terms this is pretty much the equivalent of being given a fifty pound note for a one pound fare. Experienced conductor that I was, or at least considered myself to be, I countered with the option three gambit and said I wouldn't give him a ticket right now but that I'd get back to him shortly when I had gathered enough change. This eminently sensible solution seemed to enrage him for some reason. Had he detected a note of sarcasm in my voice? Or a note of superiority not appropriate to one of my humble standing? No doubt glibness is one of my besetting sins. But sarcasm at that time of morning? I don't think so. All the same something had definitely got his goat and he threatened to report me to an inspector. I was a little puzzled that someone would be so zealous in his desire to pay 20p or whatever the fare was as to report me, but I had a busful of other passengers and a satchel almost completely devoid of change so I ignored his imprecations and went about my work. Inevitably it was a slow change day and on my way back past him I still had not assembled the necessary. In an attempt to defuse the situation I made it clear that if an inspector got on I would vouch that he had attempted to pay and that his lack of a ticket was my fault. And I made sure that other passengers in the vicinity heard me. Bizarrely this seemed to infuriate him even more as if I were singling him out for this treatment and he repeated his threat. At this point I felt my own anger kindle and we all know that that's when the red mist comes down.

By now we were trundling towards the Drummer Street stop which was a favourite place for inspectors to position themselves. I jumped out at the bus pull-in oblivious to the scrum of people forcing their way onto the bus and went around to my driver and told him to hang on while I dealt with a difficult customer though I think I might have expressed this in the vernacular. Then I got back on the bus and invited the passenger with the five pound note to accompany me to the inspector who was standing at the head of the bus bay so that he could register his complaint on the spot. Many of the passengers, as I well knew, were heading for the station and the last thing they wanted was a delay in connecting with the London train. Before I had even finished making my offer there were voices complaining about missing the train. Soon the chorus was almost universal with one or two voices from those further from the epicentre of the dispute giving voice to more vulgar utterances. In the face of this peer group pressure he subsided muttering something about having taken my number and reserving the right to make his complaint in writing. I affected not to hear this as I gave a sharp double pull on the bell to let the driver know we could continue.

Just before we got to the station I calculated that I had enough change to give Mr Grumpy his fare. For a moment I thought he was going to refuse to complete the transaction but eventually he presented the five pound note at which point I had the pleasure of carefully counting out his change in the smallest denominations possible. As he jingled his way off the bus weighed down with half a hundredweight of coppers I thought that it is not often that one triumphs over the curmudgeons of this world. Later on over a cup of tea Speedy, my driver, asked me what had been going on. I gave him an outline of the incident but professed myself puzzled as to why someone should get so enraged about something so trivial. Speedy, on the principle of *cherchez la femme*, offered the view that the bloke's wife had probably failed to provide him with any nooky the previous night. Apparently restricted access to the delights of the marital bed could put Speedy out of sorts all day long. I chuckled at the thought and Speedy slurped his tea for dramatic effect. Or it was possible that the man was a secret passenger. I wasn't quite sure what Speedy was talking about. The passenger's behaviour had been far from secret. Speedy said that he'd heard that there was another tier of inspectors who were in plain clothes and contrived difficult situations on purpose to measure the performance of the company's staff. I was a little doubtful about this and wondered not for the first time what exactly it was that Speedy sweetened his tea with. It sounded like a ludicrous conspiracy theory. On the other hand as I went back over the incident in my mind I was starting to regret having given Mr Grumpy that pocketful of shrapnel.

The other aspect of the job that was closely supervised by the company was scheduling and time-keeping. A shift would involve a certain number of return journeys of the particular route. As a passenger it had always seemed to me that the bus timetable was entirely notional summed up by that common experience of waiting for ages for a bus and then three coming at once. No doubt the vagaries of the time of day, the weather conditions, the weight of traffic, not to mention whether it was term time or not could all play havoc with the schedule. One might suppose that late-running was endemic and that the company would bend every sinew to prevent it. In fact they were remarkably relaxed about late-running. If there was absolutely no hope of catching up an inspector would eventually turn you around or instruct you to wait at the next terminus until a given time. It was leaving a stop early that was streng verboten. You could be as late as you liked, but never early. Paradoxically it was the conductor who was in charge of time-keeping even though it was the driver who had control of the accelerator. Unfortunately direct communication with the driver was limited to using the bell pull to control stopping and starting, one ring for stop, two for go. The latter in theory reserved to the conductor. Other than that one had to make do with a small repertoire of hand signals. The easiest way to slow things down if there was a risk of getting ahead of the timetable was to hold the bus at each stop a little after all passengers had boarded. A tap on the left wrist was supposed to indicate that it was a timing issue. An even better ruse was to walk around to the driver's cab as if there were some more serious problem. This was not popular with the drivers and it certainly wasn't popular with the passengers.

Most drivers were quite happy to pootle along. Inevitably the one who eventually became my regular partner gave every indication that he had aspirations in the world of Formula One. He seemed to delight in throwing the bus around, lurching through the traffic and pulling up sharply at stops. Occasionally he would overtake the bus in front of us. In itself this was not against the rules so long as you weren't ahead of schedule. In Speedy's case it was just because he saw the whole thing as a race. Walking around to his cab to tell him to slow down seemed to have no effect and as I headed back to the platform I half expected to see the bus pulling away without me, such was his eagerness to be on the move.

One early morning, though, I did have occasion to be grateful to his Stirling Moss ways. On the whole I was disciplined about getting up early enough to arrive in timely fashion at the garage. On this particular day I overslept. No doubt alcohol was involved. From the bus company's point of view late running because of the vagaries of the traffic was perfectly acceptable; but late running because of failure to start your shift on time was a disciplinary offence. When I got to the garage Speedy was in the cab revving the engine. I started to explain but he waved aside my pathetic excuses and said that he thought no

31

one had noticed yet. The question was how were we going to explain why we were so late on the first leg of the morning when we got to one of the timing points. Speedy thought that the best thing to do was not to pick up any passengers at all on our run up to the Golden Hind on Milton Road. He said that we should put up the Not In Service sign on the destination board and get up there as fast as possible.

I was fairly doubtful about this plan. What if we passed an inspector en route which was far from improbable at that time of morning. Speedy thought for a bit and then suggested that we avoid the city centre altogether. He reasoned that an inspector would have no reason to be on duty on The Backs for example. He sketched out the route we would take and then we'd resume our schedule at Mitcham's Corner. I wasn't even sure that there was enough clearance for a double-decker bus on the route he was suggesting but I could see that the longer we debated the issue the later we were likely to be. No doubt my lack of moral fibre was connected to the monumental hang-over I was nursing so I agreed weakly, put up the Not In Service sign and hid myself in the back of the bus. A Bristol Lodekka LFS 45 is faster than a Morrison Electricar milk float, but not much. Despite that fact Speedy managed to coax an impressive performance from the lumbering beast and we made up most of the time lost due to my hangover. In my bilious state I couldn't help imagining the puzzled looks on the faces of early morning walkers as they saw a double-decker bus screeching around some of the more scenic parts of Cambridge.

When we got to Mitcham's Corner we changed the sign on the destination board and Speedy having had his fix of speed for the day proceeded at a more stately pace. The only residual worry was that when the clerks in the office came to analyse my waybill for that day they might query why I had sold no tickets during the first half hour of my shift. I hoped that so long as daily aggregates were within certain bounds, no alarm bells would be set ringing. Thankfully our ruse worked and in my remaining time as a conductor I never overslept again.

Speedy's driving had a less positive outcome on another

occasion. He came into the roundabout on the Milton Road in Stirling Moss style only to find that a car coming from the right had decided to play chicken with the speeding bus. Speedy slammed on the brakes. Fortunately we didn't have many passengers on board. In fact the only person standing was me. I was on the raised deck just inboard of the platform issuing a ticket and therefore not holding onto the rail when the abrupt stopping of the bus propelled me down the aisle and slammed me into the bulkhead before depositing me in a heap on the floor with my wrist caught under my Setright machine. The only person to have been catapulted out of her seat was an elderly lady who had been sitting on the seat behind the driver. By some mystery of momentum she had ended up landing on me and so I had entirely accidentally cushioned her fall. Everyone else had been holding on tight as we were required to recommend countless times a day.

Once I had got to my feet and helped the lady back to her seat I rang the bell to indicate to Speedy to pull over at the next stop so I could made out an incident report and take statements from the passengers. I went around the bus asking people if they'd like to make a statement. A couple of people offered some inconsequential observations. I then returned to the lady and told her she had a right to make a complaint and that there might be a matter of some compensation. She replied that she was perfectly fine and that she didn't want to make a formal complaint. It occurred to me that she had quite enjoyed the brief physical contact but I immediately put this thought out of my mind especially as my wrist was starting to throb quite badly. Even worse I realised that it was my Setright winding hand, a fact which was going to make the rest of my shift a painful business. If anyone deserved compensation, I thought, it was me. But I felt sure that the company would look askance at any injury claim that came from one of its own conductors when not a single member of the travelling public felt strongly enough to complain about the incident and the only person who might be found to be at fault was the driver. So I abandoned the report. When we stopped for a break I strapped up my wrist with my handkerchief and knocked back a couple of aspirin that I had bought at a newsagent.

Later on as I was sitting in the canteen with Speedy having a greasy cup of tea I got out the book that I was carrying in my dustjacket pocket to try and take my mind off my sprained wrist which was still throbbing quite badly. It was the Penguin edition of Nietzsche's *Beyond Good and Evil*. The cover showed a reproduction of a painting by Franz von Stuck of The Sphinx. The Sphinx was shown in ghastly shades of yellow and green as a bare-breasted woman with her arms stretched out in front of her in a somewhat predatory pose. The combination of title and cover illustration was obviously working to good effect on Speedy's imagination. He nodded at the book and said 'Cor, that looks like a good read!' I could only agree. I thought he might ask to borrow it. And why not? If a black cab driver could go on to win Mastermind, I don't see why a bus driver couldn't become an expert in German nineteenth century thought. I explained that the cover was a bit misleading and gave him a thumbnail sketch of what the book was about. Speedy listened politely but the look on his face was one of scarcely concealed disappointment. Perhaps he was a Hegelian?

Despite the delights of the Setright machine and the pleasant prospect of swapping notes with Speedy on the *Übermensch* and the eternal recurrence I knew that my days as a conductor were numbered. Notwithstanding the occasional difficult customer I rather enjoyed the busy city centre routes. The day did not drag and there was always plenty of incident to chat about with your partner on tea breaks. But after a few weeks we got moved to a country run heading south out of the city via Harston and Haslingfield to Meldreth. Gaps between stops were much greater and for much of the time the bus was almost empty. Particularly at night it could be a rather dismal experience. And paradoxically it was much easier to lose track of where one was for the purposes of advancing the Setright's fare stage. What's more Speedy had made it clear that he had had enough of the course on German thought and that his interest in Nietzsche was strictly limited to Page 3 aspects. I wondered idly whether there was a monograph waiting to be written on

Nietzsche and the objectification of the female body, but then rejected the idea on the basis that Jacques Lacan had already had his grubby fingers all over it.

# Arts Theatre Casual

AND SO I STARTED looking for a new job. I have no idea what prompted me to walk into the Arts Theatre and ask at the box office whether they had any jobs. It was all the more surprising given that I had managed to avoid being involved in any of the student drama societies. I had certainly studied quite a lot of classic drama as part of my degree; Molière, Lessing, Hebbel, Corneille, Hauptmann, Brecht and so on. And Bill, my French supervision partner, and I had a soft spot for absurdist drama, in particular N. F. Simpson. But I had no desire to act. A couple of appearances on stage at school had ensured that. Nor had I ever been involved with any of the practical aspects of putting on a play; directing, set design or stage management. Unfortunately, The Arts was fresh out of box office jobs but suggested that I check at the stage door with Mike Arnold, the Stage Manager. Despite my complete lack of experience I somehow managed to persuade Mike to take me on as a casual.

The first shows I worked on were Joe Orton's *Entertaining Mr Sloane* and Pirandello's *Six Characters in Search of an Author*. The Joe Orton production seemed to have been kidnapped by the set designer. The stage of The Arts is not notably large. Even so the designer had decided in an access of symbolic over-determination to set the suburban living room implied by Orton's text in the middle of a rubbish dump which in turn was contained within the jagged embrace of a giant egg shell. The unfortunate actors were consequently reduced to a very restricted palette of moves and gestures. The text, however, is brilliant and the constraint seems to have brought out the best in them. The set for the Pirandello by contrast was schematic in the extreme. The main feature was a fountain which The Arts stage crew had been commissioned to construct at the theatre's workshop which was located in the former Festival Theatre in Newmarket Road.

When I was asked to report to the Festival Theatre on Newmarket Road I was at first puzzled. I had been up and down that road many times and never noticed a theatre. This was explained by the fact that it is set back off the road and the front elevation looks as if it is a Georgian house. But once inside you realise that you have entered an architectural gem. No one among my workmates was able to give me much information about the theatre although the guy who ran the workshop thought that Tyrone Guthrie had been associated with the theatre in the 1920s.

In fact the rest of the crew seemed thoroughly unimpressed by my amazement, almost as unimpressed as they were by the piece of scenery that I constructed that day. In the time that it took the stage carpenter to build a fireplace and mantelpiece for the *Entertaining Mr Sloane* set, I just about managed to assemble what was essentially a wooden box which was supposed to be part of the plinth for the fountain in *Six Characters*. After the guffaws had subsided I was informed that it was not fit for purpose. For a start it was not square and secondly it was far too heavy. The essence of scenery is that it should be light and easily moved. So my masterpiece was rejected. As we were clearing up, the stage carpenter suggested that if we turned it upside down it would make a good receptacle for bolts and shackles when we were taking a set down. Thereafter it was known as Eamonn's strike box. I prefer to think that this was a modest kind of accolade although I think that it was more likely the equivalent of a dunce's hat.

I soon got used to the routine at the Arts. We would get in at 10.30 in the morning and tidy things up from the night before. Mike Arnold was a stickler for tidiness and cleanliness. A theatre stage is potentially a dangerous place. There is a lot of mechanical equipment with heavy objects suspended overhead.

There is also the potential to leave sharp objects lying around for performers to step on or bang into. So sweeping and mopping the stage was something of an obsession with him. Often there would be a matinée performance which as we all know takes place in the afternoon. Between shifts the stage crew and sometimes performers would repare to The Eagle pub. The Eagle is an ancient galleried inn. At that time the rooms that front onto Bene't Street were still used as student accommodation. The main bar was at the back and its ceiling had famously been graffitied by air-crew in world war two. The smaller side bar was where the regulars congregated. The landlord was in many respects a curmudgeonly individual. He had served in the Middle East during the war and still had something of the military about him. But by one of those mysterious alchemical effects he ran a very good pub.

And it is indeed possible that the alchemy was powered by the Greene King Abbott ale that he served. At nearly 5% ABV Abbott was one of the stronger ales available, though really nothing compared to the strength of some Belgian ales. But the rumour was that there was something else in it that affected the drinker's brain in much the same way that marijuana does. The rationale for this was that it was something to do with the hops used. And some people said that hops and hemp were botanically related. I have no idea if this is true. It sounds unlikely. But it does sound like the kind of factoid that a stoned person might come up with. Whatever the truth Abbott seemed to have an effect like no other beer.

We would invite visiting thespians or stage crew to join us for a quick half between shows and then we would make sure that it was Abbott that they were drinking. Of course it was a ridiculously juvenile thing to do. But what was remarkable was the effect that it has on nearly everyone that drank it, even hardened drinkers and there are quite a few of those in the the ranks of the luvvies. Not all actors are extroverts but once they get going they know how to project. The Arts may have staged quite a few absurdist plays at the time but the more profoundly absurd performances were often to be observed in the small side bar of The Eagle.

After the Pirandello and Joe Orton there was a range of material from Mozart's *Don Giovanni*, Gilbert and Sullivan's *The Gondoliers* and Marlowe's *The Jew of Malta* to dance programmes from the Royal Ballet and the Ballet Rambert. Soon Christmas was approaching and we started getting ready for the annual pantomime. This was the first pantomime I had ever worked on and it had a particularly unruly cast. The comic (Buttons), who had a stand-up slot, and the prima ballerina were having an affair. It had got to the stage where they were rapidly falling out of love, but no doubt still rooming together. They would be bickering in the wings while waiting for their entrances but as soon as they crossed the sight lines they would snap into character, although truth to tell there is little scope for psychological insight in a pantomime.

On one fateful day they arrived for the show extremely late. As they disappeared down to the dressing rooms it became clear that the prima ballerina was sporting a glorious black eye. Trouper that she was she applied plenty of slap and pirouetted onto stage on cue. Buttons was not so fortunate. Although not visibly injured, the strain of the row had shattered his already fragile composure. It is fair to say that stand-up comedy was not his forte. A small group of children had been in to see the show on more than one occasion and knew his routine by heart. On this particular night they took delight in shouting out the punchlines to his gags before he had got to the end of them. He had no strategy for dealing with their pre-emptive strikes. He was neither able to introduce new material to wrong-foot them nor improvise ripostes. He died, as they say. The hecklers triumphed.

A number of Buttons' colleagues however were made of much sterner stuff. Pantomimes love their sound effects. And this production was no exception. The action was liberally punctuated with bangs and flashes. The bangs were provided by a kind of cracker known as a maroon which was let off in a tank mounted on the flying grid high above the stage. A great deal of care is taken with these devices because fire and the the theatre are a notoriously dangerous combination. It is not so much that there are copious amounts of flammable material in a theatre, though that is true, as that the panic engendered by the flames or indeed just the rumour of fire can lead to people being trampled to death. Consequently it is forbidden to the staff of a theatre both backstage and front of house to use the word fire if they want to inform colleagues and management that there really is a conflagration. Instead a code phrase is used. In the case of the Arts it was 'Mr Sand is in the house.' The idea here was that if a member of the public were to overhear the message being passed from one theatre employee to another, he would be unlikely to discern its true meaning, notwithstanding the fact that the phrase even in the 1970s sounded hopelessly antiquated. And yet not long ago at a London Underground station I heard a tannoyed message asking for 'Inspector Sands' to report to some location urgently. I wonder?

However on this particular evening the phrase was being used in earnest. Enough small pieces of cartridge cardboard from previous maroon detonations must have built up in the tank to create a small fire. It could clearly be smelled and the smoke was drifting down onto the stage. Somebody went to call the fire brigade and a couple of us were ordered aloft with a fire extinguisher to set to work on the smouldering cardboard in the tank. We inched out onto the flying grid and directed the nozzle of the extinguisher into the tank. Really there was not much in the way of a fire. If it had just been left it would have soon gone out.

Forty feet beneath us the Dame was continuing with her routine whilst directing nervous glances aloft. The sketch involved the Dame following a recipe on the Jimmy Young radio programme which was voiced by another actor at the prompt desk. Of course the whoosh of the extinguisher was amplified by the tank so that it was perfectly audible on stage and to some extent in the auditorium I imagine. Scarcely missing a beat the Dame mimed her apologies for the sudden attack of flatulence. At that point the Fire Brigade arrived and one of their number climbed up to join us and check that all was well. Back down at the prompt desk a whispered conference concluded that there was no need to evacuate the theatre. The show could go on.

However that was not the end of the mayhem and the

consequent need for improvising skills. We were close to the end of the run. The show was running on autopilot. One of the gags I was involved in was also part of the radio recipe sketch. The recipe that the Dame was following was for rabbit pie which in those days was itself something of a joke. We had a stuffed rabbit-skin rigged up on a wire. Each time the Dame tried to cut its head off I pulled the wire and she missed and ran some patter about being sure she'd asked for a dead rabbit. On the third attempt instead of moving a couple of feet across the table the rabbit was meant to take off vertically and dis-appear behind the proscenium arch and into the wings. This was achieved by having the wire run over a pulley above the stage then across to the flying gantry where it was attached to a sandbag. At the right moment the stagehand in the flying gan-try would drop the sandbag and the rabbit instead of moving across the table would fly into wings once the slack that I had been manipulating had been taken up.

On this particular evening however the slack of the wire got caught on something and although the rabbit took off from the table, it failed to clear the proscenium arch and hung several feet above the Dame swinging back and forth. Nothing daunted, the actor who was doing the radio voice created a news flash about a flying rabbit having been spotted over Cambridge. At the same time the Dame rushed to the prompt desk picked up the starting pistol that was there for a number of other whizz-bang gags and rushed back on stage firing at the rabbit. By this time we had managed to unsnag the line and reel the rabbit in. Those guys were expert improvisers. I doubt if anyone in the audience realised it wasn't planned like that. Not even Buttons' tormentors.

I am sure that no one who has ever been to a pantomime will be surprised that the Dame was a man. Cross-dressing seems to be as old as the theatre itself. Shakespeare's companies were famously all male, so that in many of the plays you have lay-ers of (gender) identity. Viola would have been played by a boy dressed as a girl who then dresses as a boy. This leads to all sorts of fun in the plays and has inspired Tom Stoppard to employ a similar device in the film Shakespeare in Love where Gwyneth Paltrow pretends to be a boy so that she can act and inevitably becomes the object of Will's affection.

One of my own forays onto the (amateur) stage involved my playing the part of the maidservant, Anna, in Max Frisch's *The Fire Raisers* (*Biedermann und die Brandstifter*). I attended an all-boys Catholic school and it was still considered improper for boys and girls to consort together for dramatic purposes. Presumably the worry was that in any play involving even a mild element of romance the participants might get carried away. It never seems to have occurred to these guardians of public morals that having two boys kissing each other might be just as likely to trigger certain deep-seated impulses.

I suppose that I was chosen not for my skill in reading the lines but because at the age of 16 I was still not shaving regularly and I had a far from manly face. It has even been suggested I had a rather good pair of legs. What did it take to be a woman? From a theatrical point of view; long hair, a 'figure', a dress or skirt and high heels. A blond wig with long plaits looped up on top of the head was provided. It had obviously seen better days on a Valkyrie. The figure was accomplished in time-honoured fashion by stuffing a bra with paper or cotton-wool. I no longer know where the bra came from. On reflection I shudder to think. Then it was decided that my bosom was not really in the right position. But no one really knew. The director was a priest and the designer/stage-manager was a bachelor and showed every sign of remaining such. The cast were adolescent boys to a man and, in some cases, to a boy.

Everyone seemed to have a view about my bosom. Some thought it should be higher, some lower. I really had no idea but somewhat objected to people prodding me and asking me to turn this way and that. I was starting to get some idea of what objectification was like. In those days most of the senior staff were priests. But one housemaster in a sign of the way things were going was actually married. Sure enough he had originally studied for the priesthood at the English College in Rome but had eventually decided that he had no vocation as the phrase had it. So he had returned to civvy street and immediately snagged the most delightful bride. He was probably in his mid-thirties. But of course to a 16 year old that seemed geriatric. His wife on the other hand was a mere 21 or so. And that meant she was a member of our generation and not his. And to highlight the contrast even more, where he was balding with a comb-over, crumpled suits and detachable collars, she wore short skirts, had copious amounts of dark lustrous hair piled on her head and was indubitably beautiful. Just my luck then that it was decided that she would tutor me in rigging my bra at the right level and how to deport myself as a woman. It may be imagined that in advance of our first session my feverish imagination created scenarios where she would shake her head sadly at my efforts to hoist my bosom to the right level and ask me to study her own magnificent chest closely. Unfortunately it didn't quite work out like that. I was reduced to stammering shyness at the delicious absurdity of being required to spend time alone with this beautiful woman discussing female underwear and how to create a naturalistic embonpoint.

My part was fairly meagre with few lines but quite a lot of stage business. I seem to recall that as the maid in the Biedermann household I was required to set and clear the dinner table. This required me to carry the wherewithal for the meal on a tray, tricky enough on a raked stage with several steps up to the door through which I made my entrances and exits, but a veritable nightmare in what seemed to me very high heels. I had been so focused on the upper body in my sessions with my housemaster's wife that I had neglected to gain any real proficiency in high heels. Add to that the fact that the only thing this Biedermeier family seemed to eat was sausages and you had fertile grounds for thespian disaster. Night after night the damn sausages eluded my control and rolled off the plates. Finally one evening the inevitable happened and one of the sausages not only rolled off the plate but continued its journey across the table and ended up on the floor. Unlike the pantomime troupers already referred to, we schoolboy actors were completely stumped by the contingency of the situation and could only watch in open-mouthed horror as the horrible comestible rolled slowly across the table and landed on the stage.

It looked for a second or two as if it might continue its journey to the edge of the stage. Happily it ran out of momentum and eventually one of the other actors stooped down and picked it up. There was no way in those heels and that skirt that I was going to try and catch the errant piece of charcuterie. That was the biggest laugh we got during the entire run. Louder even than the reaction to my wig. Sadly the play was not a comedy.

It says something for my naïveté that it never occurred to me at the time that indulging in public cross-dressing might expose me to sniggers and innuendoes. Perhaps at a catholic school it did not seem so strange when the majority of the teachers were priests and swished around in cassocks on a daily basis. And then again it has always been true that 'Some Like It Hot'. But the risk is that protestations to the contrary will be to no avail. When Jack Lemon's character, Jerry, reveals to the ardent Osgood at the end of that marvellous movie that he is in fact a man, it merely elicits the immortal line 'Well, nobody's perfect'.

And that is exactly the point—the disguise should not be convincing. Film routinely deals in verisimilitude—you will believe a man can fly. But with female impersonation, grounds for disbelief should always be evident. To an extent theatre in contrast to film is at pains to stress the artificiality of the representation. As with those optical illusions where we alternately see a young woman and an aged crone, illusion in the theatre is better if it is not utterly convincing. Perhaps this is more a function of the comedic vision. Certainly the movies that draw on this tradition are comedies; *Some Like It Hot*, *Tootsie*, *Victor And Victoria* and *Mrs Doubtfire*. And the inadequacy of Jack Lemon's and Tony Curtis's drag is accentuated by the 'jello on springs' beauty of Marilyn Monroe.

By the beginning of 1976 the stage work was starting to dry up. So I transferred to looking after the stage door. How much lower could I sink? The job was intrinsically boring. Apart from intercepting members of the general public in hot pursuit of minor TV celebrities, my duties also included being a kind of cloakroom attendant for visitors to the theatre's restaurant and for a brief period taking deliveries for the restaurant. Looking after people's coats and shopping was a little demeaning for one of my superior aspirations. Occasionally well-meaning diners would even offer me a tip.

When it was built the Arts Theatre had been shoe-horned into a space behind the shops on King's Parade, Peas Hill and Bene't Street. The stage door itself was located in St Edward's Passage which formed one side of St Edward's Square. The nearest point to the stage door and more particularly the stage loading bay where a vehicle could park was in Peas Hill opposite the side of the Guildhall. This was not ideal for a repertory theatre where the programme changed every few weeks, indeed at some points every week. Scenery and equipment had to be carried down St Edward's Passage often in inclement weather.

Though small, the square contains an ancient church from which it takes its name. The theatre takes up the whole of one of the sides of the square. On the opposite side in the corner next to a small second-hand bookshop was an old stable or barn-like building. This was used as a scenery store, but there was also a cellar including storage for the Arts restaurant. The wine cellar was particularly well stocked. The rumour was that the wine collection had been laid down by John Maynard Keynes and that Commander Blackwood, the General Manager of The Arts, was slowly (some said not so slowly) drinking his way through it. Given that the period in question was some thirty years after Keynes's death, I think it unlikely that much of the wine was of the appropriate quality to be drinkable that many years later. On the other hand Keynes was a noted epicure and philanthropist. I do know however that there were some very expensive truffles down there.

One day there was a kitchen delivery from a swanky Italian food suppliers. I opened up the store room and cellar as requested. The delivery man asked for the restaurant manager. I pointed out that he was away on holiday and that I was looking after the stores in his absence. The delivery man narrowed his eyes and asked if the usual arrangement was operating. I didn't have the foggiest idea what he meant. Why would the procedure change just because the boss was away? I didn't even know what the procedure was. So I replied in the affirmative with an expansive wave of the hand.

A little while later when everything had been barrowed to the store, he returned to my cubby-hole and handed me his copy of the delivery note to sign, which I did. He then gave me a tin and said he'd see me again in a fortnight. I suppose if I'd been properly prepped for the job I would have been told to check the items on the delivery note against what had actually been delivered. But innocent that I was, this did not occur to me. The tin I had just been given must have been my 'payment' for whatever little fraud was going on.

Something of the sort was starting to form in my mind as the delivery man gave me a cheery *ciao* and sauntered off. But getting paid in tinned goods seemed an odd way to collaborate in petty theft. I took a look at the tin. Finest Perigord truffles. I didn't actually know what they were. I vaguely thought they were a kind of chocolate confection. But the image on the tin looked more like a mushroom. My normal repast was probably a curry or a moussaka at one of the cheap eateries that served the student population. Little actual cooking got done in the Vincent gaff. So I decided that I had no actual use for the contents of the tin and put it back in the store where I assumed it was meant to be. I could only imagine what the delivery man's side of the scam might be. It was only later as I had a pint with a more worldly-wise friend that I discovered that truffles are practically worth their weight in gold. And much more tasty. OK, tinned truffles are not ideal, but they're still pretty expensive. No doubt if my back-hander had been a jar of caviar I would have twigged sooner what was going on. I still wonder what concoction I might have come up with had I taken the truffles home. Truffles on toast?

The compensation for looking after the stage door was that it gave me plenty of time to read—and to write. Part of the reason for getting a job in the theatre, apart from the obvious reluctance to face the real world was that it seemed conducive to the time and energy management needs of an aspiring writer. At that point I still really considered myself a poet and I was wrestling with a long poem called *Waves*, a fantasia weaving geology, English history, cell biology, physics, personal history and environmental disaster into the implied figure of the lemniscate, the mathematical symbol for infinity. By temperament I am a miniaturist and most of my pieces were just a few lines. I am still mystified as to what impelled me to write something so long-winded. I suppose it must have been my own 'periphrastic study in a worn-out poetical fashion', which was confirmed by the meagre encouragement I had received from the few readers I had shown my work to outside my close friends. In this rather crestfallen state I refocused my ambition on becoming a playwright. This had the advantage that it enabled me to pretend that my stage managerial exploits were all part of a carefully wrought plan, a way of acquiring first hand experience of the constraints of the medium and the tricks of the trade. And a way of meeting people who might be able to help me promote the dramas I was confident that I would soon be producing. My chequered academic career had also focused to a great extent on classic European drama, so I felt that there was also some intellectual credibility to this change of gears.

I had also been an admirer, though not uncritical, of Denis Potter's work for television. I was uncomfortable with his crude depiction of sexuality, but I liked his formal inventiveness. That was the direction I wanted to take. I realised that the chances of an unknown getting anything produced were limited. So the smaller the cast, the simpler the setting, the better. The brief to myself, therefore, was a two-hander, single room set and, with a nod to McLuhan, the dramatic proceedings should be a critique of the medium. All in all something that sounded impressive when you talked about it but was ludicrously tricky to realise.

And then unfortunately I made the fatal error of mentioning it to one of the regular backstage visitors. He had seen me scribbling in my notebook and had asked me what I was writing. I gave him a hesitant summary of my idea and prepared to ward off the usual mockery or scepticism. But far from mocking the idea, he was enthusiastic. It turned out that he was a published writer. His name was Fred Willets and he was connected to someone in the play currently in production. More importantly he had contacts in the drama department of the BBC and if he felt my work was up to scratch he would introduce me. I didn't take this seriously, but I did feel that having unexpectedly announced the gist of my play, I was duty bound to make a stab at it.

So after weeks struggling with this self-imposed conundrum I was delivered of a short play which I called *The Fault's In The Set*. The action takes place in the living room of a young-ish couple. The main point of view is from their TV set placed directly in front of a sofa. It is as if the camera is actually in the TV set, the key thing being that we never see the TV or its screen. The essential conceit is that the husband is more interested in what's on the TV than in his wife. Their relationship has stagnated. She tries various ways to get him to pay attention to her suggesting at one point that she might be having an affair with another man. This ruse does not work. In despair she is even prepared to humiliate herself by doing a striptease for her husband. But as she starts to remove her clothes, his interest is captured by a scene in the programme he has been watching in which a young woman is doing a striptease. The husband seems to be only able to deal with the reality of his own life if it is mediated through, or endorsed by, television. He chooses the simulation over the real. Though it was to be a few more years until I encountered the ideas of Jean Baudrillard, I was already in my own facile way toying with the precession of the simulacra.

The title of the piece was a play on the message that sometimes used to flash up on your TV screen when there was a problem with the transmission—Do not adjust your set—to deter viewers from fiddling with the fine tuning control or more likely giving the TV set a good thump on the side. The point was the problem was in the network not in the TV set, the network here standing for contemporary society and the TV set standing for the domestic relationship. On this view modern technological development is perverting the foundational relationship of human society. Looking back from the full spate of an internet obsessed era the degree of psychological deformation attributable to television watching seems decidedly limited. But sufficient unto the day is the evil thereof, I suppose.

Given the reflexivity of the dramatic structure it is little

49

wonder that the actual dialogue ended up being ponderous, but I put that thought to one side. I was just enjoying the feeling of finally having finished something. All the time I had been working on it Fred had been badgering me to see the drafts. I had prevaricated. At last I could put him off no longer. I typed it up on my portable Olivetti and waited for the inevitable criticism. There was none. He liked it. I was nonplussed. That's not the way things worked. Everyone knew that the pattern was repeated rejection and that what you had to do was bear in mind Samuel Beckett's words from *Worstward Ho!* 'All of old. Nothing else ever. Ever tried. Ever failed. No matter. Try again. Fail again. Fail better.' Of course that's a little anachronistic. *Worstward Ho!* didn't appear until 1983. But 'if at first you don't succeed, try, try, try again' is far too positive. And of course Beckettian gloom was something I had revelled in ever since I had seen a West End production of *Waiting for Godot* in 1967 or 1968.

Fred did not feel the piece needed tweaking at this stage. He felt it was ready to send off to his contact in the BBC's drama department. As I pushed the poorly typed manuscript into the pillar box I really had very low expectations. So I was more than a little surprised a few weeks later when I got a letter back from a producer at BBC East, saying that they would like to include the piece in a season of short plays by new writers to be filmed in the BBC's Norwich studios. I was amazed. In my heart I didn't really think the play was any good. It was more a technical exercise. But if that was what the ravening beast of TV wanted, that was fine by me.

At the same time my patience in holding the stage door fort was repaid when Mike Arnold recommended me for the job of Deputy Stage Manager at the Belgrade Theatre in Coventry. The job came with an Equity card, so this really was a big break in stage management terms. It seems that Mike's recommendations really meant something and were not lightly handed out. Suddenly I was in a bit of a quandary. The BBC had just accepted my first play and in the heady delight of this initial approbation it seemed certain that I would soon need to produce more work if I wanted get anywhere as a screenwriter. The prospect of toiling backstage at the Belgrade began to lose some of its lustre. After a sleepless night I came to a fateful conclusion. I would turn down the Belgrade job. I told Mike. He was not impressed. I was pretty sure I wouldn't be getting any more leg-ups from that direction. I sensed that my days at The Arts were over. Still onwards and upwards. At least that was the hope.

But instead it was backwards and downwards. Just as I was coming to the end of the period of notice I was working out I got another letter from the BBC producer. Sorry to be the bearer of bad tidings but the proposed season of new plays has been axed. The economic state of affairs, raging inflation etc. With a bound I had made myself redundant and the bubble of my literary ambitions had suddenly popped.

So I rather slunk out of The Arts with my tail between my legs. I was feeling pretty miserable because I knew I'd have to get another job pretty quickly or give up my grotty bedsit in a large corner house in Tenison Road. Not that I was particularly sentimental about what was a severely functional living space. But at least it was place to escape to, to sleep in and sometimes to write in. The house was divided into six or seven bedsits with communal toilet and bathroom facilities. I had the front ground floor room right beside the front door. There was a single bed in one corner, a table with a couple of chairs and a wooden framed armchair. There was a gas fire and in the corner furthest from the bay window a small sink unit with a gas geyser. The room looked larger than it was because there was so little in it. I spent as little time there as I could and so far as I can remember I only entertained there once.

On that occasion I had gone along to a meeting of the poetry society. I had taken a couple of poems. The format was that we met in a room in the Merton Arms  and then we each read a poem aloud to the assembled group who were then invited to respond to it. I've got a feeling that I went first. I can't imagine why. I really don't think I would have volunteered for pole position. The poem was called 'Rien Ne Va Plus'. The poem played with the image of a roulette wheel and a compass, the idea being that we are guided whether we admit it or not by chance and that what we like to think of as our self is actually like a pointer or needle that is moved by a powerful and invisible force so that in some way although death is ineluctable, the route there is not predetermined. It is possible for example to create something that only I could have made, in this case the poem I was reading which emerges from silence in the same way that the universe is created by the utterance of God. ("I / utter silence / in the centre / here.") Or something like that.

When I had finished reading there was silence, but it was awkward rather than utter. Eventually someone said that it was a rather difficult poem to digest, perhaps somewhat obscure. Another person said that she didn't think the language was particularly poetic, lacking music. I muttered something about it being more a poem for the eye but that the sounds were important too. I could have and probably should have unpacked some of the meaning. For example that the last word was both the locus of creation and an invocation to listen (here/hear). But it seemed to me that if the *last word* wasn't enough, in the sense that the poem required further explication, then the poem had somehow failed. So I stayed shtum. And we moved on with relief to the next contestant. I am sorry to say that I can't remember anything about the other poems because I was seething in a stew of irritation and embarrassment. Afterwards there was time for a couple of pints of beer and some chitchat but I had no great desire to stay, so I made my excuses. At this point another young guy said he was leaving too. He'd read something that was full of organic imagery but that was as much as I'd taken in. We walked back across Cambridge. He was Swedish and as it turned out into Rudolf Steiner in a big way. Which was fine by me. We got back to Tenison Road. I invited him in for a cup of coffee. And then I began to realise that he had the hots for me. Which was not fine by me. Just not my thing really. I eventually managed to push him out into the night. I suppose if I'd thought that it was my poetic genius that had inflamed him I might have been more accommodating, but I was pretty certain he was just after a bit of post-modern cock. I made a mental note to cross the Cambridge Poetry Society off my Christmas card list.

Bedsitter life is the antithesis of sharing a house. You each have your little space and you don't really get to know the other occupants. In fact you hardly ever see them. The upside is no one steals your milk from the communal fridge. The downside is you have no fridge. But in fact I did get to know the guy who had the attic room. I can't remember how we bonded. Down the pub probably. He was an illustrator and graphic designer and used his room as his studio. His subject was the signs of the zodiac. The style was very much based on that of Alan Aldridge's *The Butterfly Ball* and *The Grasshopper's Feast*, swirling psychedelic confections. Aldridge was a genius. My friend in the attic was not. Not only was the zodiac a well-trodden path in the field of illustration but his style was extremely derivative. It would have been churlish not to have offered some praise especially since the private view was accompanied by several joints which enhanced my appreciation. But under the influence I found his shabby curtains almost as fascinating. Eventually he completed the set and let me know one day that he was moving to London to try and get them published. I never saw him again. I hope he had chosen a propitious conjunction to make his move.

One of the annoyances of having the room next to the front door was that I had to do more than more fair share of dealing with callers to the house. I was forever taking in packages for the other residents. One day I took in a parcel from the postman for the couple who lived in the room directly above mine. Despite the proximity of our rooms and the fact that from the bay window of my room I had a partial view of the porch I realised that I had never seen them. In fact the only reasons I had for believing that they were a couple were the sounds of passion that disturbed my slumber with alarming regularity. Nor was this amorous soundtrack confined to the hours of darkness. They were certainly not averse to a bout of lovemaking in the middle of the day and I could tell from the symphony of creaks, gasps and throaty chuckles that this was one those days.

I waited until the volcano had subsided and went up to their room. It occurred to me that I could just leave the parcel outside their door but I was afraid that it might go missing. So

53

I knocked loudly on their door. Muffled sounds of confusion came from inside. Eventually a male voice asked me who I was and what I wanted. I shouted back that I was the guy who lived downstairs. I was about to tell him about the parcel and that I would leave it outside the door when he said 'OK man, but we're naked'. I was still trying to fathom this piece of information when the door opened and a naked man with a ring through his nose stood before me. I explained about the postman and pushed the parcel at him. He didn't seem convinced by my explanation but muttered what I took to be his thanks whilst scrutinising me carefully. I responded by trying not to scrutinise him at all. But it was clear from his accent that he was American and from his eyes that he was totally smashed.

A few days later I bumped into him in the little yard at the back of the house when we were both putting out rubbish. Clearly since I hadn't freaked out when I'd encountered him starkers, he felt now more at ease with me. In the spirit of entente that had now broken out I asked him what he was doing in the UK? Was he now or had he ever been a student? He glanced around suspiciously and then glared at me, 'No, man. I was in Nam'. I probably said something empathetic like 'Heavy, man,' which would have sounded a lot less fake then than it does now.

It wasn't that unusual to meet young Americans who had been in Viet Nam or who had dodged the draft. I'd drunk until dawn in Paris a couple of years before when I'd been cramming for my French oral exam with an American called Reeves who was the same age as me and was on leave from the US Navy. This was not actually the best way of improving my spoken French but it was a very pleasant way of spending a night in Paris. Reeves was immensely irritated because he had volunteered for the Navy figuring it was the safest service to be in, only to find that the Nixon administration had concluded that the war was unwinnable and had decided to withdraw. At the same time it abandoned conscription. So it turned out that those born in 1952 were the last to face the draft. Unfortunately Reeves still had some years of service before him because he was a volunteer.

But I hadn't met anyone who had been in combat and it

became clear to me that that was exactly my neighbour's experience. 'You can't be too careful,' he said. 'Keep a low profile.' I kind of agreed but wearing a ring through your nose certainly attracted attention in the 1970s. 'You never know if they're dead or not.' And then he went into a kind of spasm, gibbering about a dead Gooks on the ground. I suppose this was some kind of flashback. One look at the poor guy's face told me that he was seriously disturbed. I immediately dropped the flip posture I had been affecting and suggested we go inside. He calmed down a bit and shuffled up to his room. No doubt what he needed was another therapy session with his girlfriend.

Clearly my new friend was suffering from post traumatic stress disorder, but that was a phrase I had not yet heard. And I'm sure the dope didn't help. Michael Herr's *Dispatches* didn't appear until the following year and Coppola's *Apocalypse Now* didn't come out until 1979. *M.A.S.H* was actually set in the Korean War, but for our generation it stood for the unfolding conflict in Viet Nam. Whilst it was astute about the pointlessness of war, it was also blind to its own gender and sexuality stereotyping. We certainly didn't need much persuading about the pointlessness of the conflict in Viet Nam. But we were only just beginning to understand its toll on the participants on both sides. The guy with the nose ring might have been getting a lot of sex, but he was not in a good place as the phrase has it. I often wondered what happened to him. It was hard to see him turning into the lawyer or architect that Reeves in due course became.

This was the early summer of 1976, renowned as one of the hottest and driest summers in modern times. The grass on Parker's Piece was scorched, transforming the birthplace of the rules of Association Football into a parched dustbowl. I had found a part-time job doing the washing-up in a restaurant on Hills Road in the evenings for a few weeks. But even in the evenings the heat was stifling, exacerbated by the exhaust heat from the kitchen equipment. I spent the daylight hours sheltering from the heat lying on my bed reading. On nights off from the restaurant I would meet Mark Evans for a drink in the Six Bells in Covent Garden or the Baker's Arms on East Road and a few games on the pinball machine, though neither of us was exactly in the wizard category as players. Mark, another Cambridge graduate putting his education to unconventional use, was working as a confectionery delivery man but told me one evening that he was planning to move to London and get a proper job. I knew he was right and that I would have to do the same, so a few days later I gave notice on my bedsit.

And instantly regretted it. Fortunately I was rescued from incipient homelessness by Roger Hones, one of the longest serving casuals at the theatre. He and his wife were going to the USA for five or six weeks over the summer and they needed someone to house-sit. Suddenly I went from the dismal bedsit near the station to a comfortable three bedroom house in Magrath Avenue. Roger was also known as Butch. In the normal way of things this would have been an ironic soubriquet. But in fact Roger was a mighty man. In his ordinary life he did something heavy duty like laying black stuff. But he and his wife were also enthusiasts for the theatre, she as an usherette, he as one of the stalwarts of the stage crew. There was something of the fairground or circus about both of them. This suspicion was underlined by the dusting of Polari and innuendo that Butch applied to his discourse. To be addressed by such a brawny individual as 'Petal' was a little disconcerting as was his habit of greeting you with a cheery 'How's your cock?' He and his wife were also great party givers and on those occasions when The Scaramouche, the main after-hours gay hang-out in those days, was unavailable, the after-show party would probably be held at their house.

I whiled away the next few weeks listening my way through Butch's record collection and came to appreciate for the first time how good Buddy Holly was. Butch had a collection of early Dylan LPs too, ending with *Highway 61 Revisited*. Clearly family or work responsibilities had interrupted his habit before he could buy the mighty *Blonde on Blonde*. But the sequence *Another Side of Bob Dylan*, *Bringing It All Back Home* and *Highway 61 Revisited* are Bob at his surrealistic best. That those three albums appeared in the 12 months from August 1964 to August 1965 is astonishing, given the uniformly high quality of the material, even on the slightly less well known *Another Side*. 'To Ramona' may have been addressed to Joan Baez, but by some syllabic alchemy which equated my name with the eponym of the song I took more heed of the lyrics than was entirely necessary and, just doing what I thought I should do, wrote to my old friends Henry Jones and Jane Garner who were living in London and asked if I could come and stay for a week or two.

# Doing the Strand

**H**ENRY WAS TEACHING AT a school off Kilburn High Road and Jane was completing her medical studies at University College Hospital. They shared a flat with another couple just off the Finchley Road and both couples were kind enough to let me sleep on the sofa for a few weeks whilst I looked for a job.

I thought it unlikely that I would get another job in stage management. The lack of an equity card seemed an insuperable barrier in the more professional world of London theatre, but right at that moment I didn't have any other ideas. So I trudged around a number of theatres receiving the same negative response at each. In mounting despair I called at the stage door office of the Adelphi Theatre in Maiden Lane just opposite Rules restaurant and asked whether they had stage crew work. Of course they didn't. But in a nice reversal of events from a couple of years earlier when I had first approached the Arts, I was told that there was a vacancy in the Box Office. I was taken through to meet the Box Office manageress who after a brief chat offered me the job subject to my passing an interview with 'Father', the General Manager. Inevitably the job involved shift work but at least we didn't work Sundays. The good thing was that it was a regular job and therefore salaried.

My interview with 'Father' was arranged for the next day when I was ushered into the presence of a splendidly urbane gentleman. The whole thing felt as if I were visiting my tutor. I half expected to be offered a glass of sherry. In the absence of a coherent employment history I noodled on about my love of the theatre and that seemed to do the trick. Either that or I was wearing the right kind of jeans. It was agreed that I would begin the following week. When I got back to Henry and Jane's flat I rang a few numbers in the accommodation section of *Time Out* without any success. No matter how early I got the magazine on the day of publication by the time I phoned every room seemed to have been snapped up. But I calculated that I hadn't yet outworn my welcome and so I began the job still living off the Finchley Road and threw myself into selling West End theatre tickets.

This was the era before computers and everything was paper-based. The only piece of technology we used was the telephone. There was a large printed seating plan of the theatre for each performance. Certain blocks of seats were allocated to the ticket agencies like Keith Prowse. We spent almost as much time on the phone to clerks at the various agencies as we did selling tickets over the counter. The Adelphi was a large theatre. The latest incarnation had been built in the 1930s in the Deco style with about 1,500 seats and so had to stage productions with wide appeal. This in effect meant big musicals and long runs. So for the whole time I was at the Adelphi I found myself selling tickets for *Irene* and only *Irene*. This musical had first been staged on Broadway in 1919 and had been a huge success, famous for the number 'You Made Me Love You'. To revive it for the London stage in the era of the Sex Pistols was quite a gamble but as it turned out one that repaid its backers handsomely. No doubt this was partly due to the inspired casting. The leading actors were Eric Flynn, who was familiar to audiences from his role as Ivanhoe in the BBC's 1970 television adaptation but who also had a fine singing voice, Jon Pertwee, who had been the third Doctor Who and the Australian soprano Julie Anthony. The show ran for more than 900 performances. I sold tickets for nearly 200 of those performances but somehow never got around to seeing it.

In retrospect it was just as well that I wasn't on the stage crew. Seeing the same production 200 times must be soul destroying. Not that selling tickets can be regarded as a stimulating occupation, but the general public can always be relied upon to make things interesting, particularly if they are American tourists. One thing that they seemed to find hard to understand was that we didn't accept US dollars. There was absolutely no denying that the greenback was the most powerful currency in the world but nevertheless it was not legal tender in the United Kingdom. Even as you patiently explained this fact they seemed additionally amazed that a dollar was worth less than a pound. Despite the fact that sterling had been in decline for decades and particularly in the 1970s the value of the pound on the currency markets had gyrated wildly it had still never fallen below parity with the dollar. This seemed to be regarded as some kind of insult by some of our American customers. Surely our quaint old money was nearly worthless.

In the same way that some of our American clients didn't understand why we couldn't accept their currency, my colleague Joyce, who was a real Cockney, couldn't understand why they in return couldn't understand her idiomatic English, not that she considered it idiomatic. So as the poor tourist eager to get a good seat to see *Irene* struggled to wonder whether the odd pound was a special kind of pound he might have in his pocket before realising that it meant paying a pound more than the actual amount proffered so that he could be given change as a £5 note, Joyce sat there drumming her fingers and sucking on her false teeth.

The one consolation over the months that I worked there was the vantage point that the theatre offered for watching the Queen's Silver Jubilee parade. Normally a royal parade would not be my cup of pageantry but we were required to come into work because once the parade had passed down the Strand to St Paul's we would have to open the theatre and get on with the business of selling tickets for *Irene*. During the parade itself we were required to keep the front doors shut because of the huge number of spectators on the pavement. By way of consolation 'Father' said that we could watch the parade from the Deco canopy of the theatre which projected over the pavement. I am no royalist but Britain does pageantry rather well. Our armed forces may be a cut-price vestige of their former glory. But when there is an opportunity to dress up and get on horseback, then we are still up there with the best.

If you have ever been in Paris on Bastille Day you will know that the French have some fine cavalrymen in beautiful uniforms. But they also insist on parading their missiles and tanks and all sorts of other hardware. In the spot I was standing near the *Hôtel de Ville* once, virtually every kind of vehicle in the French armed forces was represented. This included military fire-engines (*pompes de circonstance?*), trucks and bulldozers. At the head of each section a senior officer proudly wearing his regiment's ceremonial *képi* was placed in some prominent position in the lead vehicle. Clearly the regiment of military bulldozers, for example, was determined that the *képi* of their commander should not be left out of the reckoning. But not every kind of vehicle has a hatch for the commander, so in the case of the regiment of bulldozers this meant that the commander was perched in a rather precarious position above the driver.

The British armed forces no doubt have analogous units but they are seldom in evidence at ceremonial events. Our approach is much more firmly anachronistic. No ballistic missiles trundling through the streets for us and not just because they actually belong to the Americans. Because when it comes to a parade you really can't beat gleaming cuirasses and helmets with their white or red plumes and scarlet or blue tunics depending on the regiment. And instead of tanks we have fairy-tale coaches. I think on the day of the Queen's Silver Jubilee practically all the state coaches were deployed. landaus, barouches, perhaps a phaeton or two, but not a single armoured military vehicle.

From our vantage point on the canopy we got an unrivalled view of the whole thing. It even seemed that we got a special wave from the Queen. When the last horse had clopped by Father led us inside and we celebrated in the only way the British can with a cup of tea and slices of sponge cake. And then it was back to work. The theatre was packed that evening. Though there had been many critics of the arrangements for the Jubilee fearing that the whole thing would be a damp squib, in the end central London was packed with thousands of people and there were more than the usual number of American tourists too it seemed.

That turned out to be the high point of my time at the Adelphi. My colleagues were a pleasant bunch and the work was not onerous. It wasn't particularly well-paid but it enabled me to pay the rent on a small room in a shared house in Cricklewood. One of Henry's colleagues had told him that he was looking for another person for his house share. The only problem was the room was very small indeed. But after several weeks on a sofa, I was in no mood to reject the offer, no matter how small the room. I went over to take a look and we agreed terms immediately. The house was a largish 30s semi not too far from Willesden Green tube station. Even better the incumbents were a nice bunch of people whom I saw myself getting along with. In fact Henry's colleague, Jonah Best, had been at Cambridge a few years before us and now taught maths. He also had installed a DEC minicomputer in the school which he'd been offered by a local firm for free, if he made all the arrangements to transport it and set it up. This was extremely advanced for 1976-7 and even though my own programming exploits still lay a couple of years in the future I was already fascinated by the possibilities of applying computers to language and information. So Jonah and I hit it off immediately.

We shared other enthusiasms too, notably music. Even though I was a declared music lover I had never had my own hi-fi. This was partly a reluctance on my part to shell out the necessary ackers and partly because for several years I had lived in shared houses or on the sofas of generous friends. So I had either listened to LPs on the communal machine or entertained myself on my guitar. Consequently this meant that I didn't have many LPs and certainly didn't carry them with me as I drifted from gaff to gaff. At a time when an extensive LP collection was *de rigueur* for a serious *aficionado* I owned a mere handful of LPs and most of those were stored at my parents's house.

The only records I had bought as an undergraduate were Van Morrison's *Astral Weeks*, Django Reinhardt's *Swing 35-39, The Quintet of the Hot Club of France* on the Decca Eclipse label, *Julian Bream, The Golden Age of English Lute Music* on RCA Victor (track 2, 'Fantasia' by John Johnson particularly lovely), *What Were Once Vices Are Now Habits* by The Doobie Brothers, The Grateful Dead's *American Beauty*, *Clear Spot* by Captain Beefheart And The Magic Band and a recording of J S Bach's *The Art of Fugue* played on the Hilderbrandt Organ in the Church of St Wenceslas in Naumburg by Johannes Ernst Kohler on the Oryx label. The Hilderbrandt organ was built in 1747 and had been played by Bach himself. This recording was part of two disc set. Sadly I was unable to afford the second disc and so my knowledge of *The Art of Fugue* is even more incomplete than it might otherwise have been. Perhaps I had a couple of other LPs but I doubt if most of my friends would have been able to list their LPs on the back of a postcard.

Even if I now had the funds to buy a relatively decent system the box room I moved into in Blackstone Road was scarcely big enough to contain the single bed and a small chest of drawers. So my LPs remained at my parents. In order to reduce the burden of the rent the big downstairs front sitting-room was used as a bedroom by Jonah but in a communitarian remembrance of student bed-sitter days he allowed his room to be the common room of the house. Especially for the purposes of listening to music. Many of his students were from the Afro-Caribbean community and he had become a great enthusiast for the new wave of reggae that had been unleashed by the popularity of Bob Marley. His students gave him tips as to the hot new releases and he soon acquired an excellent reggae collection. Occasionally students would come to the house and it was clear that he was regarded as an honorary rastafarian—perhaps one of the very few ginger-haired ones. His collection numbered LPs by Burning Spear, *Party Time* by The Heptones, *War Ina Babylon* (Max Romeo), *Police and Thieves* by Junior Murvin, *Heart of the Congos* by The Congos, *Right Time* by the Mighty Diamonds and most iconically *Two Sevens Clash* by Culture.

This immersion in reggae culminated in our going to hear Marley play at the Rainbow in Finsbury Park in June 1977. One of the great pleasures of going to gigs in London in the seventies was that many of the venues were former cinemas from the golden age of the silver screen, as it were. Over the years I came to associate great rock music with surreal interiors, listening to

Van Morrison or Thin Lizzy in the pared back Art Deco exuberance of the Hammersmith Odeon or Nils Lofgren or Horslips beneath the stunning stained glass of the Venue in Victoria, formerly the Metropole. And when I lived in Cross Street in Islington I was fascinated by the bingo hall on the Essex Road which had once been an ABC Cinema. The facade of the building is in the form of an Egyptian temple all lotus flowers and buds in brightly coloured tiles just like a little bit of Luxor in N1. Apparently the interior was equally sumptuous but I could never pluck up the courage to submit to a session of bingo to confirm this.

But nothing compared to The Rainbow in Finsbury Park. Built in 1930 as one of the monumental Astoria cinemas, by 1971 the building had ceased to screen films and became one of the leading music venues in London. The plain tiled exterior of the Rainbow gives no suggestion of the wonders of the interior. In the centre of the octagonal lobby is a large fountain in a star-shaped pool as you might find in the Alhambra or the Casa de Pilatos in Seville, the whole space brightly decorated in Art Deco zigzag. Extending the Moorish theme each bay of the octagon has a balcony with brass deco railings and star-shaped chandelier. The lobby itself is set at an angle to and below the main body of the building so that you must first ascend a grand staircase and then bear to the right before entering the auditorium, which is breath-taking in its scale and magnificence. The proscenium and the areas to the left and right of the stage are presented as a full scale replica of a Moorish castle and village with windows turrets and balconies. The stage itself is the main gate into this Andalusian wonderland.

In June 1977 this extravaganza was the setting for a series of performances by the combined forces of two of the biggest reggae acts of that summer Junior Murvin, whose Lee Perry produced *Police and Thieves* had broken through to a non-reggae audience and Bob Marley still the doyen of reggae, whose sublime *Exodus* was one of stand-out albums of the year. Jonah managed to get us some tickets satisfyingly forward in the stalls. It was a day I was working and I arrived a little late so that the band was already chugging along as I found my way to my seat.

65

The sound was immensely infectious and as I moved down the aisle my gait morphed into a shy skank. Sound systems might not have been as sophisticated as they have since become but the Wailers was a band at the height of its powers and Marley was one of the outstanding performers of his era able to imbue the rather wonky doctrinal ideas of rastafarianism with a compelling and humanitarian urgency.

The weirdest aspect of rastafarianism is the way in which it is focussed on the person of Haile Selassie. In fact Haile Selassie is a title. The name of the man who was Emperor of Ethiopia (1930-74) was Tafari Makonnen and Ras is a title roughly equivalent to Prince or Duke. In the rasta interpretation of the bible Zion is the Promised Land which happens to be Ethiopia and Babylon is western civilization. Haile Selassie is the Lion of Judah, an incarnation of Christ, sometimes referred to as Jah Rastafari, Jah being equivalent to the Old Testament Jahweh. So this was why the stage of the Rainbow was dominated by an image of the Lion of Judah with the face of Haile Selassie superimposed on it. In the rituals of Rastafarianism cannabis occupies a sacramental role and the pipe is sometimes referred to as a chalice. To judge from the 'natural mystic' swirling around me as I took my seat the sacrament was being furtively celebrated by many members of the audience although in an entirely undoctrinal way.

The idea of return to the promised land of Zion is linked for some in ideas of repatriation to Africa and the pan-african ideas of Marcus Garvey, famous, at least in reggae music, as the founder of the Black Star shipping line whose aim was to return members of the African diaspora to their ancestral lands. That the imputed ancestral land is considered to be Ethiopia is at odds with the fact that the majority of Afro-Caribbeans are probably of West African descent. But many in the Rasta community revere Garvey as a kind of John the Baptist figure, although Garvey was never a Rasta and in fact had become a Roman Catholic at the time of his death.

It goes without saying that it is not at all necessary to be convinced by the ideology of rastafarianism to enjoy the music. And this was one of the great gigs of the seventies. Actually

Marley was not at all well during the four nights of the Rainbow concerts. Not that you could have guessed from the passion and energy that he put into the performance I witnessed. There was much speculation at the time about what was ailing Marley including the fact that he had injured himself in a football match. It has since become clear that he had developed a malignant melanoma under the nail of a toe. Because of his religious beliefs and against medical advice he refused to have the toe amputated but agreed to the removal of the nail and a skin graft to cover the site and in due course the cancer spread to his brain and lungs and he died in 1981. The graft seems not to have responded well to the pressures of touring and by the time of the London shows seems to have resulted in serious bleeding. Consequently the next stage of the tour which was due to take in the United States was cancelled.

Despite heavy exposure to the rasta vibration I was unable to give up my affiliation to the old wave of rock artists and modestly expanded my own record collection to include Van Morrison's *A Period of Transition*, Led Zeppelin's *Presence*, 801's *801 Live* and Pink Floyd's *Animals*. But 1977 was also famously the year of punk. If, under Jonah's influence, I had embraced, to an extent, the reggae tendency, I wasn't yet ready to embrace this new wave of white popular music.

The utopian dreams of the 60s and early 70s had evaporated in the face of industrial relations turmoil, raging inflation and the running sore of Irish republican terrorism. Hippy rhapsodies and progressive rock symphonies no longer seemed an appropriate soundtrack to everyday life. But millionaire popular musicians insulated by the windfall of wealth merely ranted at the level of income tax and in many cases fled to jurisdictions with less punitive tax rates. The rage at the depredations of the taxman was not exactly new in the popular music field. The opening track of The Beatles 1966 album *Revolver* written by George Harrison was 'Taxman' ('There's one for you, nineteen for me' and references to Heath and Wilson). And also in 1966 Ray Davies had released 'Sunny Afternoon' with the opening lyrics 'The taxman's taken all my dough and left me in my stately home lazing on a sunny afternoon.' Davis claims that the song's protagonist is a feckless aristocrat. But the casual listener could be forgiven for thinking that the stately home he's lazing around in belongs to the successful pop singer.

So far as it goes the lyrics to the Beatles' 'Taxman' were accurate. The highest rate of income tax had peaked at 99.25% during the Second World War. It dropped after the war but only slightly. Through the 1950s and 1960s the highest rate of tax remained at 90%. By 1971, however, the Heath government reduced the top rate on earned income to 75% but a 15% surcharge on investment income meant that for the wealthiest the combined top rate of tax remained at 90%. And then in 1974 in response to the turmoil caused by the huge increase in oil prices and the inflationary expectations that this had unleashed the incoming Wilson administration raised the combined rate to 98%, the highest rate since the war. At the same time corporation tax was increased to 52% and even the basic rate of tax went up to 33%. Eventually in 1975 inflation hit an eye-watering 25%. In just one year rail fares had doubled, the cost of electricity had risen by 66% and coal by 47%. The roll-call of British artists heading off to other tax jurisdictions included the Rolling Stones, Rod Stewart and David Bowie. In an ostentatious act of faith in the UK, the era's most successful recording artist stayed put. Elton John had sales of 28 million records in 1975 alone. The revenue that this generated was phenomenal but after tax Mr Dwight only got 2p in every pound.

Not surprisingly it was not just rock stars who had had enough. Starting in 1974 and continuing for the next three years the number of people emigrating from the UK exceeded the number of immigrants. In fact for the first time since records had been compiled the UK's net population declined. Much of this was down to a declining birth rate but the net outward migration did not help. Perhaps most alarmingly between 1961 and 1971 the population of Greater London had dropped by 600,000. And for those that stayed the situation was pretty miserable with the median monthly disposable income of British households declining year on year between 1974 and 1977.

At the same time the number of people out of work increased

dramatically to reach 1.4 million and naturally enough a growing number of these were young people. So it was hardly surprising that there was a ready audience for a style of music that might reflect this sense of hopelessness. The standard bearers for this new attitude were of course the Sex Pistols managed with foxlike cunning by the wily Malcolm MacLaren. The definitive account of this period in English popular music is analysed in Jon Savage's *England's Dreaming*. As I stood on the canopy of the Adelphi Theatre and pretended not to be impressed by the pageantry of the Queen's Silver Jubilee, the Sex Pistols second single, 'God Save The Queen', was generating the expected outrage. To retired majors from the shires and many people for whom the Second World War was still a recent memory Johnny Rotten represented all that was wrong with modern Britain.

Typically, what was elided by the weight of the opprobrium was the fact that Johnny Rotten was merely a persona. The real person behind the mask was a young north Londoner, John Lydon. You might as well lay the blame for the decline in British public life at the feet of Mr Pastry or James Bond. The fact that a pop group could evoke such a reaction is a tribute to how well they had mastered the semiotics of the media. And in the inevitable reversal Lydon has now entered the hallowed company of English eccentrics as a kind of Artful Dodger and the song is reinterpreted almost as a defence of the Queen and the deep traditions of English culture.

And certainly the song itself is elliptical and antithetical enough to yield contradictory readings. 'Fascist regime' is not necessarily in apposition to the Queen and indeed later in the song the singer claims to love the Queen, which despite the sneering 'We mean it man' is not necessarily ironic. The fifth verse begins 'Oh, God save history' extending the benediction to a 'mad parade' not unlike the one I was observing from the canopy of the Adelphi and inviting the obvious identification of the Queen and history. Then after begging God for mercy in general the singer notes that 'All crimes are paid.' And the next verse goes on to say that when there is no future, as the singer reiterates throughout the song, there can be no sin. The absolution of past crimes and the abolition of future sins at this moment in a royal cavalcade suggest something millennial. The identification of the Queen with history is amplified by the lines 'she ain't no human being' and then later 'our figurehead is not what she seems' which is only surprising to the extent that it implies a view bordering on the mystical. Of course if you chose to, you could read this as suggesting the monarchy was finished and the Queen inhuman, which was a reading of the song popular in the mainstream media at the time. The 'flowers in the dustbin' are the rising generation for whom there are few opportunities and inevitably they will become 'the poison in your human machine' or 'a potential H-bomb', the new destabilising element in society. The crimes that will have to be paid for are those that have been committed by the establishment in blighting the future for the new generation. They will only have themselves to blame if the retribution that they face is violent and destructive. No doubt in the flickering semantics of the song both readings are valid.

The twin-pronged assault on rock music by punk and reggae set me to thinking about change in popular culture, indeed change in anything. In the ferment of revolutionary movements there is a tendency to forget the old saying—*plus ça change, plus c'est la même chose*. Notwithstanding the triteness of this insight I decided to portray the idea as it applied to popular music in dramatic form. I started to sketch out a play in my spare time. Having been knocked back by both TV and radio and inspired by the production of *The Illuminatus!* that I'd seen at The National Theatre in March I decided to write something for the stage.

Ken Campbell's version of *The Illuminatus!* made me realise that the stage was probably the medium best suited to portraying the anarchic and not just to the extent that the production might involve bad language, nudity and a non-judgemental view of the drug culture. In the event the play I wrote had no nudity, no sex and rather innocuous bad language. It did address drug usage but mostly as a metaphor. The play was called *Get Out Of It* and of course that was a phrase with drug culture connotations. To get out of it was to get stoned or to trip out. But it had other overtones. 'Get out of it' was a phrase from an earlier generation meaning 'You must be kidding' or 'I don't believe you'. In the imperative mood it is also a command to leave this place, to extricate yourself from a situation. Absurdly I wanted to write a play that picked up all these meanings through the depiction of an established mode of popular music being swept away by a new aesthetic. The rock establishment was to be represented by a Syd Barrett type figure, a genius recluse who has burnt out by, it is rumoured, having taken too many drugs. The new wave is represented by a Johnny Rotten figure. The dramatic link between the two is personified by a Jerry Hall type character who transfers her affection from one to the other, though in the case of Hall, it is arguable that her direction of travel was in the opposite direction, from new wave (Bryan Ferry) to old (Mick Jagger). To complicate matters further I wanted to portray the Syd character as a sacred king or oracular hero along the lines of Sir James Frazer's *The Golden Bough* and Robert Graves's *The White Goddess* who is replaced by his rival or, borrowing a term from Graves, his tanist.

This, of course, was entirely the wrong way to go about writing a play. The dramatic situation I had conceived was too slight to carry the freight of this imagery. Somewhere Les Murray, the great Australian poet, has said that an idea is the worst thing to start building a poem from. Not that it is impossible, but the result is likely to be rather thin gruel. The same thing holds for drama. The more schematic the structure, the less believable the characters and the less true to life the situation. The weeks went by and my compositional struggles resulted in a few weedy pages of stilted dialogue. Even worse, my characters failed to come alive on the page, so what chance had they of convincing on the stage? In time honoured fashion instead of accepting that my initial idea was a poor one, I concluded that what was holding me back was my environment. The slight demands of my job and the somewhat more insistent demands of my domestic situation i.e. non-stop house party meant that I seldom managed a sustained period of work on the play. So the obvious solution was that I should give up my job and my room in the house in Cricklewood and move to somewhere remote and extremely cheap. In effect I was going to have to apply to my own life the command implicit in the title of the play in order to get it finished.

# Getting out of it

Almost as soon as I had conceived this ridiculous plan, which was really just a massive exercise in procrastination, I stumbled on the means to realise it in the classified ads pages of Private Eye. A remote cottage near Dalmally in the West Highlands was available to rent for six months. It would suit a writer. I phoned the number immediately and spoke to a woman called Julia Keay. I told her something of myself and that I was looking for a place where I could finish the piece of writing I was working on. This made complete sense to her she said as her own husband was a writer. It turned out that the cottage was pretty basic but it was available immediately and that so far as she was concerned the cottage was mine. I calculated quickly how much notice I would need to give at work and to my housemates and proposed a date. That was also fine and no she didn't need a deposit. I put the phone down and let a curiously pleasant feeling of uncertainty wash over me. Two or three weeks later at the beginning of October found myself on the coach to Edinburgh. I stayed the night in Christina's flat in New Town and the next day got the train to Glasgow and then made my way to Queen Street station for the train to Oban.

My new landlady, Julia, had told me that the cottage was a couple of miles outside the actual village of Dalmally and then a further two miles up a track on the lower slopes of Ben Lui. Ideally I should have had good waterproof clothes and boots just to get there. But in fact I was wearing my everyday city hipster clothes, jeans and flimsy footgear. In a misguided attempt to preserve as much money as possible from my Adelphi earnings I had taken the decision not to buy any new clothes or equipment on the shaky premise enunciated by Thoreau not to engage on any project that needed new clothes. In fact Thoreau's advice is not so much about conserving one's slender means as not to pretend to be something one is not. 'I say, beware of all enterprises that require new clothes, and not rather a new wearer of clothes.' Was I that new wearer? Only time would tell.

In the meantime the little train set off from Queen Street. Initially it trundled through Hillhead keeping the Clyde on our left and then headed up towards Dumbarton and Helensburgh all the while the Clyde broadening out into a sea loch. Then the line skirted Gareloch and Faslane. No doubt I had heard of Faslane, but as we rumbled onwards I gave no thought at all to the fact that this was the home of Polaris, the UK's nuclear deterrent. But terrible as this weapon was, it was already becoming obsolete and the government now headed by Jim Callaghan since Harold Wilson's resignation the previous year was considering a replacement. The preferred option was to acquire the American's Trident system but it was not at all clear that the USA was of the same mind. A couple of years later, however, Callaghan saw his chance to put pressure on Jimmy Carter at the infamous 1979 summit in the Caribbean on his return from which he never uttered the words 'Crisis. What crisis?'

We are still living with the divisions in public opinion this decision has provoked. On the one hand Faslane employs thousands of people in the Glasgow area and the possession of Trident enables the UK to continue to consider itself a great power. On the other hand the use of such a weapon would signify the failure of a defence strategy based on mutually assured destruction, even assuming that the Americans would ever let us use the weapon without their permission. The enormous expense involved has meant the relentless withering of more conventional defence arrangements. The Falklands War was still some years in the future but the cuts necessitated by the concentration of defence spending on a nuclear deterrent was one of the factors that encouraged the Argentinian Junta to invade las Malvinas.

It is odd, on reflection, that my attempt to get out of it, to find somewhere remote to write my play, had landed me up not too far from a site which must have been heavily targeted by Soviet missiles. To think of it in *Lord Of The Rings* terms, it was as if I had set out for Rivendell only to find that I had arrived at Orthanc, the black tower of Isengard. And isn't there something quintessentially Tolkienesque about a weapon that can never be used, but the possession of which creates the illusion of security? If I had any thoughts along these lines, they were soon interrupted by the glorious sight of Loch Lomond appearing on the opposite side of the train. At the end of the loch we stopped at Ardlui and then headed on to Crianlarich where the track divided and we swung around to the west to skirt Ben Lui heading towards Tyndrum and Dalmally.

It was already late afternoon when we arrived in Dalmally and so it was completely dark by the time I had trudged up the track to Succoth. Julia introduce me to her husband John Keay and I was invited in for a drink and something to eat. John and Julia were too kind to say it but I think they had imagined I was going to be arriving in a car. My meagre pack must have seemed unlikely to contain enough to keep me going for the next few months. When we had finished our meal John took me across the estate to the cottages which were at various stages of renovation. The one I was renting was basically a two up two down. It was used mainly by walkers and climbers. There was a range in the kitchen and a couple of battered armchairs in the sitting room. Between the two rooms there was a small bathroom and toilet and upstairs two bedrooms. Perfect for my needs. In fact more space than I had ever occupied on my own. John said there was no heating apart from that generated by the range but I could gather as much firewood as I wanted, although he did warn me that I would have to cut it myself and it was likely to be quite wet. He also pointed out that Succoth was not connected to the grid. They generated their own electricity from a diesel generator in a nearby barn. Because of the cost of oil they only ran the generator for a couple of hours in the morning and then for four or five hours in the evening. Not surprisingly there was no TV in the cottage, but that was fine by me as the main reason for my being there was so that I could get on with my writing.

I then remembered that Julia had said that John was himself a writer. So I asked him what he was working on. He told me that he had travelled extensively in the Himalayas and India where he had been a correspondent for *The Economist*. The fruit of this experience was a book called *Into India* which had been published by John Murray in 1973. His second book, *When Men and Mountains Meet*, the first volume in a two volume history of the European discovery of the Himalayas, had been published earlier that year also by John Murray. He was now nearing completion on the second volume to be called *The Gilgit Game*. John was older than me but still a young man, perhaps about 35 at that time. This already seemed a formidable achievement for one so young since he was unattached to any academic establishment and had a young family to support. He courteously asked me about my own work. I admitted that I had no publishing credits but that I was working on a stage play, having worked in the theatre since I graduated. He didn't seem to find this as ridiculous as I thought it sounded. He then bade me good night and left me to my first night in the cottage. I made up the bed in one of the bedrooms and settled down to read myself to sleep.

After reading only a few pages the electric light went off as predicted and since I had not thought to bring any candles up with me, I gave myself up to sleep. Or at least tried to. For the previous few years I had been living in an urban environment and like most urban dwellers found the constant noise of human activity weirdly comforting. But perched here on the lower slopes of Ben Lui there was absolutely no sound of human activity at all. There was only the soughing of the wind in the trees, the creaking of the old house and the rattling of branches against the window. And it was very dark. I am not particularly easy to spook but once your ear starts to try and identify particular noises your level of alertness increases considerably. No doubt this is an evolutionary adaptation that helped us to survive in the countless millennia before we developed permanent dwellings, but like all innate tendencies it is hard to deactivate once engaged. Eventually I managed to drift off to sleep but in my dreams the glen which I had not yet seen in daylight was full of noises and twangling instruments. After a few days and nights I adjusted to the rural quietness and velvety dark and thereafter regained my customary sound sleep.

Over the next few weeks I got to know John and Julia and their children. They had a marvellous bohemian, intellectual lifestyle. In the mornings John would set off up the glen on a long walk with his two red setters. Later in the day he would do work around the smallholding. They had some livestock, a pig, a couple of geese and some chickens. The plan was to fatten the goose for Christmas but the goose had other ideas and refused to stay in its pen. Its wings were going to have to be seriously clipped if there were to be any serious hopes of having a plump goose for the festive table. But no one had the heart to treat it quite so harshly at this stage of proceed-ings and the magnificent beast was allowed to rule the rather restricted roost. The pig, too, was eventually destined for the table. I found this fact a little more upsetting because whereas the goose was rather an aggressive character, the pig was an extremely friendly beast and seemed to welcome my morning visits with the scraps from my breakfast. In the end I was able to resist sentimentalising the fate of these creatures who were being reared for food but who in the meantime were well cared for and living what seemed a pleasant life compared to what I imagined more intensively reared animals experienced. This blithe attitude was dented when I learned from John that the plan was to slaughter the pig on the premises. They would of course bring in a properly qualified slaughterman but John said that he would be the assistant and wondered whether I would be interested in witnessing the event. I accepted the invitation but not without some misgivings. Thankfully the fatal day was not for some time yet. So there was still time for me to change my mind or better accommodate myself to the idea.

After the family supper John would withdraw to his study and work through the evenings on his next book. How I envied the way that he had constructed his life; a beautiful wife, delightful children, an idyllic habitation, physical work, proper exercise and sustained intellectual endeavour. My own life seemed chaotic, insubstantial, almost fraudulent by comparison. From my little living room window I could see John in his rustic but impressive book-lined study. I imagined him as a two or three thousand words a day man. Not only that but he was a writer of non-fiction, predominantly historical and geographical subjects so there was a huge amount of research involved too.

As many a writer knows only too well when the blank page beckons almost any research no matter how obscure and tangential seems to have an irresistible allure. Well, I speak for myself, of course. And that was why, in a feeble attempt to counter my procrastinative tendencies, the only book I had brought with me was the hard tack of Defoe's *Robinson Crusoe,* a book about getting lost, but perhaps not one to get lost in. In fact whilst *Robinson Crusoe* is not without interest, it is perhaps not the best text to stimulate the composition of a new work of poetically tinged drama. I might have been better advised, following the rubric of Desert Island Discs, to have brought a copy of the works of Shakespeare or a copy of the Bible. In retrospect I think that almost anything would have been better than *Robinson Crusoe*. Part of the problem was that it is so eminently readable that I had finished it within a couple of days of arrival. What I really needed was something that might have offered more resistance, *Bleak House*, perhaps, or *Great Expectations*. Or *Moby Dick* or *Ulysses*. Or even *Finnegans Wake*, God dammit. I prided myself on having read a fair few unreadable books whilst having neglected most of the classics that should stock a well-read mind. But here I was having read *Robinson Crusoe*, which was both eminently readable and a classic to boot, twice or perhaps thrice. Not good. Not good at all for the hipster credentials.

Meanwhile having despatched Robinson's adventures in short order I had little choice but to resume work on the play which was after all my reason for being in that beautiful but desolate spot. But it was a terrible struggle. It would be a good day if I managed to complete more than a page of serviceable dialogue. I wondered what the secret to John's huge productivity was and decided that it must be his routine, particularly his daily walk and I thought I would try and emulate him. But I was thwarted by my lack of proper equipment. The one pair of shoes I had brought with me were far from waterproof and would soon have disintegrated once I deviated from the main track up from the road. I decided that I would have to go into Dalmally and see if I could buy some boots. The following day I bumped into John and asked him if there was somewhere in the village that sold boots. By way of reply John asked me my shoe size and said that he had an old pair he thought might fit me. So the next morning as soon as there was enough light I walked up through the forestry commission plantation to the deer fence which I walked along until I came to a gate which let me through into the tussocky, peaty slopes of Ben Lui.

Once out of the trees and high enough up, the views were spectacular. Over the years Henry had tried hard to persuade me of the pleasures of the uplands but I had always maintained that I saw nothing wrong with a fenland sky nor come to that a site of urban archaeology such as I might be guided around by Tim Mars. The people I knew who were keen on hillwalking and mountaineering seemed to be almost as interested in the acquisition of specialist kit and the completion of obscure rituals like Munro bagging. But once I got up above the deer fence and the view across to Ben Cruachan opened up I began to get an inkling of what attracted people to the high places of the Earth.

When I next saw John he asked me how I had got on with the boots and I described to him as best I could where I'd walked to and perhaps I waxed a little lyrical about the magic of the mountains. He said that in that case I might be interested in reading *When Men and Mountains Meet*. I accepted his kind offer enthusiastically. I certainly needed some relief from my own halting dramaturgy. A little later when John brought over a copy of the book I wondered whether I might have got myself into an embarrassing situation. Despite the fact that I had made a couple of sorties beyond the deer fence, the truth was that I hadn't got very high or very far and I feared that detailed accounts of base camps on south cols would soon exhaust my interest. I would then have to work out a way of saying something nice about the book. The author would no doubt expect not just approbation but a telling reference to that one recondite detail which would show that I had read with my attention fully engaged. But I needn't have worried. The book was irresistible and I read it in a few days.

John seemed to appreciate my comments about his book and said that he had just completed a draft of *The Gilgit Game*, the second volume in the sequence. Would I be interested in reading that in typescript? I was in fact delighted by the suggestion. Not just because I had found the first volume so interesting. It would be instructive to see a professional writer's work in embryo. When I agreed John asked whether I'd also be prepared to do a degree of proof-reading, bring to his attention any typos or obvious omissions. As it turned out the draft was remarkably clean and my proofreaderly comments were few. Either John's first drafts were very polished or I was an inattentive proofreader. Nevertheless John said he'd found my notes useful and gave me a signed copy of *When Men and Mountains Meet* in recompense. This volume still occupies a place of honour on my bookshelves.

I was starting to enjoy the texture of life, working my way methodically through John's typescript, increasingly adventurous walks through the woods and glens and a few lines of dialogue added to the play every day. The only cloud on the horizon was the parlous state of my bank account. It was clear that despite my thriftiness I was soon going to run out of funds and wouldn't be able to pay my rent. Though it had not been part of my original plan, it now occurred to me that I might be able to sign on at the local Labour Exchange or Job Centre as it was now known. I wasn't sure what the attitude would be to a theatrical refugee from London signing on in Dalmally with little likelihood of being able to get to a place of work unless it was located in one of the surrounding Forestry Commission plantations, but I thought I'd give it a go.

Not surprisingly, there was no Job Centre in Dalmally. The nearest one was in Oban, a few stops further up the West

Highland line. I assembled the documents that I thought I might need and one grey day in early winter made my way to Oban. No doubt Oban is attractive in the summer with lots going on in the harbour and holiday makers milling around. But in November it presented a fairly forbidding appearance. I also imagined that the local bureaucrats who, I nervously assumed, would be of a Calvinist disposition might look askance at my registering as unemployed and perhaps in need of supplementary benefit as it was then called. But I needn't have worried, everyone behaved as if it were the most natural thing in the world. There was not even the slightest suggestion that I might have to present myself for a job interview somewhere. This was after all 1977 and the unemployment rate was approaching 1.5 million, the highest it had been in terms of headcount since the thirties. Of course in percentage terms the thirties had been much worse. In 1933 nearly a quarter of the workforce was unemployed. But although not on anything like that scale the figures were still shocking in that they had doubled since 1975. The jobs were simply not available especially in a remote rural area like the West Highlands. Even better, from a selfish perspective, I was only required to present myself every other week to sign on.

So began a period in which I would tootle into Oban once a fortnight and having made my mark in the register, picked up my giro and cashed it, nip into one of the pubs on the front for a quick pint. This was not quite as reckless as it might seem because for the remainder of the fortnight I was effectively teetotal. One curious feature of the pub that I frequented was that it was presided over by a Mynah bird with an extensive range of phrases. Clearly the phrases had been acquired from different regulars because whilst the predominant accent was West Highlands, there was also a certain amount of variation and even one or two phrases in Received Pronunciation. The uncanny effect was that a virtually empty bar might at times sound reasonably full. As I sat there sipping my pint it occurred to me that the absurdist dialogues the bird was generating had an *élan* missing from my own laboriously crafted lines. For a while I toyed with the idea of abandoning the play and starting a new piece which would in effect be a transcription of the bird's utterances. I even devised a title for the piece-—*Mynah Variations*. In the end I didn't have the bottle, but in a parallel universe I am a noted avant-gardist with a highly productive aviary.

Towards Christmas John mentioned that he and Julia and the kids had a social event to attend in London. They would like to be away for several days but there were the dogs to be walked and the livestock to be fed. Was that something I would be prepared to do? And in general keep an eye on the place. The dogs were a pair of Red Setter sisters. I had already made friends with them and they would often come into my cottage, but John thought it might be a good idea if I took them out a few times whilst he was still around. John warned me that they fancied their chances chasing deer but that in reality they were never going to get close. Nevertheless it was a wonderful sight to see them bounding through the woods their beautiful red coats streaming in the wind. Taking them for a walk was actually something of a misnomer. At first I was worried that I might lose them. But they knew the paths and routes much better than me and clearly expected a proper walk, the kind they got from John, not half measures. They must have sensed that I was not as confident or as firm in my handling of them and the walks seemed to get longer and longer.

The only real concern I had was that one of the bitches was a bit of a killer. She had not been allowed to have pups like her sister, perhaps because she was rather more neurotic. But it is also possible that the neuroticism was a consequence of her barrenness allied to the fact that Red Setters are quite highly strung. I was not enough of a dog wrangler to be able to determine the matter. The result was that she liked to terrorise the chickens and occasionally kill one. No doubt *pour encourager les autres*. Throughout my tour of duty I worried that the Keays might return to a depleted flock of chickens but thankfully there were no poultry casualties during my short time in charge. I also became even better friends with the pig because I was now providing it with all its food not just a few scraps. Sadly the end of this deepening relationship was presaged when the Keays returned to Succoth with John telling me that he had booked a date with the local slaughterman to kill and butcher the pig.

In the end my curiosity overcame my squeamishness and I decided to witness the event. Traditionally a pig is bled whilst it is still alive, but it had been decided to modify this approach slightly in the interests of a more humane procedure. The pig was led out of its pen to the barn where an old bath had been set up with a block and tackle securely attached to one of the rafters over the bath. The pig seemed calm and not at all apprehensive. Gently the slaughterman produced a rifle put it to the head of the pig and pulled the trigger. The pig fell over to one side at which point John put the hook end of the tackle through the rear hock of the pig and the two of them swung the sizeable beast into the air over the bath. The slaughterman then cut the pig's throat and there seemed to be enough vitality in its body to pump out a huge amount of blood into the bath. Copious amounts of boiling water had been prepared and with this and sharp blades the pig's bristles were shaved off. The bath of blood was moved out of the way and covered and the slaughterman got ready to gut the beast.

I suddenly realised that this was the point at which my curiosity had been satisfied and I announced that I had an urgent appointment with a blank page. John and the slaughterman worked on for some hours until the pig had been neatly deconstructed. When I dared emerge again from my cottage I was amazed at the transfiguration of my old friend. I wasn't particularly surprised at the full hams that were going to be hung to cure or the chops and steaks. I wasn't even particularly surprised at the noble beast's sightless head looking at me because I had taken part in a Boar's Head feast in the shared house I was briefly living some years before. But I was surprised at the way the intestines were being neatly cleaned. This was the first time that I realised that the traditional material for sausage skins was in fact the pig's own intestine. John was planning to make his own sausages and salami and so he was making as much use of the carcass as he could. Even the blood was going to be used to make black pudding or highland boudin. I had some of the sausages in due course and they were delicious.

A few days later I received a letter from my parents wondering if they might see me at Christmas and so I missed the less poignant end of the goose. Despite the fact that it had not been fattened as tradition demanded, it had been pronounced good eating. When I returned to Dalmally a few days after New Year the snow had fallen and the temperature had dropped considerably. It was as if some alpine transformation had taken place. I wondered if the Keays had a toboggan. I was also looking forward to resuming my forest walks with the dogs. But the change in climactic conditions did present the problem of keeping my living space at a reasonable temperature. I had failed to stockpile any wood before I went away and now conditions were not ideal for gathering new fuel. I consulted John and he said that there was a coal merchant in Dalmally and that I could use the phone to place an order. I apologised to the person who answered my call that I would not be able to collect the coal myself. It turned out that the price included delivery even when I explained that I lived at Succoth.

The next day I looked out of the cottage window to see a mighty figure in a kilt, with bare legs and hob-nailed boots trudging up the snowy path to my cottage with a bag of coal on his shoulder. It was the coal merchant. He had only been able to get part way on the track to Succoth because of the snow and had come the rest of the way on foot. I was uncomfortably poised between embarrassment that my small order had taken so much personal effort and the realisation that a bigger order would have involved him in even more improbable physical effort. I thanked him profusely and offered him a cup of tea but he seemed not in the slightest dismayed by the situation, declined my offer politely and set off back to his truck in the snow. I came to realise that this was the standard attitude to service in the Highlands. The postman adopted the same approach during the bad weather. Even if there was only one letter to deliver he would get as far he could in his van and then come the rest of the way on foot to deliver a billet-doux from Christina or a surreally decorated envelope from Tim Mars.

One service which was less than equal to the weather conditions, however, was the supplier of oil for the electricity generator. The fuel for the generator was about to run out and the suppliers said that they would be unable to get a tanker up the track. The best they could do would be to drop off a 56 gallon barrel at the bottom of the track. John agreed to this and asked me if I would be able to help him get the barrel up to Succoth. I was happy to help but puzzled as to what he had in mind.

The idea was that we were going to drive the Land Rover to a loading platform belonging to a farm just off the main road where the barrel had been left, roll the barrel into the back of the Land Rover and then drive up the snowy track in low gear using four-wheel drive. Land Rovers are famed for their sure-footedness and really he only needed my help to get the barrel into the back of the vehicle and then off again when we got to the barn in which the generator was located. As we went down the track I think we both realised that it might not be such an easy job. There had been a lot of snow and even in four-wheel drive the Land Rover was sliding around quite a lot. Once we saw the barrel we were even more sure that it was going to be tricky. But we soon managed to manoeuvre the barrel onto the back of the Land Rover because the loading platform was at exactly the right height and we didn't have to do any lifting. John got into the driver's seat and suggested I get in the back and try and keep the barrel steady. That was easier said than done. Part of the problem was that the barrel was heavy and all the weight was over the rear axle. Because of its size and shape we had been unable to secure it and at times with the incline of the hill the barrel would roll back and lift the front of the Land Rover reducing the amount of grip from the front wheels. John shouted at me to try an keep the barrel steady but I was reluctant to get right behind it. Eventually we reached a flat part of the track and John pulled over for a breather and to review the situation.

As we caught our breath he asked me whether I drove. I said I was an experienced driver and had passed my test within a few weeks of my seventeenth birthday. Thereafter apart from the family cars I had driven tractors and dumper trucks during vacation jobs and of course I was something of a whizz on milk floats. He didn't seem convinced and as it turned out my milk float credentials were of little relevance to what he had in mind. Would I be prepared to drive whilst he got in the back and tried to stop the barrel moving around quite so much? I gulped and agreed even though I felt that I'd much rather do the job in the back. I wished I hadn't mentioned tractors and dumper trucks. The fact was that I had been sacked from that particular holiday job when the dumper truck I was driving had gone over the edge of a steep bank on a building site and smashed into a pile of roofing tiles.

Whilst I was wondering whether in a spirit of full disclosure I ought to allude to this particular incident or not John jumped in the back and nodded at me to get the Land Rover on the move. I was feeling a little panicky because I knew that the track got steeper and that we also had to cross a bridge over the river. I put the Land Rover in gear and accelerated slowly. John shouted that I'd need to give it more gas if we were going to get up the slope. I did my best but innate caution and the way the Land Rover squirmed in the snow and slush prevented me from being as bold as the situation demanded. When we came to the bridge the camber of the track took us perilously close to the low wall of the bridge. John shouted something, I gulped, pushed the accelerator hard and we shot over the bridge. This was of course too fast and as the barrel jerked backwards John nearly fell off. I thought I could hear him cursing me but by now my one goal was to get the Land Rover to the top and hand back the ignition keys. Eventually more by luck than driving skill we reached the barn and the only damage was to my reputation as on off-road driver.

The problem now was how to get the oil into the reservoir of the generator. The tanker had a pump, but we were pumpless. Whilst we had a cup of tea John thought about it and decided that the only thing to do was to try and siphon it. He found some tubing, got himself in position on the generator tank and then very bravely sucked on the end of the tube until he tasted oil. Fortunately this got the flow going and he was able to transfer enough fuel to see us through until a tanker was able to get up the track. I realised then if I hadn't before that he was just the sort of guy you wanted to have around when you were in a tight spot.

The snow lasted for quite a few more weeks and despite the acquisition of more coal, conditions in the cottage deteriorated. One night I woke up and realised that there was frost on the bed covers and my feet felt numb. I decided that I'd better go downstairs and sleep in front of the range. Even so it took quite a while for the circulation in my feet to return to normal. For the next few nights I camped downstairs and decided that I wouldn't return to the bedroom until the icicles had disappeared from the ceiling. During this period Succoth started to look like something from *The Lion, The Witch and The Wardrobe*. There was a burn at the back of the cottage fed by a small waterfall. It was too fast-flowing to freeze completely but a section of it had become a giant icicle. I wrote to Christina to tell her about the landscape and she decided she would like to come and see it for herself.

A few days later she turned up together with her watercolours. I protested that it was far too cold to attempt any kind of pleinairism and told her about the frost on the counterpane but she was not impressed by my arguments and over the next few days completed several pieces despite the risk of chilblains and frostbite. Some of those paintings still exist and you can see the frost flowers in the layers of paint.

And then suddenly as if by some Narnian miracle the snow disappeared and the play was finished. I seemed to have woken from a trance. I put the manuscript to one side for a few days and decided that I would lose myself in someone else's writing. John allowed me to choose something from his library and I took down Laurence Durrell's *Alexandria Quartet*. Having steeped myself in Durrell's steamy prose for several days, I then gave the play a final read through.

I was pleasantly surprised. It was certainly a chamber piece and understated. But within the constraints I had set myself I felt I had achieved something especially with the imagery and the language. And if I'd had something Beckettian or Eliotesque in mind while writing it, there was little trace of nihilistic absurdity or Christian mysticism in the finished product. No doubt it was lacking in dramatic tension and was unlikely to have theatrical agents queuing up to produce it. But that had never really been the intention. I felt that I had completed some self-imposed work on myself and now felt ready to rejoin the hurly-burly.

And of course it had been a great pleasure to get to know the Keays and to share their lives for a few months in that beautiful location. But now it was time to move on. Or perhaps time to get back. It wasn't entirely clear to what, but I was pretty sure that it would involve going back to London and finding a job. The only problem was that I had rather dramatically severed any continuity in accommodation and employment in that city. I outlined my predicament to Bill Reed in one of my letters and he suggested that I come and stay with him in the spare room of his flat in Northampton on my way back to the Smoke. I needed no second bidding and a few weeks later found myself packing up my still meagre belongings only slightly augmented by my slim notebook containing the completed play.

# Deferred Gentrification

LOVELY THOUGH IT WAS to be hooking up with Bill again it was not quite like the old days. To begin with he had a proper job which involved wearing a suit and a tie and using terms like marketing. And he still had parental responsibilities although they were now at arm's length. In any case Northampton, notwithstanding its many attractive qualities was not exactly my cup of Middle England. I saw it more as a staging post on my way back to the delights of the capital. So as light relief from typing up the final draft of *Get Out Of It*, I would go down to the public library and scan the situations vacant columns in the national papers. It was time once again to restore the Vincent finances and for that I needed a 'proper' job too.

Unfortunately in the race to get interesting and lucrative employment I had been rather slow out of the blocks. Those of my contemporaries who had been more ambitious or at least more sensible had used their time at University to work on student publications or get involved in student drama. Famously, Footlights was seen as a stepping stone to opportunities in television, and Varsity to jobs in journalism. I had in fact applied to Varsity in my first year when Jeremy Paxman was editor. He had asked me to report on something like a third division hockey match. No thank you. Now, not only did I not have any relevant experience—I still didn't know one end of a hockey stick from the other—but I had let several years slip by since I had graduated. Consequently my spasmodic attempts to apply for jobs with prestigious organisations were met with indifference.

Rather late in the day I was coming to understand that getting a job was in fact a sales pitch. That meant that you had to understand what your customer (the prospective employer) was looking for and you had to present your product (yourself) in a way that made your product the best solution to the customer's problem. Therefore there was no such thing as a standard curriculum vitae. Completeness was completely beside the point. The point was relevance. The CV needed to be crafted for each specific application even to the extent of suppressing certain details. And context was important too. A period of unemployment, even in the service of art, immediately prior to an application for a job which by its nature is likely to attract strong applications is not a winning hand. To dust down another truism, you needed to set a sprat to catch a mackerel. Which meant I needed the sort of job, which whilst being relatively humble, might provide a springboard to get a better job. In other words forget the milk round and so on. At the same time whatever this job was going to be, it should be one where my months in Dalmally would not be a disqualifying factor. And ideally that job would be in London.

A couple of weeks passed by and nothing particularly enticing appeared until one day I spotted an ad for a position teaching English as a foreign language to business people in Kensington. The job would suit a modern languages graduate. I had never really considered myself any kind of teacher, but this looked like something I could have a shot at. I copied down the details and showed it to Bill that evening. His response was a little unexpected. He felt that the job actually suited him better than it suited me. He had in fact already had some experience of teaching English as foreign language when he had still been based in Cambridge and since then he had also acquired a modicum of business experience. I had to admit that he had a point but I hadn't realised that he had been considering changing jobs or in fact leaving Northampton. When it became clear that he was serious I deferred to his greater determination and consoled myself with the thought that, from a personal perspective, London would be hugely improved by his presence there. He phoned the number in the ad, secured an interview and in due course the position.

Well, at least one of us now had a job in London. The next problem was to find somewhere to live. Once again Henry and Jane came to the rescue. Jane was now a junior doctor at University College Hospital which provided her with a nice flat in Huntley Street. The question was how would they feel about putting up not just one waif but two for a few weeks. Henry seemed delighted and if Jane wasn't, she didn't show it. Of course Bill had an assured job and I promised Henry and Jane that I would find something immediately and that we would be out of their hair forthwith.

True to my word the day after we arrived in the Smoke I signed on with Manpower and for a couple of weeks I was on a team that specialised in moving heavy objects. I felt that this assignment was a somewhat literal interpretation of the name of the company. More to do with the fact, I imagine, that they thought that someone who had worked on a stage crew must be practical and not a little bit muscular too. Neither was exactly true in my case and these non-existent qualities were put to an extreme test one day when I was involved in moving a heavy cast iron safe. Fortunately the other blokes on the crew seemed to know what they were doing. And the good thing was that once we moved the designated object, we'd done our shift for the day. Unfortunately this was not the finest implementation of my new strategy. It was hard to see what moving safes might be a springboard to, other than a visit to the osteopath. Eventually I pointed out to my manager that moving stuff wasn't really my forte and the following week I was given an office job in an Iranian bank in Kensington High Street. The downside of the new gig was that it was nine to five and required wearing a tie and a jacket; the upside was that I was unlikely to give myself a hernia.

This was 1978 so the Iranian Revolution was little more than a year away. My job was to help send out statements to the bank's UK customers. I was well enough informed about current affairs to understand the extent to which the actions of OPEC following the Yom Kippur war had affected the price of oil but it had never occurred to me that for a minority of people this development was far from being a disaster. And so far as I could tell from the statements with which I was dealing quite a few of them were our customers. For the first couple of days I kept a mental note of the record positive balance that caught my eye. And even though the scale of these balances was far beyond anything I could imagine, they soon became just the texture of everyday life.

At the end of my first week at the bank Bill spotted an ad in *Time Out* for a house share in Islington that needed two more people. We phoned to see if the rooms were still available and on finding out that this was the case made an appointment to go and see the place. The house was in Cross Street which runs between Upper Street and Essex Road. On one side was a series of small shops and Victorian light industrial buildings and on the other was a row of Georgian town houses in varying states of repair, one of the nicer of which was the address we had been given.

We presented ourselves and were interviewed by a friendly Scot called Graeme Matheson Bruce. There were five bedrooms and currently three tenants. There was a small box room on the top floor and a larger room on the third floor. Graeme was a tenor in the chorus of the English National Opera and was just starting to take bigger roles. The other housemates were a female lawyer and a theatre director who specialised in youth theatre. As soon as we had seen the house we were pretty sure we wanted to take the rooms. The question was would Graeme and the others like the cut of our jibs. This was not the kind of house share we were used to. There was a well-equipped and tidy kitchen diner on the first floor and an elegant reception room with sofas and a piano on the first floor. Up until then we had been more beanbags, paper lampshades and squalid facilities. But I think that Graeme was more concerned about whether we were good for the rent than whether we were house-trained. Bill could give a good account of himself in respect of his financial position and in a moment of inspiration I said that I worked for an Iranian bank. I thought it sounded a little more impressive than saying that I was temping for Manpower. I certainly didn't tell him that I was little more than an envelope stuffer. And I suppose we did stress a little more than we really needed to the fact that we were Cambridge graduates. Graeme said that he would talk to the others and get back to us.

The next day we got the good news. We had been accepted subject to payment of a deposit. It was not until we moved in that we realised that two, and possibly all three of our new housemates, were gay. And it seems possible that at least to begin with they thought the same about us. Perhaps we overdid it trying to pretend not to be too uncouth. Although we were close friends, we weren't *that* close. Whether or not there really had been any initial misunderstanding, it proved to be a good base for the next couple of years and the occasional clash of cultures was, for the most part, handled in good grace.

The house we now moved into was an example of the gentrification that had been going on in Islington for some time but in 1978 it had not yet turned it into the monoculture it now is. There were plenty of property developers in evidence. The squares and streets off Upper Street were being transformed. But not every Georgian house had been turned into a des res and there were still pockets of shocking poverty. Indeed cab drivers were often reluctant to take you to certain areas. This was a little surprising since the Public Carriage Office, the body that supervised cabs and cabbies and administered The Knowledge was located on Penton Street. There were some rough pubs too but at least they still had their traditional names. And there was still the sense of an authentic community with greengrocers, bakers, haberdashery shops and the like in Upper Street. Not that Bill and I were regular patrons of any of those establishments. I suppose that's what happens. As the new wave moves in, the old businesses perish because of declining patronage. Cross Street itself was the frontline between the advance guard of Upper Street gentrification and a kind of proletarian resistance focussed on Essex Road. Consequently it had a schizophrenic character, rag trade workshops on one side squaring up to Georgian porches on the other.

We did at least frequent the local pubs. Our actual local was The King's Head which was already a well-established theatre pub with the added distinction of still charging in pre-decimal money. It goes without saying that that put it squarely in the gentrification camp. Most pub goers in 1978 had been brought up in the pre-decimalisation era of course, so we rather prided ourselves on our ability to render the appropriate amount in new money without batting an eyelid. No doubt it was a little puzzling for tourists but a lot about British pubs was puzzling for tourists, the opening hours in particular. The theatrical entertainment in the back room of the pub was varied and on the whole of a high standard and there were often Chas and Dave type musical acts in the front bar. But if we wanted to listen to loud music in a sweaty basement we tended to go to the Hope and Anchor further up the road which was a major venue on the burgeoning pub rock circuit. I remember going to hear Charles Shaar Murray's band there one night and finding myself standing next to Lee Brilleaux, the singer in Dr Feelgood. That was quite a tribute in its way. I hope Charlie knew he was there. The Hope was also a rather nice place to resort to on a Sunday lunchtime. It had a well-stocked jukebox and one could leaf through the Sunday papers over a couple of strong Bloody Marys in an attempt to appease the hangover from the previous night. Another haunt of ours when food was in question was the Roxy Diner, which did good hamburgers. Which was just as well because we made infrequent use of the rather nice kitchen in Cross Street.

Shortly after we moved in I decided that I had had enough of my rather menial job at the Iranian bank. It was also becoming apparent that I needed something better paid if I was going to avoid getting into arrears with the rent. Once again I set about scouring the situations vacant columns. The classic problem with landing a job is that many require some minimal period of experience in the particular discipline. But how do you get that experience in the first place? In my case I knew a bit about milk delivery, the buses, stage work, box office work and stuffing envelopes in a bank. Even if I'd wanted to reprise one of these functions, which I didn't, there weren't any ads for that kind of thing in the newspapers and magazines I was checking. And in any case none of those jobs had the appropriate springboard quality. No doubt I was being somewhat optimistic perusing titles like *Campaign* and *Marketing Week*, but finally I saw an ad that wanted a graduate to work on a computerised marketing campaign for a media monitoring business. I had little idea what any of that meant, but I had already worked out that marketing was a kind of umami for the more ambitious job seeker. And crucially the job didn't seem to require any previous experience. This was perhaps because the likelihood of anyone having the kind of experience required was low.

Bearing all this in mind I decided that rather than calling the number from a callbox after work or in my lunch-break I would use the phone on my desk. Personal calls were strongly disapproved of, but I thought if I chose my moment I might get away with it and it would give the impression that I was in an established position. I decided to stress the fact that I had been a management trainee and was now working for a bank and gloss over the years since graduation. If the questions got too searching, I'd probably come unstuck. But if I could get an interview, I figured I had half a chance.

Surprisingly I got straight through to the director in charge of the project. I did my pitch and then stopped talking. When you are pitching there is a tendency to feel that you should keep talking until you have hooked your prospect. In fact this can feel like a hard sell and is often counterproductive. Conversation is a collaborative process. The baton of speech is handed back and forth between the parties to the conversation by various markers; eye movement, prosody and silence. In a phone conversation, where there are fewer markers, silence is particularly powerful. I made my pitch and then shut up. The silence became uncomfortable. I was on the point of making a supplementary comment, when to my delight, the director invited me to an interview. At the interview I concentrated on my time in Germany and Cambridge and talked vaguely but briefly about oil wealth. I let the interviewer do most of the talking.

I started the following week.

The company I was now working for was called Tellex Monitors. Tellex was a media monitoring service. It had been set up in the

1950s but with the rise of independent radio and local news stations made possible by the Sound Broadcasting Act of 1972 its activities expanded considerably. All large companies retained PR companies. The promotional functions of these organisations is self-evident but they were also in the business of 'rapid rebuttal' on behalf of their clients. When news was a centralised and largely printed matter this was a fairly straightforward business. But with the advent of local broadcast news programmes the process became much more difficult. Tellex provided a service which responded to this need by taping the entire output of local radio stations and transcribing news items that were of interest to the big PR agencies.

The trouble was that this required someone to read the transcripts and know which companies might be interested. An experienced account executive could get through quite a few stories in a day but it took time to train such individuals and then that expertise remained locked inside their heads. It was not easily transferrable to others in the organisation. And indeed these account executives had no interest in sharing their hard won knowledge not least because it gave them a certain amount of bargaining power when it came to discussions about pay in what was otherwise a cut-throat environment.

The solution the directors at Tellex came up with was to categorise news stories using what was called the Standard Industrial Classification. This provided four digit numbers for every conceivable industrial trade or occupation. For example shipbuilding which was much in the news at the time was 3730. The idea was that someone could tag each story with the appropriate codes and then an account executive could check a list of companies and PR agencies which had been tagged with codes that would be of interest to them. That way an inexperienced account executive could phone just those agencies which had an interest in news relating to shipbuilding.

In itself it was not such a bad idea. In fact it was distinctly far-sighted. Unfortunately neither the software nor the hardware of the era was up to the task. In 1978 Tellex's artificial brain of choice was a Burroughs B80. This behemoth which looked like an overgrown dot-matrix printer boasted a tiny 64K

of RAM. On the plus side this was about the size of the computer on Apollo 11 which landed the first men on the moon. On
the negative side it was also about the same size as the Apollo 11
module. By contrast my iPhone 6 which is by no means the most
current iPhone has more than 15,000 times as much memory.
Of course the Burroughs had been bought to do the accounts
and for that 64k was enough. Then someone had decided that
it might be a good idea to get it to solve one of the hardest contemporary computational problems in its spare time.

The absurdity was that no one on the team seemed to be a
programmer. I certainly wasn't at that stage and even though
I had presented a highly selective account of my work experience, at no stage had I claimed to have programming skills. So I
found myself having to try and work out *in situ* what it was that
a systems analyst did. Despite misgivings that I was completely
out of my depth, I was at the same time intrigued and I decided to sign up for evening classes in programming at the City
University. These classes were conducted on the mainframe of
the university. No screens for us, just teletype terminals and
print-outs. But as the course progressed it became pretty clear
that whatever aptitude I had for programming I was never going to acquire enough experience within a few months to help
rescue the Tellex project.

Worse still, we realised as we started to build a prototype
that the SIC categories didn't really fit our needs. The SIC could
distinguish between brass screws and steel screws but it didn't
know about mesothelioma. Not surprisingly in a way. This was
a time, however, of rising concern about the health effects of as-
bestos. The public affairs representatives of Turner and Newall
were clients of Tellex. So we were going to have to adapt or
expand the SIC codes. This was when the real madness set in.
Categorisation ought to be simple. But it's not. And there is a
tendency to try and create a taxonomy *de novo*. The trouble
with this approach is that no matter how rigorous you are in
creating the model, later on you always find an exception or a
value that needs to be in more than one category or decide that
you need to remodel the whole damn thing.

What we needed was a proper understanding of information

architecture but this was a discipline that was still in its infancy. If we had had even a glimmer of the possibilities afforded by relational databases we might have had a better idea of the direction in which to take the project. But the principles of the relational approach had only recently been published by Edgar F. Dodd, and Oracle, the first commercial product, to exemplify these ideas did not appear until the following year. If time travel were an option I'd pop back to 1978 with copies of Linux, Apache, MySQL and PHP, the so-called Lamp stack, and have the problem sorted in a trice. If I could take my colleague Stu McLellan with me we'd also be able to automate the transcribing and categorisation of new news items using machine learning techniques. Of course that would result in the universe imploding in a big logical paradox.

In the absence of time travel the best we could have done was to have had multiple taxonomies but this seemed to offend the tidy-minded souls who had conceived the project leading to many bad-tempered discussions about whether a particular item was fish or fowl. Woe betide the snivelling assistant who raised the matter of penguins.

It didn't take a genius to see that sooner or later there was going to be a nasty crash and I didn't really want to be around when that happened. It was time to spring again. So once more I found myself hunting for a job. To begin with there was nothing that seemed an advance on what I was already doing. After a couple of weeks, though an ad looking for people to take part in brainstorming sessions caught my eye. If my understanding of the basics of marketing had been slight, my understanding of what was involved in brainstorming was non-existent, so of course it was irresistible. The ad had been placed by a firm of trademark lawyers who had offices not far from the Tellex offices. I phoned the number and was invited for an interview. A few evenings later I found myself taking part in my first brainstorming session.

I was introduced to a group of seven or eight other people in their twenties. The group was led by a slightly older American woman. We sat around a large conference table. There were refreshments including alcoholic beverages, which we were encouraged to drink. The atmosphere was relaxed and friendly. The group leader gave a short introduction for the benefit of new participants and then she read out our first brief of the evening. Our task was to generate words suggested by the brief that might serve as a brand name. We were not informed as to the identity of the client, although once I'd been doing the job for a couple of weeks, it was occasionally possible to make an informed guess. The process was undoubtedly weird. It was like a group free association session. It was made clear that the measure of our productivity was the number of words each of us came up with. It was about quantity rather quality. It was not our job to come up with one or two perfectly crafted words. In fact the more unexpected or oblique one's contributions, the happier our manager seemed to be. If I have one weakness, it is that I am glib. And voluble. And I quite like the sound of my own voice, or so I've been told. Is that still one weakness? Well, anyway in this context it was a distinct advantage.

Perhaps it sounds as if it was money for old rope. In fact it was quite hard to maintain the flow of ideas. You'd start out with lots of good words but as the evening wore on you'd find yourself drying up or repeating words you'd generated earlier or at a previous session. I soon realised that those people whose output was consistently on the meagre side weren't asked back. The turnover of participants was actually quite high and there'd be at least one new face at most sessions. It was rather like being a member of a combat unit, another familiar face missing each time we went into action. It turns out that it is quite hard to be spontaneous to order. Even in the world of free association it is possible to get stuck in a rut.

I realised that my time as a member of this strange group was likely to be short, but at least this was work additional to my day job and in itself it was rather pleasant way to spend an evening and get paid. I actually lasted several weeks longer than I expected to. Inevitably our moderator decided that she had heard enough of my Robert Graves and Van Morrison tinged contributions. Sadly I have yet to encounter a fragrance called *White Goddess* or *Madame George*.

In the meantime I had spotted a potential new full-time job

in an ad that linked the phrase 'analysing sales and marketing data' with the phrase 'the music business'. I felt I could make a case for an easy familiarity with the two words beginning with M. The other words suggested some grasp of statistics but I decided to understand them in the most general terms. This was a considerable extension of the approach I had used to get the Tellex job. It's one thing to highlight the skills and experience that you actually have, quite another to let it be thought that you were competent in techniques about which you had no knowledge. On the other hand the Tellex job had required me to deploy skills that they knew I didn't have. So why wouldn't that be the same for any job at this level?

# Chart Antics

SOMEWHAT SURPRISINGLY I GOT the interview and presented myself at the offices of Radio and Record News one Friday evening just before Christmas 1978. R&RN occupied one floor of a 30s building at the junction of Beak Street and Carnaby Street in Soho. R&RN was what we would now call a start-up established to disrupt the way that popular music sales were reported. At that point the charts, as they were called, were controlled by the British Market Research Bureau, the BBC and *Music Week*, the leading music business trade paper. A group of young entrepreneurial types on the fringes of the music business had pooled their scant resources to launch a new magazine into this crowded commercial space. The aim was to provide independent market intelligence for the various stake-holders in the music business.

I was shown into a room furnished with chrome-plated furniture, more like the vestibule of a dodgy discothèque or club than an office. The Chief Executive was Greg Thain, a hyper-energetic guy not much older than myself. I'd decided that I was going to keep discussions about my skill-set tightly focused on the Burroughs and the SIC. I was relying on the fact that computers were such a rarity that anyone who had actually seen one, let alone worked with one, must be some kind of boffin. But I needn't have worried because Greg was much more interested in painting me a picture of the glittering future of *R&RN*. This should have given me pause for thought. Who exactly was pitching to whom here?

The other thing was that he wanted me to start immediately.

Steady on, Tiger! I needed to give some of sort of notice to Tellex and Christmas was coming up too. I was a little worried that there might be another candidate who could start immediately but I really did feel that I had to show Tellex a modicum of respect. Greg furrowed his brow and then agreed on condition I start immediately after New Year. Deal. I learnt then that if you are about to close a negotiation, the strongest play is to make it clear that you can still walk away. The desperate seldom land the deal, or at least not the deal they think they've made. Come to think of it. . . Hmm.

No doubt the (literal) mood music had got to me. Blondie's 'Heart of Glass' from the *Parallel Lines* LP was just about to be released as a single and a review copy was on continuous replay on the office hi-fi. That was the kind of office in which I could see myself working. In my admittedly limited experience of working in offices hi-fis had not featured prominently. Here a state of the art hi-fi was front and centre. If I hadn't been so intoxicated by the disco vibe of 'Heart of Glass' I might have noticed the unmistakeable odour of burning as I jumped neatly from the frying pan into the fire.

*R&RN* was a controlled circulation trade publication. This meant that it depended for its income on advertising from the industry that it served. It was therefore vital not to offend potential advertisers. So forget about investigative journalism or satire. This also meant that the snarling or bilious reviews of the kind carried by the weekly consumer papers had no place in the columns of *R&RN* so far as Greg and the business guys were concerned. This was a source of immense frustration to some of the editorial staff, especially those who also freelanced for the weekly music press or who aspired to do so. It was one thing to generate a sparky, independent voice but not at the expense of offending advertisers. The trick was to find another source of revenue, a way of providing added value to our readers as the jargon has it. Oddly this is where I came in.

In the golden age of pop music radio had been the main vector of discovery for most buyers of records. This meant that the pluggers and hustlers who represented the record companies tended to home in on Broadcasting House in Portland Place.

Clearly the existence of such a monopoly and a client group who had access to considerable funds bred an unhealthy atmosphere. The only challenge to the BBC's hegemony had come from the so-called pirate stations. The BBC's response to this challenge in 1967 was the creation of Radios 1 and 2 from the old Light Programme. But the pirate stations were not so easily deterred. The Heath government realised that the whole regulatory framework needed overhauling and decided that the best way of doing this was to license commercial radio. In effect they co-opted the pirates under the guise of providing greater choice. And so The Sound Broadcasting Act of 1972 entered the statute book, broke the BBC's monopoly over radio broadcasts and opened the way to commercial radio in the UK. By 1978 there were around 20 commercial radio stations in the UK.

Even though most of the radio stations were regionally based and therefore their transmission ranges did not overlap there was still an understandable tendency to create a station identity by offering a distinct mix of music. This meant that by 1978 there were something like 20 playlists. If a particular record was getting a lot of airplay in Liverpool, say, it made sense for the record company to support this greater exposure with a greater supply of that particular record in local shops. The *R&RN* founders had decided that what the industry needed was a comprehensive and timely list of all the records on UK radio playlists. Thus was born the *Monday Report*.

The *Monday Report* also aimed to produce a better singles chart. Though the *World In Action* documentary exposing the corruption within the singles chart system did not appear until 1980, it was common knowledge, certainly within the industry, that the charts were to a large extent manipulated to put it in the most anodyne terms. Producing a better chart, however, was much easier said than done. It was one thing to get un-manipulated data, quite another for an un-hyped chart to have any credibility, not least because if the chart was being manipulated, it was being manipulated by those who had the power to withhold advertising revenue from this impertinent upstart of a magazine.

Our goal might have been to try and disrupt the cosy world

of record sales charts. But if we'd raise our gaze just a little we would have realised that the world economy was going through one of those intense periods of perturbation which are the hall-marks of capitalism. We were the never-had-it-so-good genera-tion, but things had started to go wrong in the 1970s. Suddenly we were living through strange days indeed. In 1973 OPEC had started to flex its muscles and the oil price more than doubled within a year. This had an inevitable impact on inflation which climbed to more than 25% by the end of 1975, higher than it had ever been in peacetime. At the same time growth stalled, unemployment rose and trade unions in an attempt to protect their members's jobs clashed repeatedly with the government. It also turned out that our economic competitors had managed things much better. The *Wirtschaftswunder* in West Germany, *les trente glorieuses* in France and the *miracolo economico* in Italy had left those countries better placed to weather the storms of the 1970s. Piloting any kind of business through such treacherous waters was no easy thing and so those who were foolhardy or unlucky enough to operate outside traditional cor-porate or professional structures could expect a bumpy ride.

*R&RN* may have been a piffling publication but it brought to-gether an interesting group of people. This was partly because no one who was mad enough to work for such a fragile outfit could be said to be on a career path. Indeed the *R&RN* staffers were anti-careerists to a man and woman. Or perhaps it would be more accurate to say that we all saw our ultimate careers elsewhere and this was just a none too secure stepping stone.

Paul Phillips, the magazine's editor, had been a successful producer with CBS but he was a talented musician in his own right and had wriggled out of the corporate embrace to write and perform his own material and edit *R&RN*. Indeed at the point at which I joined the magazine he had just had an actual hit record with 'Car 67'.

The pop trivia history books call it a novelty record. But to call 'Car 67' a novelty record is really to do the song a disservice. It is witty, well constructed and beautifully played and appears to be based on his own real life experience as a minicab driver in Birmingham. Following an appearance by Driver 67, the name of band, on *Top of the Pops* the single was expected to go number one. Unfortunately a bottleneck in the supply chain either at the pressing plant or at the wholesaler meant that the single peaked at number seven. This was no mean achievement but Paul's relationship with his record company deteriorated. There were disputes about royalties or the degree of support he got from the label who, he felt, were much more interested in a new band on their roster called The Tourists.

As it happened I had seen The Tourists play at the Nashville. They were supporting The Gang of Four who pretty much blew them off the stage. But then The Gang of Four could do that. It was their stock in trade. Not quite punk they were musically muscular and ideologically hard-edged. The Tourists by contrast were channeling a gentle hippie mode which had already been rendered irrelevant by the punk explosion. I seem to recall they also featured a flute in their line-up. Ditto. Despite the mauling they received that evening in this ad hoc battle of the bands, two members of The Tourists stood out, Annie Lennox and Dave Stewart. Both were talented musicians and had real stage presence. The record company had also spotted the same thing and began the process of repackaging them as The Eurhythmics.

In the normal scheme of things this shouldn't have made any difference to Paul's fortunes. But Logo was a small label with only limited resources. Paul felt he had generated considerable revenue for the label but they were concentrating on The Tourists rather than Driver 67. Of course all creatives want the undivided attention of their publisher/record company/fast food sponsor. It all gets a bit complicated, however, if the artist is also highly knowledgeable about music business matters as Paul undoubtedly was. Inevitably he and Logo parted company but not before a follow-up single had bombed as did an album on which 'Car 67' was re-recorded for an American audience minus the Brummie accent. All in all a disaster. Sadly for Logo there was no compensating success with Lennox and Stewart. It was left to RCA to capitalise on the alchemy between them backed by a crack team of krautrockers for The Eurhythmics's first album, *The Garden*.

Paul's deputy at the magazine was Jamie Jauncey. He was a refined individual who gave the impression of coming from a rather superior background. He looked as if he'd be much more at home in a legal chambers or the senior combination room of an obscure college. But no one fetched up at *R&RN* without having some unconventional aspect to his or her personality. In Jamie's case it was that he was actively involved in trying to reboot, as the phrase *du jour* has it, Peter Sarstedt's career. In 'Where Do You Go To (My Lovely)' Sarstedt had had one of the huge hits of the late 1960s. He was not strictly a one-hit wonder, 'Frozen Orange Juice' was a top-ten hit a little later, but he came close. More particularly his style was completely antithetical to the mood of the 1970s. Despite that fact Sarstedt has managed to keep touring and producing albums to this day. Jamie was a guitarist so presumably he appears on one or more of his albums.

The idea that the entire editorial team at *R&RN* was moonlighting as musicians is unfortunately disproved by those further down the batting order. The sub-editor, Nick Higham, ended up as the BBC's media correspondent, while Adrian Hodges who worked on my team became a leading screen writer. His film credits include *My Week With Marilyn* and *Tom And Viv*. And his TV credits are too long to list. But before he got his breakthrough in writing for the screen he was a film reviewer. Occasionally he would invite me to join him at a screening. In this way I got to see the previews of a number of classic films including *Apocalypse Now*, the first *Alien* movie and Nic Roeg's *Bad Timing*. I am no cineaste but I realised from the opening frames of *Apocalypse Now* that this was a remarkable film. Strangely screening times for previews seemed to be early in the day. It was a strange experience to step into lunchtime Soho with one's heart pumping having just seen *Alien*. Adrian's breakthrough came in classic fashion. He had been working for several years in film development and funding, first at Thorn EMI and then at British Screen. Lyn Golbey, the producer, was having difficulties finding a suitable screenwriter for an adaptation of *The Bridge*, Maggie Hemingway's novel about Philip

Wilson Steer. Adrian said that he knew someone who could do it. Lyn asked him who that might be. Of course that person was Adrian. It says something for Lyn's judgement that she gave him his chance and the rest is a glittering career.

Sometime before his breakthrough as a screenwriter I had mentioned my own efforts at writing for the stage. Adrian suggested we collaborate. His idea was a TV play based on The Talking Heads song 'Life During Wartime' from their *Fear Of Music* album. The mood of the song is decidely paranoid. It is not clear from the song's narrative whether there actually is a war going on, but there is a distinct sense of threat and social breakdown. One infers that the song's protagonist is caught up in some kind of urban guerrilla activity *à la* Baader-Meinhof or the Symbionese Liberation Army which in 1974 had kidnapped Patty Hearst, an heiress of the Hearst publishing empire, and co-opted her into their exploits to the extent that she eventually joined in a bank robbery. It is a brilliant song and captures the weird 1970s mood of alienation very well. At the same time it is a great pop song with the memorable hook 'This ain't no party, this ain't no disco, this ain't no fooling around.' Adrian and I spent the best part of an afternoon trying to build a narrative around the song. Eventually we wrapped up for the day and slid off for a pint. Our *Life During Wartime* project never went any further but perhaps something of the mood that informed it resurfaced in Adrian's remake of *The Survivors* for the BBC many years later.

Another member of the editorial staff with whom I became friendly was John Gill. John was hugely productive writer. He was possibly the fastest typist I have ever seen. Many journalists are of the two finger school, literally and metaphorically, but John had been trained by the GPO in their Telex department. You never saw John using the backspace. He could type as fast as he could think. He produced news pieces, reviews and the weekly gossip column, *Hype*. This was the most enjoyable part of the whole magazine. John had a great talent for getting people to spill the beans and he was refreshingly indiscreet. This of course was not ideal material for a trade magazine and Greg and Paul would often have to deal with complaints from industry bigwigs threatening to withdraw their advertising if we did't stop lampooning them. Despite, or more probably because of, that the column was extremely popular with the general readership and so somehow, although almost permanently under the axe, lasted as long as the magazine.

The *R&RN* gig was John's day job but he was also a star contributor on *Sounds* magazine. Eventually he became music editor and then books editor for *Time Out* in its heyday. Then he and his partner, Graham Collier, the jazz composer and educator, moved to Ronda in Andalusia and John turned to travel writing and book length projects. Once again his author credits are too long to list. But that was all in the future. At the time he and Graham lived in a flat in Earls Court Square. Graham was hugely respected in the jazz world. He had been the first British graduate of the Berklee School of Music. He had composed numerous highly advanced pieces for big bands combining scored and aleatory sections. But since it was hard to pay the rent with jazz commissions he also composed film and TV music. He also taught and eventually became director of the jazz course at the Royal Academy of Music.

In the early days of teaching one of Graham's private students had been Manfred Mann. No doubt if this information had found its way into the public realm as Mann was establishing his pop career it would have been a matter of embarrassment. But in fact Mann never actually looked like a pop star. He looked more like 50s beat existentialist who had wandered into the wrong decade. It says something for his professionalism though that he was prepared to take music lessons from a practitioner as rarefied as Graham Collier. It certainly wasn't in the conventional pop or rock spirit which failing the prodigious innate talent of a Jimi Hendrix merely required the mastery of three or four chords and bags of chutzpah. You were highly unlikely to get the principle of the three chord trick in one of Graham's lessons. But you would get a thorough grounding in harmonic progression.

So it was very unwise of me to mention to Graham that I had been teaching myself to play jazz guitar and that I could now bash out a few major sevenths and sixths. He gently pointed out that there was a little more to jazz than that. By way of illustration he invited me to one of his gigs at the Roundhouse, a performance of his piece based on Lowry's *Day of the Dead*. In the context of my earlier claims the complexity of the music and the brilliance of the musicians was nothing short of dismaying. After the gig Graham asked me to join the band for drinks and something to eat. We went to a Greek place in Camden. He sat me next to his guitar player, Ed Speight, which was a great thrill because I knew that he had been involved in Ian Dury's Kilburn and the High Roads and had played on *New Boots and Panties*. What I hadn't realised before the concert earlier that evening was that he was also a superb jazz guitarist and played on many of Graham's recordings. As Ed and I chatted over the kebabs I decided to keep quiet about my prowess with major seventh chords.

One of the perks of working for a music magazine even one as unglamorous as *R&RN* was that there were a lot of invitations to gigs and music biz events floating around. Given the back room nature of the job I did, I seldom got personal invitations but I would sometimes get other people's cast-offs. As a reviewer John used to get lots and he would sometimes invite me along. On one particular evening there was a big party to mark the launch of a new record label and the event was to be held at London Zoo in the elegant banqueting suite of the Zoological Society of London. This was still in the boom years of the popular music industry when excess was the music business's middle name. On this particular evening there were free bars, pretty girls who might also have been free for all I knew and much more extravagance besides. I made the mistake of hitting the whisky bar straight away. Pretty soon I was flying. I lost track of John but was fascinated to spot Phil Lynott of Thin Lizzy. He swept around the main room red rose in his button hole. Of course I was far too cool (or not drunk enough) to talk to him. And in any case I doubt I was his sort. I wasn't particularly a Thin Lizzy fan but prompted by this glancing encounter I subsequently managed to hustle some Thin Lizzy tickets for a gig at the Hammersmith Odeon. It was one of the best live concerts I have ever seen. At that point Gary Moore was still in the band. I was lucky to catch this line-up because Moore left the band shortly afterwards. The sound was immense with Moore's passionate bluesy playing and Lynott's thundering bass. Lynott was exactly what people describe as a magnetic performer. He certainly seemed to exude star quality as I watched him work the room at London Zoo that evening.

The rest of the evening is and probably was a blur. Eventually I decided that I ought to head home. I staggered towards the exit and saw a long line of limousines waiting to pick up those lucky members of the glitterati. As I hit the cold air I realised just how drunk I was. I am no big drinker but I have always relied on some kind of autopilot to get me home or get me out of trouble. But on this particular occasion I was having great difficulty working out exactly where I was even though Parkway was only short way away. In my befuddled state I might have been on a different planet altogether. And I was having difficulty putting one foot in front of the other. I made my way up to the road that exits the park in the direction of Camden because I thought I might be more likely to get a taxi there. Some corner of my mind that was still working figured that there might be more cabs heading back into the West End so I sat on one of the illuminated bollards on a traffic island and settled down to wait feeling in equal measure queasy and cold.

Eventually a cab appeared and the driver took pity on me. On the whole cabbies are not particularly sympathetic to drunks. But this guy must have been a part-time angel. He got me back to Cross Street in Islington. He was also understanding enough to accept my explanation that I had lost my wallet but my girlfriend would have the money for the fare if he would just wait for two minutes whilst I knocked on the door because I couldn't seem to find my keys either. Christina had already gone to bed but she rustled up the cash as I propped myself against the front door jamb. After she had paid the cabbie she pushed me inside and ticked me off for coming back in such a state. Just about the only thing I was able to say was Phil Lynott. She was trying to unravel this conundrum when the door bell rang and it was the cabbie at the door. In my addled state I imagined that we must have underpaid him or I'd been sick in the back of his cab and he wanted to point out the error of my ways. In fact he had found my wallet in the back of the cab and he was returning it to me. Clearly he was a full-time angel.

The way I felt next morning has been mercifully scrubbed from my memory. We all know what those mornings are like. But the conversation I had with John at lunchtime remains crystal clear through the alcoholic haze all these years later. He asked whether I had enjoyed the party. I nodded but mentioned that I had had a difficult time getting a cab. He was incredulous. Why hadn't I taken one of the limos? He explained that the limos were for anyone at the party. Just because I hadn't been invited in person, it didn't mean that I couldn't avail myself of the facility. As I nursed a half pint in the time honoured hair-of the-dog ritual I kicked myself for being so naïve but consoled myself that it was unlikely that any angels were on limo driving duty that night.

However I had not been hired for my meagre skills as a ligger nor for any potential I might have as a writer of novelty hit singles. I had been hired to conjure a disruptive model of record sales and radio airplay charts out of thin air. The 6th January 1979 issue of *R&RN* introduced me to its readership who were no doubt all agog as to how I was going to achieve this remarkable feat.

The essential problem was that information about the forthcoming week's playlists wasn't available until late in the week. If the magazine was going to be on executives' desks it was going to have to be in the post before midday on Saturday. This meant that it had to be coming off the printing press early on Saturday morning. In turn this meant that the typesetting and page make-up had to be finished before midnight on Friday. But as I was to discover we would be lucky if we had assembled all the playlist data by 6pm on Friday. OK, still doable except someone would have to see the pages through the typesetting process and the typesetters were in Chatham because we couldn't afford London based type and print. And that person would be me. Hang on. When I took on this job I hadn't agreed to give up my Friday nights for the foreseeable future.

This was of course in an era before email, the internet, desktop publishing or office computers of any kind. I am not sure we even had an electric typewriter. The titles of each song appearing on a playlist were typed out, cut up and then pasted onto a grid having been put into alphabetical order by hand where the rows were the song titles and the columns were the radio stations. Then if a particular song was being played on a particular station a Letraset bullet point (a large dot) would be inset into the appropriate cell. This was a problem that was crying out for spreadsheet technology. The scope for error when doing this kind of thing by hand was considerable. It didn't really matter too much if the alphabetisation was a little off. But it did matter if you transferred a Letraset bullet into the wrong cell and that was easily done. The truly randomising factor was that the typesetters then reset the whole thing from our grids. Proofreading tabular material under time pressure late on a Friday was no joke.

Then Greg had the bright idea to get a fax machine. I was familiar with telex machines, but a fax machine was a new one on me. If you'd popped into the pub next door to the office and taken a straw poll to see who knew what a fax machine was, you wouldn't have got many right answers despite the fact that machines for sending so-called wire photos had been in use by Associated Press since the 1930s. The idea was that we would fax our grid pages empty except for the list of song titles to the typesetters who would fax back copies of the typeset pages so that we could Letraset onto fax versions of the proof pages. That was fine except that the paper used by those early machines was shiny and grey and curled because it came off a heated roller. This meant that the pages were extremely hard to read and it was even harder to get the dots to adhere to them. The other drawback was that each page took more than a minute to send. Oh, and the machine would break down with alarming regularity.

That first week it was starting to look as if the *Monday Report* ought to be called the *Tuesday Report*. Paul Phillips, and I went down to the typesetters and we eventually signed off the pages in the small hours of Saturday morning. Getting a train back to London was not easy. I got back to my gaff in Islington around 8am on Saturday morning. I went straight to bed and slept for most of the weekend. We eventually refined the process and after a few weeks I was able to get back to London before midnight. But for the next year Friday evenings were not my own and this was when I was at an age when Friday night was the big night out.

The bigger problem was how to give the sales charts any credibility. We had a panel of shops, some of which were in the BMRB list. One of the problems we faced with hype was that when it was successful it resulted in increased real sales across the entire distribution network. So if we merely produced a chart that was more or less the same as the BBC chart, but ranked records in a slightly different order, who would care? In any case it was the top five slots people were focussed on. What we needed was some way of differentiating our chart from the BBC chart but still making it relevant. Our first step in this direction was to produce specialist charts serving the country music, folk and jazz communities. Whilst not mainstream, country and folk fans were much more proactive consumers than pop music fans and they were always pleased to see their music taken seriously.

Eventually we were nominated for an award by the Country Music Association. The awards dinner was held at the Grosvenor House Hotel. Greg booked a table and several of us went along for a bit of laugh. We were laughing a bit more sincerely later on when it was announced that *R&RN* had won an award for services to country music. I assumed that Greg would go and and accept the absurd plexiglass object but he pushed me to my feet and I stumbled to the podium to be presented with the ridiculous bauble by none other than Boxcar Willie. Who? Quite. That was my problem too. Well, OK, I knew his name because it appeared in our chart week after week. His 1978 album, *Daddy Was A Railroad Man* was pretty much a permanent fixture but the sad truth was that I'd never even heard one track from it. And I still haven't. Fortunately this revelation is unlikely to upset Boxcar seeing that he somehow managed to sell more than

100 million records. Oh, and he's dead too.

The award seemed to be big news on the British country music scene and I was invited onto the radio to talk about the new chart. I was asked a series of questions about how we compiled the charts. I waffled on for a bit about a panel of specialised chart shops. Of course, I said knowingly, I couldn't reveal where they were because that might distort future reports. The presenter seemed fascinated by the process. I couldn't imagine why. I just hoped that the questions didn't get too probing because the shameful fact was that the chart was really more a work of fiction than a statistically rigorous study. Boxcar Willie's 100 million sales notwithstanding, actual sales volumes of country albums were low compared to the pop chart, consequently the composition of these charts changed much less frequently and individual records might drop out and then reenter weeks later in response to a television appearance or the announcement of a tour. A certain amount of gentle manipulation was required to make the charts tell a coherent story. Of course I couldn't actually say this on the radio or our recently acquired plexiglass object would be promptly snatched back.

As ever I resorted to obfuscation. I talked airily about qualitative as opposed to quantitative research. (God knows where I got these concepts from. No doubt from an idle glance at *Campaign* or some such.) My sentence started out magnificently, lost its footing on those pesky alveolar plosives and collapsed in an embarrassing stutter. It must have sounded far from convincing. But the presenter was an old hand and he teed up a Willie Nelson track. As he did so he asked me whether I was a fan. The easy thing would simply have been to affirm but I was still squirming with embarrassment and the brain just wouldn't engage. If I said yes I might have to say something intelligent about Willie Nelson and if I demurred I might have to justify my position and at the same time piss off countless Nelson fans. The fact was I was as ignorant of Willie Nelson as I was of Boxcar Willie. As the intro to the track played I wondered if all country artistes had to be called Willie. Finally I mumbled something indecipherable. The presenter smoothed over my ineptitude and said 'Well, partial' and faded up the track. By the time the interview was over I was a nervous wreck. As I slipped out of the studio one of the charming BBC assistants handed me a cassette of my segment of the programme. I was pretty certain that I wouldn't be playing that to colleagues or friends any time soon.

Clearly the creative approach to sales statistics which we used for the specialist charts wasn't going to pass muster for the mainstream chart. Well, that's not strictly true since for the first few weeks in the job I had such meagre returns that publishing a completely unfiltered set of returns would have had us laughed out of the business. Eventually Greg had a brainwave. As in most businesses the retail tier was served by a wholesale tier. In this respect the record business was no different. The record companies supplied a relatively small number of wholesalers who fulfilled orders to retailers. If a surge in demand cascaded back up through the distribution chain the wholesalers were going to know about it before anyone else. And they in turn might need to increase their supply from the pressing plants. The process of responding to the increased demand for a particular title might take several days before the increased supply was available in the record stores. So adjustments in the wholesale positions for particular titles was a good indication of retail sales the following week. In other words if we could get this information we would have a good idea of the aggregate flow of key titles.

The problem was how to get hold of this information. I started to try and build up contacts at the main wholesalers. Understandably they were suspicious of our motives. Eventually we encountered a young guy who was extremely knowledgeable and happy to give us a few nuggets each week. Suddenly we were in the position where we were regularly publishing the number one a few days before the BBC chart came out. In effect we were predicting what was going to happen at the retail end. Sometimes we got it wrong. But we got it right enough times for people in the business to notice.

And we got better. The guy who had been feeding us the information joined the team and started to provide us with a detailed picture of what was happening across the wholesale end of the business. This led to an enquiry from BBC Scotland as to whether we could produce a chart for sales in Scotland. They were keen to differentiate themselves from the Sassenach Top 20. I flew up to Glasgow and was shown around the studios and an outline agreement was drawn up. As I sipped my gin and tonic on the flight back to London that evening I felt rather pleased with myself.

As I have since experienced on more than one occasion such self-congratulatory moods inevitably presage disaster. Within little more than six weeks *R&RN* was no more. The reality was that the magazine had never been properly capitalised and despite all Greg's ducking and diving the magazine was perennially strapped for cash. Eventually a knight on a white charger was found in the shape of an investment by a local newspaper group. But the price for that was the departure of Greg. It would be true to say that he was not everyone's favourite person, but at least he was one of us and no one doubted his commitment. With his departure an executive from the newspaper group was foisted on us as Managing Director. He was an amiable enough guy, and had a strong background in periodical publishing. Unfortunately he had no real idea about the music business. And ultimately he didn't really make the decisions. They emanated from head office wherever that was.

Accounts of what happened next differ. The standard explanation is that the new owners realised belatedly that they had acquired a financial black hole and that there was little point in throwing good money after bad so they decided to close the publication. But the conspiracy theorists amongst us were convinced that the new owners were mere proxies and that they were doing a favour for third party who had a vested interest in seeing this pesky upstart strangled in its cradle. Who knows?

What I do know is that for the first time in a year I decided to take a Friday off. I had a heavy cold and I had decided that the *Monday Report* production process was so streamlined now that it would work without my nannying and cajoling. So I was a little surprised to get a phone call at my place in Islington from the new MD asking whether I really couldn't make it into the office. I bridled at the implication that I was malingering, but he hastened to assure me that that was not the purpose of his call. He had summoned all staff to a meeting that afternoon. It was extremely important and it would be better if I was there. I snuffled something to the effect that I'd do my best.

Later that afternoon we all assembled in the main office. He told us that head office had decided that the magazine was not commercially viable and had decided to close it down. The current issue which was about to go to the printers would be the last one. We were all redundant with immediate effect and we should clear our desks and leave the premises in an orderly fashion. We were then each handed a brown envelope with our final pay. I don't think anyone was entitled to any redundancy pay. We were all pretty stunned. A number of people expressed their anger. But it was made clear that this was an irrevocable decision.

In the immediate aftermath somebody found a bottle of Scotch and we raised a sardonic toast. People started clearing their desks but as the hooch took effect the clearing became somewhat destructive. The conspiracy theorists seemed to think that the existing staff were being removed so that scab labour could be brought in to produce future issues of the magazine. This was hardly likely as we were being paid well below union rates and in fact few of us were actual members of a union anyway. Just to make sure people started tearing up and binning editorial material that had been lined up for future editions with considerable enthusiasm. Mayhem is not my style. Or perhaps I was suffering from an overdose of Benylin and Scotch so I did not join in. In fact what I wanted to do was make a last minute change to the front page to let our readers know what was going on. I sat down at my desk and typed out the copy and then faxed it to the typesetters whilst a Beak Street bonfire of the vanities raged around me. I still wonder who our Savonarola was.

Despite the fact that it was a December evening a number of the iconoclasts opened the windows that looked out over Carnaby Street and started throwing the ripped up editorial material into the street below. The mood got uglier until eventually a typewriter was pushed out of one of the windows. Carnaby Street is a busy thoroughfare. It is a miracle that no one was hit by the falling typewriter. Clearly someone was shocked enough to call the police who soon arrived and put an end to our attempts to trash the office. As I got the 38 bus back to Islington I concluded that if that's what came of taking a day off, I would make sure to think carefully before ever doing so again.

It is one of those irrefutable truisms that Christmas always seems to loom at moments of financial instability. I realised that my small savings were not going to pay the rent indefinitely. So reluctantly I signed on with an employment agency. I assumed that it might take the agency some time to match my peculiar talents to a suitable vacancy. But employment agencies specialise in the art of banging square pegs into round holes. The round hole that they had unearthed for me was a company called Kiver-Patterson which published a number of technical journals, among them *Electronic Production* and *Underwater Systems Design*. I protested that my knowledge of matters electronic and submarine was extremely limited. Now, if they had a nice vacancy where knowledge of matters literary and musical was required, that would be much more like it. Of course, as I was only too well aware, there are very few of those kind of vacancies and those that do exist are hotly contested. I somewhat resented this naked hustling, but decided to go along with the process to buy time in the hope that something else might turn up. I felt pretty sure that I could undermine the electronic and underwater interview process.

My master plan was to make little or no effort to present a businesslike demeanour. To this end I eschewed the suit that convention might dictate. I even left off the tie. I presented myself at the appointed hour at the offices of Kiver-Patterson in St John Street in an open-necked shirt and jeans. I rang the buzzer and I was asked to go upstairs to the reception area where I was told that Mr Patterson was running a bit late but that he would be with me directly. I sat in the waiting area and leafed through the recent editions of *Electronic Production* and *Underwater*

*Systems Design* which were displayed on the little table. I was far from impressed. The subject matter was incomprehensible and the layout was execrable.

Eventually a thin, balding man appeared and introduced himself as Ed Patterson. He showed me into his office. The building was an early Victorian or Georgian house. The office would have been the main reception room when the building was a house. A desk was in front of the fireplace. At right angles to the desk was a long table with several discrete piles of paper scattered about it. On the mantelpiece was a model of a sailing ship. There was nothing you could really call office equipment in the room. In itself this was not unusual. In those days the offices of executives might be hard to distinguish from the study of a university academic or the comfortable sitting room of a gentleman's club. The encrustations of information technology had yet to breach the executive calm.

Ed asked me to sit down and started to look at the copy of my CV which the agency had sent him. I gazed around the room and studied the details of the model ship. I thought I recognised the ship from the outstretched arm of the female figurehead. He noticed the direction of my gaze and asked me if I knew the name of the ship. I said I thought it was the *Cutty Sark*. He seemed impressed and asked how I knew. Rather than admit that it was a guess, I said that I had been born in South East London and the *Cutty Sark* in its dry dock at Greenwich was a familiar landmark. I also told him that my father had a penchant for reciting verses from Robert Burns, so I was familiar with a number of the poems including 'Tam O'Shanter'. Ed was curious about the Scottish connection and I explained that my father had done his RAF training in Scotland during the Second World War. I then asked him what the *Cutty Sark* signified to him. He said that his grandfather had been the ship's carpenter.

'Look,' he said 'I've kept you waiting and now it's lunchtime. Do you fancy a pint and a sandwich at the pub up the road?' Well, I've seldom turned down an invitation to have a beer. And it was not as if I had a crowded diary, what with being redundant and all. So we strolled the few yards up to The Crown and Woolpack passing The Empress of Russia on the way. The

Empress of Russia sported a fine inn sign depicting a double headed eagle. I was vaguely aware of the the Empress as a folk music pub, though my own local was The King's Head further up Upper Street. I asked Ed why we weren't going into The Empress. He shrugged and replied that he didn't really like Whitbread beers. Whitbread no longer brew beer, but it is one of the great names of English brewing, indeed at the time you could still see their Shire horse drawn drays in the Islington area.

The Crown and Woolpack is on the junction of Owen Street and right behind it was the handsome red-brick building of the old Dame Alice Owen grammar school. Ed and I went into the back bar. I wasn't quite sure what the etiquette was going to be. I assumed he would be buying, but ought I to offer to go a round? It also occurred to me that this might be some kind of test and that a prudent circulation and marketing manager of *Electronic Production* would undoubtedly make sure to only consume non-alcoholic beverages at lunchtime. Then I reminded myself that the whole point of my approach was that I didn't want the job, so when he asked me what I was drinking I ordered a pint of best bitter. Despite my affected insouciance I was relieved to see that Ed ordered the same for himself.

Ed was evidently well known in the pub from the jocular greetings that were exchanged and I was subsequently to discover that he had his lunch there nearly every day. Those were the days. Shortly after this period lunchtime in British companies was abolished. As the 80s unfolded it became *de rigueur* to grab a sandwich at your desk. At the same time it became considered appropriate not to knock off at 5.30. Oh no, the thrusters stayed on well beyond that, another hour or even two. And if you wanted to really impress, then you'd better make damn sure that you were in before 8.30am.

We settled at a table and started to chat. There was nary a word about electronic production or underwater systems design. Nor did he ask me to account for myself, my present unemployed status, my career ambitions, my educational background or my life circumstances. It was just regular pub chat. He seemed pleased that I knew about the *Cutty Sark* and that my father had been in the RAF. That particular detail set him off on his own Second World War experiences. He'd been a Dakota pilot in Burma. After completing training he'd been posted to the Far East. He'd eventually been given command of a small airstrip in the jungle. The thing that shocked him most on taking over his command was the amount of paperwork involved in fighting a war in the jungle. He had already decided that he was unlikely to survive the tour of duty and so acting in a manner calculated to achieve promotion was futile. His first act on assuming command therefore was to burn the majority of the airstrip's paperwork. So far as he was concerned the only vital paperwork was that needed to requisition fuel and ammunition.

Having spoken to a number of people who have survived combat it seems to me that those who came through the horror relatively unscathed were the ones who had decided from the outset that their lives were already lost. It is almost as if hope is the thing that drives you mad. In Ed's case he seems to have taken this approach to extremes. Not only did he conduct the administrative aspects of his command in a way that might have got him court-martialled, but he actually flew without a parachute. His reasoning was that if he got hit, he would either come down in the jungle which was largely held by Japanese forces, or he would come down in the sea which was reputed to be shark-infested. He didn't fancy either eventuality. As it turned out he avoided the Japanese, the sharks and court-martial but he retained the same disdain for paperwork and formal procedures. Thirty-five years later he was running a small magazine publishing company specialising in technological subjects, not an airstrip in the jungle, but the approach was much the same.

We finished our drinks and got ready to leave. I said that I had enjoyed the lunch and I assumed that we were heading back to the office to do the interview proper. 'Oh no,' he said 'We've already done the interview'. I must have looked a bit puzzled. 'What I'd like you to do,' he continued 'is to go home and write to me telling me why you want the job.' I thanked him and drifted back up to the house in Cross Street. My initial reaction was one of relief. I had turned up for the interview and I hadn't actually been offered a job. I had achieved the goal I had set myself. I was square with the agency and I could wait a bit longer until they found me a job which really fitted my talents. But I found it difficult to shake the idiosyncratic nature of the 'interview' from my mind. The things that Ed had said intrigued me. I felt I ought to write to him as he had suggested, at least to thank him for the pleasant lunch.

The next day I started to feel guilty—not *vis-à-vis* the agency, but *vis-à-vis* Ed and before I knew it I was drafting a letter telling him why I wanted the job. My first draft drew on the approach I had adopted with the Tellex and *R&RN* jobs and I listed all the ways in which I could make a difference to Kiver-Patterson. As I read over my draft and reflected on the conversation in the pub, I felt uncomfortable about its crass tone. So I redrafted the letter to the effect that working at Kiver-Patterson would be a great opportunity for someone of my limited experience in periodical publishing. I wasn't sure why I was abandoning the hard-nosed approach, but something about Ed intrigued me. In the event I got the job and what a great experience it was.

I somehow imagined that since the company published five periodicals there must be a reasonably large editorial team. Not at all. The editorial department was Ed and his business partner Sheila. The long table in his office with the piles of paper was the clearing house for future editions of each of the company's titles. As PR releases and technical reports came in Ed would mark them with a highlighter and a pen and plot them into the page plan for the appropriate issue. There were specially commissioned articles on specific subjects but these were always written by external experts. When enough material had been assembled the pile of paper was sent to the typesetters. Once the issue had been proofed and laid out the pile of paper was consigned to the wastepaper basket.

Ed extended this hyper-efficient approach to the management of the company. He had no secretary. I don't think he even had a typewriter. Perhaps Sheila did. Most correspondence that he received went straight into the wastepaper basket. If something was sufficiently important to warrant a reply, he would scribble a brief hand-written note on the letter and return it to the sender. He would only keep a copy of the correspondence if he considered the exchange to be of the highest importance. In those cases having penned his response he would photocopy the annotated letter and put the copy into a small filing cabinet.

His personnel management techniques were interesting too. The Advertising Manager was a big guy from Yorkshire who in his younger days had been in the Navy. As is common in sales jobs his pay was a combination of a basic salary and a performance-related bonus. The annual pay round for him focussed on the bonus metric. But, as Ed confided to me towards the end of my stint there, he would have been better advised to have negotiated harder on his basic as this was a cumulative metric. An important lesson.

Ed was not an ungenerous man. He wanted people to behave rationally and he felt that that was what should be rewarded. After I had been with him for a year I applied for the position of Marketing and Circulation Manager at the Architectural Press and unexpectedly I was offered the job. The only problem was that I was therefore going to miss out on the annual bonus. On the other hand the new job paid much better and because it was a bigger company the prospects for advancement were better too. I was due to start the new job immediately after the New Year's holiday. Towards the end of the Kiver-Patterson staff Christmas lunch Ed came over to me and said how disappointed he was that I was leaving. I mumbled something about the wider opportunities that were available in a larger company. I reminded him that when he had asked me to write to him after the interview in the pub I had talked in terms of what I could learn from Kiver-Patterson. He acknowledged this and then handed me an envelope. I asked what it was. 'It's your bonus,' he said. I replied that I thought that by resigning I had forfeited it. He said it was a reward for work I'd done, not a bribe for work I might do. When I opened the envelope later it contained a cheque for a thousand pounds. What a decent employer he was. I felt slightly guilty, but only slightly.

124

# The Bride of Denmark

S O A LITTLE MORE than a year after I got talked into the Kiver-Patterson job, I talked my way out of it. The Guardian's situations vacant pages used to focus on so-called creative and media jobs one day a week. In the late autumn I saw that the London Review of Books was looking for a publisher.

One of the casualties of Rupert Murdoch's dispute with the print unions in 1979 had been the *Times Literary Supplement*. Publication was suspended for a year or so. A number of titles emerged to fill the gap including the *London Review of Books*, immediately establishing itself as a confident new voice in the cultural debate. I was an avid reader of periodicals. I took the *New Statesman* and *New Society* every week and I was probably still reading the *NME*. I now added the *LRB* to my reading list. From the start the *LRB*'s tone was serious but light-hearted in contrast to the *TLS*'s smug hauteur. I sent off my CV and a letter of application with little expectation. I was pleasantly surprised when I received a reply inviting me for a interview.

The interview was with the incumbent publisher, an Australian academic. We hit it off pretty well and he said he would recommend me for the position, but I would have to be approved by the editorial troika. This comprised the editor, Karl Miller, who was also professor of English at University College, London. Mary-Kay Wilmers, who had been an editor at the *TLS* and Susannah Clapp, who'd been at the *Listener*. At the second interview Professor Miller asked me to sit down and he made the introductions. I suppose when his name had been mentioned at the first interview I'd thought there might be some German influence in his background so I was surprised by the elegant Scottish lilt in his voice. Not that a Scot couldn't have German forebears of course. He started off by saying that my letter of application was surprisingly well written. I am sure that he meant this as a compliment but for some reason I felt irritated. Did he mean that he didn't expect a degree of literacy from an applicant for the business role? Was there an implication that the editorial team were the free-born nobles and the business staff merely useful serfs? No doubt it was just the idiosyncratic way he stressed certain words and perhaps there was an element of gentle roughing up in these introductory remarks but it certainly punctured the entirely inappropriate equanimity that I had been feeling on arriving for the interview. In a foolhardy attempt to regain the initiative I set about trying to establish my intellectual credentials by displaying how thoroughly I had read recent issues of the magazine and spattering my remarks with references to the other titles on my weekly reading list, being careful, of course, not to mention the *NME*.

It then occurred to me that I was in fact applying for the publishing role and that I really ought to make it clear that I had appropriate experience and skills in that area too. I started talking about economic realities, the need for budgetary discipline and referred to the bottom line. This provoked a furious reaction from Miller. I needed to understand that the 'bottom line' (the phrase was enunciated with melodramatic stress) was editorial quality. For the *LRB* the only thing that mattered was excellent writing and it would live or die by that approach. I replied that there wasn't much point in employing someone like me then. What they needed was someone to stick stamps on the envelopes and make the tea (which, to be fair, I was pretty good at). I am seldom so impulsive.

Looking back on the encounter I am still shocked at my self-defeating behaviour. I had landed an interview for what would have been the perfect proof of the springboard theory of jobs that I had envisaged a couple of years earlier. And I was screwing it up. If I had been offered the job I would have moved from a world intrigued by soldering machines and submersibles to one excited by books and ideas. And even more absurdly

I actually agreed with Miller. I didn't actually think that the financial bottom line was all that mattered. I was pretending to be a hard-nosed business type and I think Miller suspected that this was just a pose. Perhaps he was even inviting me to reveal my authentic self. But something in his spiky manner got my goat.

Rather dramatically I stood up and said that there wasn't any point going on with the interview rather as if I had convened it in the first place. God knows what had come over me. I suppose I must have thought I was being impressive, whereas in fact I was just being petulant. I picked up my coat, thanked the members of the troika for their time and headed for the door. Miller followed me out and offered an apology and asked me to return. I declined. What an idiot I was! No doubt Miller was a difficult character but he had a proven track record as a literary editor and the *LRB* is a great testament to his acumen. It has taken me a long time to learn that not only should one accept compliments, one should also accept apologies. As I discovered later Miller was himself a great resigner. But here was I resigning before I'd even got the job.

It also became apparent that my callow obsession with the bottom line was entirely misplaced when it came to the LRB. Mary-Kay Wilmers was the beneficiary of a great fortune. She has subsidised the magazine to an eye-watering extent over the last 30 years and subsequently became editor, a role she continues to perform with distinction to this day.

One factor which might have played a part in my mishandling of the encounter was that I was in the running for another job. I had also recently applied for the post of Marketing and Circulation Manager at the Architectural Press and had had a preliminary interview at the company's administrative offices in Wimbledon and been invited for a second interview at the head office in Queen Anne's Gate. These two interviews neatly straddled the second *LRB* interview and I had rather shamelessly at the first Architectural Press interview mentioned that I was also being considered for the *LRB* job. In my rather arrogant way I thought that it might enhance my desirability. Perhaps it did. It seems to be human nature to want what others have. If I hadn't lost my composure so early on I might have tried the same trick at the LRB.

The AP's administrative departments were based in rather humdrum commercial offices in Wimbledon. And Wimbledon was not an easy journey from Bounds Green, which was where I was now living. I was also dismayed that there was such a rigorous functional split with the accountancy, circulation and general administrative staff based in the Wimbledon offices, whilst the editorial and production staff and the executives were based in central London. I assumed that if I got the job I would be based in Wimbledon which was not really optimal. Still, having had a bit of a freak-out at the LRB interview, I decided that I'd better take the second interview at the AP seriously. When I eventually presented myself at the magnificent Queen Anne's Gate offices, I was even more certain that being based at Wimbledon was a deal-breaker. How I wished I'd been more sensible at the *LRB* interview!

The offices were located in a row of Queen Anne mansions between Petty France and St James's Park. The style was at once classic and funky. I was asked to wait in an area that overlooked a small patio garden. Eventually I was shown up a staircase that was crowded with a large and heterogenous collection of paintings to an elegant study complete with armchairs and sofas. My interview was with the commercial director, George Dunn. He asked me to sit in one of the armchairs and we started to chat. It soon became apparent to me that rather than having to pitch for the job the meeting was to discuss the position that the company found itself in and my role if I joined them. It was being assumed that the job was mine if I wanted it.

I found this surprising but it encouraged me to be bolder. So I started to enumerate the drawbacks to my taking the position, the length of the journey from Bounds Green to Wimbledon, the fact that if I took the AP job I would forfeit a bonus from my current employers. Mr Dunn looked a little shocked at this ungentlemanly conduct, but perhaps decided that this was the kind of young thruster that the company needed. The first problem was easily solved he announced. The AP was moving the administrative functions out of the Wimbledon office and integrating them in the Queen Anne's Gate site. And as for the missed bonus, they would simply enhance the starting point of my salary on the pay scale by the amount of the foregone bonus. I realised at that point that I had got the job and it would be foolish of me not to take it.

All that remained was to agree a starting date. I was in no great hurry to begin, but it became clear that the constraint on the AP side was the imminent retirement of the person I'd be taking over from and it was felt that I might need a week or two working with this person so as to be able to pick up the reins more easily. So once again I found myself relocating over the Christmas break.

The Architectural Press was the publisher of the Architect's Journal (*AJ*) and the Architectural Review (*AR*). The company had been set up in the 1880s and for most of its existence had been run by the Regan and Hastings families. The Hastings family had supplied one of the *AR's* great editors, Hubert de Cronin Hastings, though the editor who had established the magazine as the leading English language architectural magazine in mid-century was Sir J. M. Richards (1937–71). Richards was able to count on the talents of writers like Nikolaus Pevsner, John Betjeman, Reyner Banham and Ian Nairn. By the time I arrived, though, the *AR* and the AP in general had lost their way somewhat.

Shortly before my arrival Peter Davey had been appointed editor of the *AR*. He set about reinvigorating the magazine and bringing on a new generation of exciting young writers. These included Dan Cruikshank, Jonathan Glancey and Lance Knobel. The AP's other title was the *AJ*, a weekly for the practising architect focusing on the nuts and bolts of architectural practice. If the *AR* saw itself as an analytical and critical journal actively involved in the aesthetic debate, the *AJ* saw itself as an invaluable technical resource. The *AJ* was edited by Leslie Fairweather, who had a strange enthusiasm for collecting images and figurines of owls. I was dimly aware that the owl was sacred to Athena (Minerva in the Roman system) and by extension the

129

city of Athens. But I could never work out what connection owls had to architecture. Peter Davey and Leslie Fairweather reported to Colin Byrne, the editorial boss who was a member of the board of directors along with George Dunn, my boss, and Michael Regan, a descendant of one of the founding families who was the managing director. The fourth executive member of the board was Godfrey Golzen who ran the AP's book publishing division.

One of the aspects of moving into a larger and more traditional company that I hadn't anticipated was that I got my own office and a secretary, Yvonne. OK, Yvonne shared the office with me, so I couldn't do the whole Don Draper thing and kick off my shoes and lie down on the sofa for a nap. And indeed I didn't even have a sofa, let alone a drinks cabinet. And sadly we were on the top floor under the eaves, so there was a lot of running up and down stairs. But it was definitely a step up from the shabby open-plan offices I was used to.

The Don Draper power aesthetic did, however, apply to the offices occupied by the four directors and the editors. Michael Regan, the managing director, occupied one of the principal rooms on the first floor. Undoubtedly in the house's heyday this would have been a salon or main reception room. It was beautifully proportioned with high ceilings, tasteful paintings and immaculate cornicing. It was in the same mode as Ed Patterson's office but several notches better. Certainly there was a conference table and a certain amount of utilitarian furniture, but the chairs and the desk were classic pieces of furniture and the desk looked as if it was 18th century. The one incongruous note was an Eames Lounge chair behind the desk. Regan was a tall man and had back problems. He claimed that the tilted but not tilting seat helped his back. But I think it was also a hint to the collective bohemian intelligentsia of the AP that inside this rather conventional English gent there lurked a bit of an existentialist.

Colin Boyne, the editorial director, had a gammy leg and perhaps for this reason he had a rather beautiful office at the back of the building on the ground floor with french doors onto the patio garden. So not only did he have a sofa to snooze on, but he could also nod off in his own patch of the garden. Not that I have any evidence that he did take an afternoon nap. My own boss, George Dunn, had a lovely study sitting room in the upper reaches of the building. The general ambience was of higher academe, fragrantly polished surfaces, leather upholstery, solid dependability. I had many meetings here over the next couple of years, few of which took place at the conference table. Mostly we sat around a coffee table and once settled in the warm embrace of a leather armchair it was all I could do to keep my eyes open. The office of the final member of the quartet was high up at the far end of the range of houses. It was undoubtedly the hippest of the four directors's rooms. It was all monochrome with black leather Poltrona Frau sofas and white painted louvre shutters dividing the main part of the room from a narrow outer office. This was a room I loved and had hopes of one day occupying.

One of the other delights of the AP was The Bride of Denmark. The Bride was that contradiction in terms, a private public house. It had been created in the basement of the AP's offices with items assembled from the ruins of the blitz. The walls were dark brown, the ambiance snug and homely in the vein of Tolkien's Hobbit holes or the Edwardian comfort of Mole's house in *The Wind In The Willows*. There were many Victorian pub mirrors, a lovely mahogany bar and a plethora of curiosities. One that particularly amused me was a framed print of a temperance poem vividly describing the perils of drinking alcohol. But undoubtedly the most remarkable item was the front half of a stuffed male lion with a magnificent but moth-eaten mane in a glass cabinet. Apparently it had been acquired by Niklaus Pevsner whilst rooting around Lord Moyne's estate. If you had clients visiting you could let the general office administration know and sandwiches and drinks would be provided. It certainly impressed the few newstrade representatives I invited, though whether it resulted in a better service from them was not so clear.

Another feature of The Bride was that one of the beautiful mirrors beside the bar had been signed with a diamond stylus by many of the the great architects of the 20th century including oddly enough Le Corbusier. It is difficult to imagine the high priest of modernism feeling comfortable in the haphazard bricolage of The Bride of Denmark. But it seems that there were few modernist greats who hadn't crossed The Bride's threshold. I seem to recall that there was a photograph of Frank Lloyd Wright holding court at the bar of The Bride. Yes, the eponym of the lines 'Architects may come and architects may go and never change your point of view.'

So the image projected by the AP was bespoke, sleek, understated elegance. There was a sense of well-heeled assurance. But it was not long before I came to realise that this was a rather thin veneer and that the company had been badly affected by the economic turbulence of the 1970s and was in an accelerating state of crisis. To make matters worse because the shareholding was concentrated in the hands of the two founding families, rather than retaining a higher proportion of profits for diversification or contingencies there was an understandable pressure to declare a dividend. The shareholding structure also meant that it was difficult to raise new capital because it would result in the dilution of the existing shareholders. Furthermore this complex of problems coincided with a generational change in the upper reaches of the AP already mentioned.

The AP did what many companies do in this situation. They tried to cut costs. But it is not uncommon for cost cutting strategies to result in extra costs, at least in the short term. And if your cost cutting strategy involves commissioning a computerisation project, you are almost certainly looking at big trouble. The decision to install a computer to handle the accounts had been taken before I joined the company. IT projects where the solution is bought in from an external contractor with no senior executive on the client side with the appropriate technological experience nearly always end in disaster or at the very least in horrible time and cost overruns. What seems to happen is that instead of commissioning a system which will handle a discrete task, say, the pay-roll or the accounts, more and more sub-tasks get added. Why don't we tack on the advertisement booking system and the subscription system, not forgetting the system for ordering sandwiches in The Bride? Yes, it sounds logical, but in reality the project will never get finished or at least will not operate as anticipated.

It was a pity that nobody in the upper reaches of the firm's hierarchy was aware of Fred Brooks' *The Mythical Man Month* which had been published in 1975. The key insight of this landmark work is that adding more manpower to a late project makes it later. Furthermore errors are inevitable and the process of correcting those errors will introduce new errors. Brooks also stresses that a system should have conceptual integrity. You cannot just bolt on optional modules. In fact a successful system will deliberately provide fewer features than it is capable of. This is achieved by freezing the code at an early stage in development.

This thorough-going pragmatism is at odds with the can-do attitude of the alpha male. Shouting and screaming and banging heads together will not advance a misconceived project. God knows, we've seen enough of them now in large-scale public sector IT projects in the UK. Admittedly all this was completely new to the executives at the AP. They had been formed in the ramshackle never-say-die crucible of the World War Two. The rise of the coolly ruthless technocrats in the shape of Bill Gates and Steve Jobs was only just beginning. And the fact is that even if I had been sufficiently influential in the company my own reading of that seminal text lay ten years or so in the future.

I ought to have known that not all was well when, a day or two after I had started, a large man with a small dark beard walked into my office and introduced himself as my boss. I was a little taken off my guard. Another thing I had omitted to do, because basically I didn't know such things existed, was to ask for an organisation chart. I muttered something to the effect that the only person that I reported to, so far as I knew, was the commercial director, though of course I recognised the seniority of any member of the board of directors. His response was simple. All business functions were being computerised and he ran the computer so it had been agreed that anyone running a business function would report to him. I said that I was all in favour of technological advance but I would clarify the situation with my director. When I did so it was clear that Mr Dunn did not share that interpretation of what the policy was. Furthermore as we talked it became clear that he had serious reservations about the whole computerisation project anyway. I decided to keep out of the computer guy's way until I had a better feel for the real state of play.

In itself the project made sense. A high proportion of the AP's circulation was fulfilled by postal subscription. This amounted to many thousands of copies. Each copy was put into a plastic envelope to protect it in the post at an automated mailing facility in Bedford which the AP also owned. It was a substantial operation and handled mailing operations for a number of other publishers including *Which?* magazine.

The labels that were affixed to each envelope were produced in the Queen Anne's Gate offices. The actual subscription records were maintained on a card index system by 3 or 4 women in a room next to mine. This office was supervised by Victoria. She had a military bearing and often sang rather beautifully to herself. If she wasn't a member of a chorus or choir, she ought to have been. Even though she was already beyond the state retirement age, she worked twice as hard as anyone else in the department. She had an immense loyalty to the company. For her, being an employee of the AP was more than just a job. So she had absolutely no faith in the computer proposals and she was determined to continue running subscriptions manually as long as she was able. She clearly thought that I was a young whippersnapper. But at least she didn't hold me responsible for commissioning the computer.

The actual subscription labels were printed on a large machine called an Addressograph which was located in one of the basement offices. Addressograph had been around since the 1890s, and therefore was of much the same generation as the AP itself. In effect the machine was like a giant John Bull printing set. Aluminium plates on which subscriber addresses had been embossed and which were stored in metal trays were fed into the frame of the machine. The roll of labels was fed onto a platen. An ink impregnated ribbon as wide as each aluminium plate was deep ran between the platten and the address plate feeder. As each plate came into line with a blank label the operator depressed a foot pedal to bring the embossed plate into contact with the label with the inked ribbon in-between. The machine was ingenious but could in no way be described as quiet or compact. And each time there was the addition of a new subscriber to the list or an existing subscriber changed address a new plate had to be produced. This was created on a large intaglio printer with a keyboard which punched the letters into a blank aluminium plate. Again not a quiet process. Bert, the man who operated these machines, was a cheerful fellow but he was as deaf as a post. It is hard to imagine in the light of modern understanding of industrial deafness that the machine wasn't the cause of his deafness. But between Bert in his hephaestian basement and Victoria in her attic office the subscription system ran faultlessly.

Interdepartmental communications were almost as antiquated and conducted via typed memoranda which were distributed internally by office messengers. So there was a leisurely feel to information exchanges including the inevitable management feuds. On one occasion the credit control manager who for some reason had taken a hearty dislike to me sent me a memo which basically said that I couldn't run a piss-up in a brewery. And the bastard had copied it not just to any old director, but to the managing director. I was aghast. To begin with I naturally felt that he was wrong about the substantive issue, whatever it was. Piss-ups in breweries were my forte. I felt that I should respond if only to make sure that future brewery duties were not denied me. At the same time I was reluctant to get into name-calling and hair-pulling and I was vaguely queasy about the idea that others might share his view of my piss-up skills.

Yvonne could see that I was troubled by his missive. Her advice was to ignore it. I pointed out that it might colour the MD's view of my abilities. I was still the new boy on the block and I had so far not had much opportunity to demonstrate the panoply of my talents and I thought that first impressions were important and so on. After letting me work through all the reasons why I should respond she said that Mr Regan would simply

not see the testy memo. 'Doesn't he read them?', I asked naively. She smoothed her cardigan and patiently explained that in
all probability he would never receive the cc'ed memo. Almost
certainly the carbon copy was in the bin, in fact it had never
been produced in the first place. I was doubtful at first. But her
conviction was persuasive. And then I realised that it wasn't
a guess; she actually knew. Of course. All the secretaries exchanged notes about their bosses at coffee time and it was well
known who the operators were. So I took her advice and resisted responding. Nothing happened.

It didn't take me long to realise that Yvonne was much more
capable of running the department than I was. She had worked
for my predecessor for many years and knew the appropriate
response to most situations. And this was probably true for
most of the company's departments. They were really run by
the secretaries; not by the titular managers. So after the fake
memo imbroglio I swallowed my pride and resolved to ask her
advice about everything to do with running the department. It
was a marvellous liberation. I moved pretty quickly from saying
'What do we do here, Yvonne?' to giving her blanket permission to respond as she thought fit and then I would just add my
signature to the pile of correspondence at the end of each day.
Perhaps I felt a little disempowered but I eventually rationalised
to myself that this left me the time and the energy to attend to
the things that really mattered. Like spending more time in The
Bride.

God knows what Yvonne really thought of me. I imagine
she saw me as some kind of milksop. In our discussion about
the memo from the nasty credit controller (they're meant to
be nasty, aren't they?) she pointed out that the internal mail
distribution system was part of my domain and that the messengers were useful people to get on the right side of. Whilst
she wasn't suggesting that they might be persuaded to make
certain awkward memos disappear, though, she hinted, that
had happened in the past, they could certainly give you early
warning of many a memo storm and they could also be persuaded to deliver memos in a particular order which might just give
a manager enough time to get his retaliation in first.

I took this advice to heart and made sure that when we recruited a new messenger, he understood that he was my guy. As with so much to do with the AP many of the incumbents were old retainers. This meant that they were loyal and reliable but not necessarily speedy or adaptable. So when I got the chance, I appointed a youngster. Yvonne tutted a bit and said she didn't think he'd stay long. I pointed out that there were lots of stairs and no lift and the vacancy had developed because the longterm holder of the post had developed breathing difficulties. It was not often that I felt I had won an argument with Yvonne. Despite the logic of my case she looked unimpressed.

The new boy started well. He zoomed around the buildings and he was personable, though one or two of the more senior staff thought he erred on the side of overfamiliarity. He started in the summer months and after a few weeks we had a bit of a heatwave. The building had no air-conditioning and with the amount of office equipment and office lighting it felt quite uncomfortable. I was sitting at my desk with tie loosened and jacket over the back of my chair when I got a call from the secretary of one of the directors. Did I have five minutes to spare? I slipped on my jacket and went downstairs. My boss was incandescent. A member of my department was wearing shorts in the workplace. It was the new messenger. I pointed out that he had an active job and it was very hot and we might assume that he would not dress like that every day. It was made clear to me that he would not dress like that any day. See to it at once. I called the boy into my office and told him that I had just discovered an ancient AP rule that shorts were not allowed. Please take note. He started to try and persuade me and I made it clear that the situation was not negotiable. He shrugged in that youthful way and said he understood.

The next day was even hotter. I awaited his first delivery of the morning and was relieved to see that his legs were demurely clad. It was then that I noticed that he was wearing a t-shirt with the words NO WUCKING FURRIES emblazoned on his chest. As Yvonne predicted he didn't last long. But then neither did I.

A few months after I started at the AP, Christina and I decided to get married. It wasn't going to be a big do, just immediate family and a few close friends. After all we had been living together for quite a few years, but more significantly Christina was now pregnant. It was as well, then, that it was going to be a modest affair because the company asked me to assist Godfrey Golzen, the head of the books division, on a trip to the United States. In the normal course of events this would not have been part of my responsibilities and certainly during the interview process and subsequently there had never been any mention of foreign travel. But Godfrey's marketing assistant who was the person who was meant to be accompanying him had done something terrible to his back and was scarcely able to get out of bed let alone fly across the Atlantic. So Godfrey asked my boss if he could borrow me. This was agreed subject to the proviso that I should be allowed to do some business for the magazine division too. This meant that I was going to have to visit four cities over a period of two weeks, a not inconsiderable challenge for a first business trip. The other problem was that I was due to fly two days after our wedding. I talked to Christina about it and she said that it was too good an opportunity to miss and in any case we had not planned a proper honeymoon partly because she was at the stage of pregnancy when she was not feeling very well. So I spent what in better run relationships ought to have been our honeymoon on my own in the US.

I'd only been at the AP for a few months so I didn't really know much about Godfrey and really nothing about the book publishing side of the business. I was apprehensive because a couple of colleagues hinted that he was difficult to work with. He could be impulsive and unpredictable. But in fact he turned out to be brilliant and charming. When he had joined the AP he had expanded the book list beyond the narrow focus on architectural matters to topics of social policy and trends. He had had a number of crossover successes, one notable one being *Paint Magic* by Jocasta Innes. He had even managed to publish a book by the celebrated anarchist Colin Wood. Godfrey as I was to learn on this first trip was a considerable bon vivant and knew everyone who was anyone in the world of books and publishing. He was also deeply cultured and very generous. We only worked together for a relatively short time, but he had a profound effect on my approach to how to operate in the creative industries.

As I flew out of Heathrow I knew none of this. The rider imposed on me by my boss meant that I had meetings in New York and Washington DC in the week before the convention. My purpose in going to New York was to visit our US distributors. More than half of the *AR*'s circulation was overseas and a high proportion of that was in the USA. But we made little money on these export copies. In particular our news stand and bookshop sales were woeful. So I had made appointments to see the wholesalers and the mailing house.

For some reason Yvonne had booked me on a flight to Newark, New Jersey. And the idea was that I would get a bus from the airport to the Bus Terminal at the junction of 5th Avenue and 42nd Street. It had seemed to make sense to book into a hotel in the vicinity of the Bus Terminal. So Yvonne had booked me into a mid-price hotel on 42nd Street itself just a stone's throw from Times Square no doubt influenced by vague memories of Broadway musicals. This turned out not to be a great idea. In 1981 the Times Square area was still pretty rough. There were hustlers, hookers and pushers everywhere. It felt authentic but a little threatening. The hotel was faded and run down. You could probably rent rooms by the hour. But I had a great view from the window of my room across the roofs of Manhattan dotted with those odd cylindrical water tanks with conic tops and the room itself was extremely spacious by European standards and could have accommodated four people without difficulty.

The first thing I did when I got into my room was to switch on the TV and I immediately felt disorientated by the number of channels. This was at a time when there were still only three channels in the UK. TV-AM and Channel Four were still a couple of years away. As I flipped through the channels I came across a screening of *Summer Holiday* starring Cliff Richard. I had been to see this film at the Regent in Bishop's Stortford in 1963. There was something surreal now about seeing the youthful and clean-cut features of Cliff and his chums driving their red double-decker London bus through Europe to Greece whilst I sat on the edge of my bed in a shabby 1980s Manhattan hotel. I sat down and watched it through to the end before I went downstairs to get something to eat. In the era of the Internet we have become used to having frictionless access to media from all ages and places. But suddenly coming across this extremely significant movie from my childhood in such an incongruous spot felt a little like travelling in time.

On the other hand Manhattan still felt like a city you could walk in. Over the next few days I criss-crossed lower Manhattan on foot shooting several rolls of film. Greenwich Village still had an authentic bohemian vibe. I spent a great day there hanging out in Washington Square Park and found a Van Morrison bootleg in a record shop. Even more delightful was discovering Noho. I found a great bar, all stained wood, offering a dizzying array of beers from breweries I'd never heard of. The camera I was carrying with me was a 35mm Yashica DX-1 single lens reflex. Cameras had metal frames and together with the wide-angle lens and the telephoto lens my camera bag weighed a ton so I really needed that drink.

I tried to kid myself that this quartering of the city was to check out the availability of the *AR* in bookshops and on major news-stands. And I was not entirely surprised to find that the *AR* had an extremely low profile. I decided to ask the sales assistants in the various book stores I visited for their impressions of the magazine or indeed whether they knew it at all. Generally they seemed to suggest that there was a reasonable level of demand for the title, but it occurred to me that they might have been conflating impressions of *AR* sales with those of other titles like *Domus* and *Architectural Digest*. Or that they were just being courteous as Americans so often are.

Publications for these outlets were supplied on a sale or return basis. Clearly it was absurd to gather together unsold copies and ship them back across the Atlantic. By the time they got back they would be far too dog-eared for resale, not to mention seriously out of date. So instead the top part of the front cover with the date and edition number was torn off and sent back to the wholesaler as proof of the number of unsold copies and then we would receive an affidavit in London attesting the number of unsolds which was usually uncomfortably high. The result for the AP was that the cost of printing and shipping thousands of copies of the magazine far exceeded the rather meagre revenue we got from bookshop and news-stand sales.

I thought that if I made it clear to the current wholesalers that there had been a change of management in London that they might raise their game. But when I presented myself at their office in New York I was left in no doubt that they were not particularly impressed by this fact. They pointed out that no European magazine sold many copies through these outlets. It was better to consider this strand of the circulation to be a form of advertising, the trick being to convert the single copy sales into annual subscriptions which was how the periodicals were typically distributed in the USA given its vast size. There was a certain logic to that. But it didn't explain why it was so difficult to find copies for sale. Clearly I knew nothing. There wasn't the space to display every publication to the extent that the publisher wanted. The competition for display space was intense. The ambitious publications had sales teams who visited key outlets and—how could one put this?—offered inducements to get a more prominent position. I blenched a bit I hope. It sounded like they were suggesting that a little bribery might help. Well, they weren't saying that exactly. Surely it was the same the world over? These things needed the personal touch. But that's the problem. I am not going to be able to persuade my directors to fund a sales team in New York. Of course. They understood. They could arrange representation for us on a very reasonable basis. So what this boiled down to was that if I wanted to improve the visibility of the magazine in New York City I could pay the wholesaler to do a better job. Hey kid, what you're paying for at the moment is distribution. What you need is sales promotion.

I'm sure they were right, but it didn't feel right to me. To use the American parlance the whole thing felt like a racket. I asked to see the director with whom I had been in correspondence. That wouldn't be possible. OK, I could come back. No, he's out of town on a business trip to Atlanta for the American

141

Booksellers Convention. Well, well. Just where I was headed myself. But I thought I'd keep that fact to myself.

So the next day I found myself travelling to Long Island City in Queens. These days the incessant gentrification that has transformed Brooklyn has reached Queens, but in those days to say it was scruffy was an understatement. The guy I was on my way to see was Herb Cohen. I liked him immediately. He exuded old world charm. He represented a lot of European publishers. And he had been operating in the New York magazine market for more than 40 years. He couldn't do much about our visibility but he could give us an independent view of the sales position and how it compared with other European publishers. At least that was a start. I felt pleased with the day's work.

Later I flew out of NYC headed for Washington DC for a meeting at the American Institute of Architects. I was staying in a hotel on the river in Georgetown. I'd worked out that there was a metro stop not too far away from the AIA's offices which in turn were only a stone's throw from the White House so I could have my meeting before doing a bit of sightseeing. The metro was ultra-modern and put the contemporary London Underground to shame. Lights flashed along the edge of the platform as a train arrived and there were sliding glass safety barriers rather as we now have at some stations on the Jubilee Line.

I emerged at what I thought was the correct stop but I'd clearly got something wrong. I couldn't be at the stop for the White House because of the scene of dereliction that presented itself. There were people—mainly black—sleeping in the street. Not just that but there was broken furniture on the sidewalk. I couldn't work out how I'd managed to end up in the ghetto because the DC metro system wasn't exactly extensive. And now I was going to be late for my meeting. I saw a cab and hailed it. I told the driver where I wanted to go and he said I was so close I could walk there. I replied that I was late for a meeting and I wanted him to take me there. I climbed in the cab and he did a U-turn and skirted the White House and dropped me at my destination. All in all a few hundred yards. It was only later when I was reading up about DC that I understood that more

142

than two-thirds of the DC population was black and that a significant number were defined as living below the poverty level. This was a shock to find this kind of racially skewed poverty in the capital of the richest country in the world.

The other puzzle was the street plan. The south-westerly stretch of New York Avenue on which the AIA building is located is interrupted by the White House and its grounds. Though Washington has the street grid aligned to the cardinal points of the compass as in most US cities, there is also a grid of avenues aligned NW-SE and NE-SW. The axes of the latter grid are not orthogonal so the street plan is more complex than in many other North American cities. In New York the main aleatory component of the street plan is Broadway which drifts across the main grid producing acute angled intersections which in turn give rise to anomalous structures like the Flatiron building which I had snapped with my Yashica. In Los Angeles that role is played by the Hollywood Hills which forces the Santa Monica Boulevard to deviate to the south-west. Otherwise the grid in those cities is definitive. Not so in Washington. This seems to have been another gift of the French to their republican cousins in that the original plan of DC was drawn up by a French engineer called Pierre L'Enfant who had served in the American Revolutionary War.

Despite my flustered state the meeting was a success. The *AR* was greatly admired and the AIA was happy to help us promote the publication to their members. For a fee, of course. In particular they thought we ought to attend their annual convention. Even better we should take a booth and stock the booth with our publications. I said I would recommend this to my directors and asked where the next convention was being held. Hawaii. Hmm. I couldn't see my bosses saying yes to that one. I felt I might have more luck getting them to agree to a policy of greasing palms in NY than underwriting a jolly to Waikiki beach for their newest middle manager. Nevertheless I assured my host that I would do my best to persuade my colleagues.

As I flew down to Atlanta to the ABA convention I was starting to realise that this was the way that a lot of commercial life was conducted, a never-ending circus that wandered from city to city, some of which seemed to exist solely for the purpose of holding trade fairs and conventions. That at least was my first impression of Atlanta. The ABA convention was being held in the Peachtree area of downtown Atlanta. This was a deeply weird place. In an attempt to regenerate the city a convention centre and several high-rise hotels had been built. The scale of the development was so massive that the organic streetscape had been completely destroyed. Many of the buildings were linked by aerial walkways so you encountered few pedestrians at street level. I was staying at the Hilton a couple of blocks from the Convention Centre. Whilst not quite as spectacular as some of the Peachtree hotels, it was still by some distance the most impressive hotel I had ever stayed in. One of the features of hotels in this period was the huge internal space. Where there had once been lobbies, there were now atria complete with internal balconies and glass lifts.

But impressive as the Hilton was it was not a patch on the Hyatt Regency where I was due to meet Godfrey the next day. The Regency was designed by John Portman Jnr and was one of the first atrium hotels. The atrium rose up inside to more than 20 floors with the interior balconies cascading with sub-tropical planting. Glass elevators rose around the atrium like 'Victorian rocketships' as Jim Morrison of The Doors described them in a 1970 interview. The space-age vibe was continued with a re-volving restaurant under a blue dome on the top of the building. There was also a circular structure in the atrium that looked like an enormous parrot's cage. It was so designed that it ap-peared to be hanging on a steel hawser from a glass ceiling. This structure was in fact a bar and it was where I was due to meet Godfrey.

When I arrived he was deep in conversation with a group of people. I hovered on the edge of the group until I caught Godfrey's eye. He greeted me and invited me to join the group. He introduced me and I realised with a bit of shock that I was joining the bosses of a number of the biggest publishing houses for a drink, including Peter Meyer of Penguin/Viking. Meyer was born in London but was an American citizen and had been educated at Oxford. He had had a hugely successful career in US publishing, but in 1978 became the CEO of Penguin Books and promptly set about restoring that venerable imprint to commercial health. He and Godfrey were clearly great mates and the conversation was light-hearted yet deeply cultured. It was like being an apprentice listening in to masters in the ancient art of making books

If the Hyatt Regency was spectacular then the Peachtree Plaza was insane. It was another Portman hotel and it shared a number of features with the Hyatt, a cylindrical tower and a revolving rooftop restaurant. But the Plaza was more than twice as high as the Hyatt and had an external glass elevator shaft running the full height of the building on one side. In terms of vertical interior space the Plaza was not as impressive as the Hyatt rising only to 17 floors. But where the Hyatt went for a mid-century space-age rainforest vibe, the Plaza went for a full-blown lagoon fantasy. The lobby bar sitting areas were a series of islands that rose up out of a half-acre lake complete with fountains, waterfalls and dozens of trees. It looked great, but finding your way across the lobby was about as easy as getting off the island in the TV series Lost.

The effect of these preposterous hotels has completely eclipsed any memory I have of the business that I did or was supposed to be doing. But I got on well with Godfrey. Though there was a considerable difference in age, we shared a number of interests, and over meals and drinks identified a shared interest in German literature and thought. In his case it was clear that this was accompanied by a certain amount of ambivalence and it soon became obvious why.

He had been born in Berlin in 1930. His family was of Jewish descent but at some point had assimilated to the Lutheran faith to the extent that Godfrey's father, who was also a hero of the First World War, in which he lost an arm and was awarded the Iron Cross had become a well-known Lutheran theologian. After the war he entered the law and eventually became a judge. The family was fortunate enough to be able to leave Germany in 1938 and settled in Edinburgh in 1939. In the way of these things Godfrey's father was interned as an enemy alien. Godfrey went to school in Edinburgh and then studied English and German at St Andrew's University. After university he did military service in the Manchester Regiment and then went into publishing in the early 1950s eventually rising to run the AP's books department. After the war Godfrey's parents and his sister had returned to Germany.

We also discovered a shared interest in Thomas Mann. We both admired *Buddenbrooks: Der Verfall einer Familie*. The novel portrays the decline of one of the leading commercial families of Lübeck through the course of the 19th Century. I know that Godfrey reread and enjoyed the novel shortly before his death. He was in fact fascinated by the way that a family's standing in the community can rise and fall in just a few generations. Given the vicissitudes suffered by his own family it is hardy surprising that this theme attracted him. On more than one occasion I heard him use the expression 'clogs to clogs in three generations'. Not that he had been reduced to clog bracket so far as I could see.

I think Godfrey saw parallels between his own father and Thomas Mann. Mann was born into a Lutheran family though his mother's background was Roman Catholic. His father died when he was 16. His own wife Katja Pringsheim was from a wealthy Jewish family. As we have seen Godfrey's father was a war hero whatever his private views of the conflict might have been. Notoriously Thomas Mann's own initial reaction to the outbreak of war in 1914 was almost one of joy ('I feel as if I were new-born' *Gedanken im Kriege*, 1914), a stance which was heavily criticised by his older brother Heinrich, whose views were more radical and much less jingoistic. Heinrich accused Thomas of using the war as a way of establishing himself as the literary voice of the nation. Meanwhile Thomas accused Heinrich of in effect being anti-German.

One of the themes running through much of Mann's work is the tension between the artist and the bourgeois. Though he had committed himself to the artistic life, he never felt like a radical and his innate conservatism made him hunger for the trappings of the lifestyle of the haute bourgeoisie. In the event his marriage to Katja had taken care of the financial side of things. Now the outbreak of war offered him the opportunity to establish his bourgeois credentials in the public realm. Maybe Godfrey's father too was tempted by the siren voices of bourgeois conformity. Whatever the truth of these matters by 1938 both these men and their families despite their efforts at assimilation found themselves forced to leave Germany, Mann for the USA and Golzen for Great Britain.

As our friendship developed, reflections on Thomas Mann and his family were woven into our discussions. A few months after the Atlanta colloquium Godfrey and I travelled together to the Frankfurt Book Fair. We drove in Godfrey's car so that we could take the books and the publicity material with which to deck out our booth which as it happened was directly opposite the Weidenfeld and Nicholson booth. My job was to remain at our booth and field enquiries while Godfrey negotiated contracts in meeting after meeting over a not inconsiderable amount of alcohol. Clearly Lord Weidenfeld was doing exactly the same thing as Godfrey. But every so often he would return to the booth to catch his breath. He was an imposing figure and between meetings he would sit at the front of his booth puffing contentedly on a large cigar. I don't suppose that would be allowed now, but this was still the era when there were smoking carriages on the London Underground and all office desks came equipped with ashtrays. Weidenfeld and Godfrey acknowledged each other though I don't remember them doing any direct business on that occasion. Weidenfeld was ten or so years older than Godfrey but had made the same journey in 1938, in his case from Vienna.

As I have already mentioned in relation to the USA trip international business seemed to be one long round of drinks parties. The Frankfurt Book Fair week was no different. As an old hand Godfrey had plenty of invitations whereas I had none. But I was not particularly disappointed. Not having been back to Frankfurt since I worked there in 1971 before going to university I was looking forward to seeing how the city had changed in the intervening years. The offices of the company I worked for had been located just behind the bombed-out ruins of the old opera house, Die Alte Oper. But to my surprise when I got there the building had been beautifully restored, though now its role in the city's cultural life was as a concert hall. The main opera house remained the beautiful glass-fronted building built in the 1960s.

An even bigger surprise was to greet me when I walked around the back of the Alte Oper where the Bockenheimer Anlage meets Reuterweg to find a huge tower looming over the neo-classical elegance of the Metallgesellschaft head office. As its name suggests (*Metallgesellschaft* actually means metal company) the company had originally been involved in the manufacture and trading of various metals. By the time I worked there it had extended its range of activities and had become an ambitious conglomerate. This ambitious streak was eventually to result in disaster when its futures hedging strategy in refined oil products in the USA went badly wrong in the 1990s. Following this disaster which was on a par with the Barings fiasco the company was essentially bankrupt and was swallowed up by a more conservatively run conglomerate. But when I worked there in 1971 and still in 1981 the company was proud of its heritage and its independence.

I had been taken on as a management trainee in the scrap department (*Schrottabteilung*) where my job initially involved processing invoices for the value of the component metals in scrapped car radiators imported from the USA. The reference price for each of the metals was established daily on the London Metal Exchange, one of the open outcry commodity exchanges for which London was famous. But the proportion of each metal would vary from consignment to consignment. The majority of the metal came into Rotterdam on transatlantic freighters. Before onward delivery to the smelting plant an assay core would be taken analysed and then divided into two samples. One was sent to the seller and the other was sent to us in Frankfurt. So it was not possible to finalise the invoice until we had the assay report which would then have to be correlated with the LME prices for the agreed contract date, an immensely tedious task in an era before the widespread use of computers and electronic calculators.

I may have won a place at Cambridge to read German but read was the operative term in that formulation. My inability to conduct a simple conversation in the local (Hessian) dialect made me feel like a simpleton. The fact that I could recite Goethe's *Heidenröslein* by heart didn't cut much ice in the *Schrottabteilung*. Goethe might have been the national poet and a local boy to boot but what was more important were the proportions of tin, lead, zinc and antimony in the latest consignment of American car radiators. It would be some weeks before my command of the local dialect was good enough to point out that some of Goethe's characteristic pairs of rhyme words showed a Hessian influence. When I did eventually advance that theory the information was received with complete indifference. It did however result in a request for more examples of Cockney rhyming slang for which my colleagues seemed to have an inexhaustible appetite. What particularly seemed to intrigue them was that the rhyming part as often as not would be left out. They discerned in this something intrinsic to the British character. But that of course is a load of old cobbler's.

In 1971 the Frankfurt skyline had been fairly uniform, three or four storey apartment houses and office buildings with here and there a church or larger public building protruding. In fact the only tower I can remember from that period was the Henninger Turm in Sachsenhausen, the other side of the river. The Henninger Turm was actually a grain silo for the Binding Brewery and sported yet another revolving restaurant on top of a cylindrical tower. It was reputed to be the tallest grain silo in the world, a curious distinction, which I suppose tells you something about the amount of beer the Germans drink. But by 1981 the era of the gigantic glass tower was in full swing. The Marriot hotel near the Frankfurt exhibition centre was nearly 50 stories high and there was another huge silver tower towards the main railway station. As I wandered around my old haunts, it scarcely seemed to be the same city. A mere 10 years had passed but we had well and truly moved from a modern to a post-modern era.

The next day on the booth Godfrey asked me what I had

done with myself the night before. I told him that I had had a nice time mooching around my old haunts and marvelling at how the skyline had changed in just ten years. He apologised for having left me to my own devices the previous evening. I protested that I had in fact enjoyed the experience. But he declared that I must accompany him to one of the industry functions to which he had been invited later that same evening. I wasn't sure if this was an order or an offer. Either way it was no hardship to join him. So later that evening I found myself in the bar of the Frankfurter Hof standing near Martin Amis who was holding court. He was in Frankfurt to promote his latest book, *Invasion of the Space Invaders.*

This particular book is that oddity in the Amis *fils* canon, a repudiated publication. At some point the title ceased to be acknowledged in the list of his previous publications in the front matter of subsequent books. It is now extremely difficult to find a copy of the book and in the perverse way of the market copies are starting to fetch ludicrous prices. At the time of writing dealers on Abe Books are asking a little under $200 for copies in good condition. No doubt we have all committed youthful indiscretions. But for those who have placed themselves in the public eye so squarely and from such a young age the scope for embarrassment is considerably greater. Inevitably by suppressing the title from his acknowledged literary offspring, he merely draws more attention to it.

Before the era of the Internet the dynamics of the book publishing industry and the exigencies of the copyright laws meant that the possibilities for the general reader to encounter the text were limited. This is no longer the case. The blogosphere has caught on to the matter and there are a number of sites where one can get a feel for the substance of the book. The ones I have seen are really quite respectful. To begin with it seems to be agreed that Martin knows his stuff. His tips for successful play are apparently on the money (as it were). And it can't be that he is ashamed of having spent time in the arcades. After all he has at different times rather foregrounded a variety of pastimes including pool, tennis and darts. That's what we liked about the boy wonder, the convergence of high and low culture.

Perhaps it is because with the rise of first the Super Mario and then the Internet generations the ambiance of the video game changed. The sleazy arcade is pure Amis, the dad playing Super Mario with his sons is not. No matter that he may well have done so. And then with the rise of the Internet you feel that here is a demotic realm which evades his powers of analysis and animation. Creeps and jerks he can do but perhaps not nerds and geeks. Still he shouldn't feel too sore about this. If the mighty Thomas Pynchon with his background in engineering and physics can't get his head around the web, *Bleeding Edge* really only deserving of a beta query plus, then what chance has a purely literary novelist. Your chances of convincing insight into the realm are perhaps greater the less literary you are. William Gibson or Neal Stephenson are writers that come to mind in this respect. But Amis has never made any claim to be a science fiction writer. Amis's approach is to observe low life through the lens of high culture. Each crafted sentence makes that clear. Gibson's prose has its felicities but what really impresses is the stunning prolepsis of his ideas. With Stephenson you are only too aware that he has spent more time at the command line or in the labyrinths of massively multiplayer online role-playing games (MMORPGs) than is good for anyone.

But this was a long time before repudiation. And I felt I might be one of the few people in that room who shared an enthusiasm for shooting down pixelated aliens, in my case evidenced by a number of high scores on the Galaxian consoles in an arcade just outside Victoria station. I was looking for an opportunity to strike up a conversation and ask Martin about his own experience with Galaxian. Unfortunately just as I was getting into the circle immediately around Amis, I felt a hand on my shoulder. It was Godfrey. He was finding the whole thing pretty boring. I'm not sure he knew what a video game was and in any case I suspect he was more of an Amis *père* man. He suggested we go somewhere else. I assumed he meant to another Book Fair event, but when we got outside he said that he had spotted that the film *Mephisto* by the Hungarian director, István Szabó, was playing at a local cinema. I am not much of a film buff but when Godfrey told me that the film was based on the novel

*Mephisto* by Klaus Mann, oldest son of Thomas Mann, my interest was piqued.

The novel is a critical portrait of Klaus Mann's erstwhile brother-in-law, Gustaf Gründgens, considered by many to be the twentieth century's finest German actor. The novel which was published in 1936 follows an actor, Hendrik Höfgen, who with the rise of the Nazis is portrayed as abandoning his previous political views to further his career. As with many of the artists and intellectuals who remained in Germany after the Nazi seizure of power, distinguishing those who merely accommodated the regime from those who actually collaborated continues to be a controversial issue. In fact in 1966 in a posthumous libel case Gründgens' heirs successfully sued Mann's publisher, a judgment which was upheld by the Federal Constitutional Court in 1971. By 1981, however, the novel had been republished in the Federal Republic and this time no action was taken by Gründgens' estate. Godfrey sketched all this in for me as we strolled to the cinema. Having made so much of my knowledge of Thomas Mann's work in my initial conversations with Godfrey, I was reluctant to admit to my ignorance of the biographies of the Mann clan.

In the film Höfgen is played by Karl Maria Brandauer. The theatrical company of which he is a member embraces the kind of engaged aesthetic pioneered by Bertolt Brecht. No one is more enthusiastic for this approach than Höfgen. Höfgen's signature role is Mephistopheles in Goethe's *Faust*. If *Hamlet* is the quintessential English drama albeit ostensibly set in Denmark, then *Faust* is the quintessential German drama. His portrayal of the character in a work that the Nazi's appropriated to their list of approved works attracts the attention of the Minister Präsident (Göring). After a gala performance Höfgen is asked to attend the Minister in his box. He is given no time to change out of costume so he is observed by the rest of the audience *en masque*. The Minister maintains an icy hauteur. For a moment it seems possible that Höfgen might be condemned for his deviationism. But eventually the Minister stops toying with him and, allowing his own mask to slip, publicly bestows his approval. Thereafter

Höfgen seems to have privileged access to the highest levels in the Nazi hierarchy and is even able to intercede on behalf of his black half-caste lover so that she is permitted to leave Germany for Paris which is also where his wife has fled. On a visit to Paris his wife begs him to leave too. But he can see no future for himself outside the culture, and specifically that of the German theatre ('I need the German language.') Inevitably his confidence that he can manipulate the representatives of power is misplaced and the régime appears set to destroy him. Höfgen is summoned to a meeting with the Minister at a stadium, empty but for the Minister and his thugs. Höfgen is thrust towards the arena. It looks as if he is about to be gunned down at which point the film ends.

The film is clearly a critique of those artists and intellectuals who appease totalitarian regimes and turn a blind eye to atrocity in the belief that the cultural is somehow disconnected from the political. In the classic text by Goethe it is Faust who is seduced by Mephistopheles. In Szabó's film Höfgen is identified with Mephistopheles and any explicit reference to Faust seems to be absent. In fact Höfgen plays the part in white face departing from the conventional iconography of a goatee-bearded figure in red and black. The white makeup is so thick that it suggests a mask with the implication that the real face is covered. And indeed this doubling is fundamental to Höfgen's character. He is both revolutionary and reactionary, hero and villain, husband and reprobate, Mephistopheles and Faust. In his pitiful defence that he needs the German language Höfgen is subscribing to the same perverse nationalism that is at the root of the fascist ideology. And even if Höfgen's conscience is satisfied by his own casuistical reasoning, his confidence in his ability to manipulate the representatives of the state apparatus is misplaced.

It didn't take much insight to recognise that the film reflected Godfrey's own ambivalence to his mother tongue. He must have been eight or nine years old before he learned a single word of English. Even so his English was accent free in the sense that it was perfect upper middle class RP. But as we had arrived at the Book Fair car park on the first day I had observed how engrained his *hochdeutsch* really was. A parking attendant was haranguing a pretty French woman who had undoubtedly broken some minor parking regulation. Godfrey, ever the gallant, sprang to her defence and dressed the attendant down in a style of locution that was decidedly pre-war. The attendant looked shocked but immediately stood to attention. You could almost see him click his heels as he grumpily acceded to Godfrey's demands to let the mademoiselle be. I have no doubt exaggerated the stereotypes at work but, as anyone who has ever tried to get served in a German restaurant knows, discreetly lifting a finger or trying to catch the waiter's eye is seldom a successful strategy. It is a brave Brit, however, who is prepared to bellow '*Herr Ober*'.

The next day we dismantled the booth and hit the road. Godfrey was a believer in soulless modern hotels when travelling on business and certainly the executive bunkhouses we had been staying in could have been in any country or none. As we were leaving quite late in the day we weren't sure how far we were going to get along the Autobahn before fatigue set in so we had made no booking. In fact we got to the ancient city of Koblenz and the only place we could find in which to stay was a gothic pile squatting on the precipitous banks of the Rhein. This place was far from soulless if that meant that it lacked ensuite shower and lavatory, trouser press, minibar and multi-channel TV. The decor was pre-war and we're talking World War One here and the dishes listed on the restaurant menu were of similar vintage. Neither of us much fancied what was on offer in the hotel restaurant. So we decided to stroll into the town and find something there.

Eventually we found a *Stübchen* which was offering plates of ham and onion tart (*Zwiebelkuchen*) and more importantly the new season's wine. This is called *Federweißer* because it is still foaming. It was delicious and we drank far too much. In the way of these things we became firm friends with the couple behind the bar, my German becoming more fluent it seemed, the drunker I got, only to discover that whilst she was *echt deutsch*, he was a Brit. He had been stationed nearby as a member of the British garrison. They had met, fallen in love and he had decided to stay and run a bar. What a topsy-turvy world. The German convivialitywas being supplied by an innkeper who was British, whereas the upper-crust English customer was actually German.

That was the last trip that Godfrey and I made together but not the last trip that I made on behalf of the AP. Changes were afoot. A management consultancy had been commissioned to analyse the business and make proposals to restore the company to its previous rude health. Godfrey was far from being the weak link in the executive team but perhaps he felt that his buccaneering style would not go down well with the MBA types that soon descended on Queen Anne's Gate. Whatever the precise details of the report it was clear that there would be changes at the top. Godfrey jumped before he was pushed, but more surprisingly Michael Regan stood down as managing director. A new man called Ron Norbury took the helm. Actually Ron was not altogether new. He ran the mailing house which was the one part of the AP empire that was prospering. Ron was seen as someone who had a commercial head on his shoulders. He immediately set about dismantling the urbanity of the Regan regime. No directoire desks and Eames lounge chairs for him. His desk was a conference table devoid of papers. The only things on the table were a drum shaped box of cigarettes and a glass of orange juice. He chain smoked the cigarettes and rinsed his smoky tonsils from time to time with the orange juice.

With the departure of my mentor and of the kindly and patrician Michael Regan I was none too sure what my own future might hold. In fact Ron made it clear that he saw a key role for me in the new dispensation and he kept me on the reconstituted management committee. All current and proposed expenditure was to be closely scrutinised. This was embarrassing because on my return from the ABA and AIA trip I had recommended that we fund a significant presence at the 1982 convention of the American Institute of Architects which was to be held in Honolulu, Hawaii. To my surprise this project got the green light. The only difference was that Godfrey would not be involved. This saddened me because I had been looking forward to observing his moves in a tropical setting. In his stead my real boss, George Dunn was going to head up the delegation.

George and I got on perfectly well, but where Godfrey brought cosmopolitan flair to everything he did, George's forte was stolidity. The other member of the party was Peter Davey, the editor of the Architectural Review. Peter's style was decidedly English eccentric. He had a magnificent pair of mutton chop sideburns. Think Joaquin Phoenix playing Doc Spotello in Paul Thomas Anderson's take on Thomas Pynchon's *Inherent Vice*. He also wielded a deft cigarette holder. So at least my front man had a strong visual image. Of course it helped a little that in a gathering of architects from all over the world Peter already had a reputation as a fine analyst and critic.

Even as I was putting in place the arrangements for the trip I was dragged once more into the festering dispute about the new computer. It was now more than a year since I had arrived at Queen Anne's Gate and the project had run into the sand so far as the subscription system was concerned. One day shortly after Ron had taken over I was asked to go down and see him to be informed that the system was ready to go live. Whilst I was recovering from my surprise he added that that meant we could reduce the head count in the subscription department. He pointed out that Victoria was beyond the state retirement age for women and that she should be informed that it was now company policy for staff members to retire at the appropriate age. I tried convince him that Victoria practically ran the whole thing on her own and that it might be better to keep the old system up to date just in case there were teething troubles. He waved my protestations aside and told me to arrange for her retirement.

With a sinking heart I went back to my office and talked it over with the redoubtable Yvonne, but this time she had no solution. So I asked her to call Victoria in. The situation was ridiculous really. I was not quite 30 and Victoria was 63. She had been in the Wrens and had probably been responsible for sinking quite a few Nazi U-boats in the Second World War. I asked her to sit down and told her that it was now company policy for staff to retire at the state retirement age and of course she was now some years beyond that. She said that she absolutely refused to retire. She was fit and strong, did much longer hours than practically anyone else in the company and she was the only person who knew how the whole system worked. All this was perfectly true. As I twisted a paperclip I realised how some Rear-Admiral might have felt when he outlined his misguided plans for sinking the Tirpitz to his wren aide-de-camp. A mere flag officer would have been no match for this dreadnought.

I tried to point out the pleasures and advantages of retirement although I really didn't have the faintest idea what they might be. She remained obdurate and said that she wanted to speak to the managing director. Clearly this was her right though it did suggest I had about as much authority as one of my messengers. I said I would arrange a meeting with Ron and slumped back in my middle management chair.

A week or so later I found myself once again in Ron's office with Victoria beside me. Ron smiled benignly at the two of us and asked what the issue was as if he didn't know. Victoria recounted our earlier conversation emphasising that not only was she implacably opposed to the decision but that she also thought it to be short-sighted. I was about to say that it was now company policy and so on but Ron cut me short with a wave of his hand. He praised Victoria's commitment and suggested that I was being a little overenthusiastic. You and I Victoria know what these ambitious young men are like. I gasped in astonishment but bit my tongue. He thanked Victoria for her resolve and said that he would persuade me to defer my decision at least for the foreseeable future. Victoria glanced across at me in triumph and went back up to her room.

When I was sure that the door was shut I expostulated that the whole thing had been his decision not mine and that everything that Victoria had just said I'd said to him in our first conversation on the subject. He told me to stop being so sensitive about it. The policy would go ahead but not just yet and I would have to learn to take a few more knocks if I wanted to be the future managing director of the AP. I gasped again. It was news to me that any such thing had ever or would ever be contemplated. He chided me for lacking belief in myself, a view I vehemently rejected. He expatiated a bit about how running an organisation was largely about managing people and that there wasn't a one size fits all approach. I wasn't convinced. From my point of view his behaviour smacked of cowardice and I felt undermined. I went back to my room in a foul mood. Looking back on it now I think Ron was probably right. It's taken me a hell of a long time to get that perspective on the matter. I suppose my approach was to present myself as a benign manager united with my colleagues against the tyranny of the boss. In fact it is probably better if an employee feels that he or she has the right to appeal over the head of an intransigent manager. Napoleon was famous for interacting directly with the enlisted men. Of course I was never really going to be the managing director not least because Ron had other plans for the company, namely to find a buyer once he had stabilised things. But I think he was suggesting that by taking ownership for the company as a whole one would make better decisions. At the time though I let my wounded sense of pride get the better of me.

In any case I had more immediate things to deal with, notably completing arrangements for our the trip to the AIA Convention in Hawaii. This was our big chance to remind the American architectural profession of the quality of AP publications. The AP prided itself on the quality of its graphic design, and not surprisingly its core readership was extremely discerning in these matters, so I was lucky enough to get to work with Bill Slack, the *AR*'s legendary art editor, on the display materials for our stand. We were of course taking lots of copies of the current edition of the *AR*. There was no doubt that magazine was its own best advertisement. We were also planning to take several boxes of back issues and copies of our most important books. This meant the consignment was quite large. One tip that Godfrey had given me early on was that when shipping materials abroad make sure to split up the consignment and send it in at least two batches. It was not uncommon for consignments to go astray and it wasn't much fun being on an empty stand for three days while you tried to get hold of the expediter. Godfrey was absolutely right. One of the batches failed to turn up. At least we had enough material from the one that did arrive to make a decent showing.

The flight took 16 hours with a layover in San Francisco. We were flying economy so we were all a bit frazzled by the time we arrived at Honolulu Airport on the island of Oahu. When the doors of the plane opened the humidity, for those of us who had set off from a rather chilly London, was quite a shock. There was also a beautiful scent from all the flowers in the gar-lands, or leis as they are known, that some passengers were being given as they left the plane. Unfortunately for me this precipitated an immediate sneezing fit. I used to suffer terribly from hay fever and hadn't anticipated that I might need some-thing stronger than my usual medication.

The shuttle bus from the airport to the hotel seemed to be full of Japanese honeymoon couples. Despite this fact the driv-er who was giving us a guided tour over the bus's PA seemed to feel no qualms about providing a detailed historical account as we passed Pearl Harbour. The Sheraton was right on the beach and all the honeymoon couples seemed to be heading there. For a moment I wondered where all the architects were. Had I booked into the wrong hotel? But of course the Sheraton was huge and we had arrived a little early to give us time to pre-pare things. I headed to the exhibition centre to start setting up. Later that evening there was a reception on the beach at a preposterous pink building called the Royal Hawaiian which was right next to The Sheraton. The Royal Hawaiian hinted at an era before mass tourism. There were lots of waiters cir-culating with drinks which matched the colour of the Royal Hawaiian for preposterousness. It seemed to be hard to get one that didn't have a chunk of pineapple in it. Even the food was garnished with pineapple.

Next morning was an early start so thankfully my pineapple avoidance technique meant that I hadn't overdone it with the cocktails. Once again my job was to mind the booth. Over the next couple of days we actually had more visitors than I re-member at the ABA in Atlanta or the Buchmesse in Frankfurt so at least the time didn't drag. But then this was actually a convention for architects, not one for the general book and publishing trade so it shouldn't have been quite so surprising. Quite a few of the visitors to the stand were pleased to see the AR. A number of them seemed to think that it had gone out of business some years before. I wasn't sure if this was evidence of American parochialism or the result of the AP's lack of attention to marketing.

Peter in the meantime was booked into a number of the conference sessions. When I saw him later, he seemed to be pleased with the meetings he'd had. I am not sure what George got from the event. No doubt he would have been trying to contact potential advertisers. But I have no idea whether he landed anything significant. If he did, he didn't mention it. On the other hand he was not obliged to report back to his subordinate. I also thought rather uncharitably that Ron might be planning to nudge him towards retirement and the trip was a bit of a consolation prize. At the end of the first day's proceedings I declined to join my colleagues for dinner saying I wanted to look around Honolulu. Eating with Godfrey had always been a pleasure but with George the fact that he was my boss seemed to get in the way of easy conversation.

I wandered around for a couple of hours to get a feel of the place. It felt just like any other American city. What was strange was the weather. Apart from the heat and humidity that I had noticed on landing there was an almost constant but very pleasant breeze. This was accompanied by brief showers, which didn't actually seem to make you any damper than you already were from the humidity. But I did notice that the breeze and the showers unfortunately exacerbated my allergy. Eventually I found a nice diner and had a burger and fries. What better way to underline the fact that despite the tropical setting I was in middle America. When I'd finished my meal I realised that it was already dark. Hawaii is pretty much right on the Equator so there isn't much variation in the length of the day. For those of us from higher latitudes the sun seemed to go down alarmingly quickly there.

Part of the convention schedule was a trip to a Polynesian cultural centre located on a beautiful sandy cove to experience 'real' Hawaiian hospitality. Dancers in hula skirts dancing to

160

slack key music, more preposterous drinks, leis being handed out. The cove was in a rural location and we were all bussed out there. I realised as soon as I got off the bus that the proximity to so much vegetation was setting off my allergy again. Pretty soon my nose was streaming and I had run out of dry handkerchiefs. I apologised to my colleagues and said that I would have to get back to the hotel. At least the air-conditioning there had filters. I managed to get a cab and made it back to the hotel where I shut myself in my room for the rest of the afternoon.

On the last day of the convention George congratulated me on having managed the logistics of the event successfully and said that he would like to take me out to dinner. He suggested we eat on the top floor restaurant of the hotel which had beautiful views out over Diamond Head, the extinct volcano cone that dominates Oahu. I was still feeling exhausted from the hay fever. George suggested we start with a couple of cocktails. I said I was fed up with mai tais and pineapple. He suggested a classic martini. As I took my first sip I realised that it was the driest martini I'd ever had. But it certainly perked me up. The meal was excellent and George was doing his best to deepen our relationship. Unfortunately the alcohol just encouraged me to give vent to my frustrations with how things had developed at the AP and in particular the computerisation project and the relationship with Ron. He was sympathetic and clearly thought I was just a bit burnt out and suggested I stay on in Hawaii for a few days. He would be happy to authorise it. I thanked him for his kindness but said that I had decided to resign. He was quite shocked. Actually this was a shock to me too because I hadn't allowed myself to entertain such thoughts. As we headed back to our rooms I vaguely thought that if I'd had the mai tai I'd probably still have a job. So much for pineapple avoidance.

When we got back to London I asked to see Ron and handed him a letter of resignation. He took one look at it and said that he wasn't accepting it. I said that even so I was giving three months's notice. Both Ron and George behaved decently in the remaining time that I spent at the AP and Ron wrote some complimentary words about me in a memo to the staff. I don't know why I was being so obdurate. Undoubtedly the issue about

161

Victoria's retirement had annoyed me and I had let it fester. I should have just shrugged it off. Dimly I realised that how I was reacting to Ron was how I would have reacted to Karl Miller if I'd got the job at the *London Review of Books*. Perhaps I had some issue with authoritarian male figures. At the time however I explained it to myself as a desire to run my own show, which is what I set about trying to do.

I felt that I now knew a lot about periodical publishing and what I had in mind was a magazine that carried reviews of paperback books. It seemed to me that the mainstream press only reviewed hardback books, but the majority of people actually bought paperbacks. I even had a title for the publication—*Softcover*. Of course this was misguided on so many levels. But as I worked out my notice I started writing a business plan and I put out feelers for freelance or consultancy work which would provide me with some kind of income whilst I looked for backers for the project.

# Blueprint & Tribune

SOMEONE MENTIONED TO ME that Peter Murray, the head of the Royal Institute of British Architects publications division, was looking for a person to sort out things with the subscription system for the *RIBA Journal*. This was precisely the kind of thing that I was trying to get away from. But beggars can't be choosers. And I found Peter Murray to be an easy person to work with. At least in this case the subscription system was more advanced than the card index and Addressograph system at the AP.

On the other hand I was being asked to coax an editorial copy and word processing system into handling subscriptions. But this time I was doing the technical work myself and the evening classes at the City University made me feel that I now had the skills to sort it. Within a few months I had managed to get something running and even more amazingly it actually seemed to work. I do not really know how robust this farrago was nor how long it lasted, but Peter seemed reasonably pleased with it. Over Christmas drinks at the end of 1982 I had mentioned to Peter my plans for launching a magazine. He replied that he too was in the process of launching a new magazine. Why didn't I join his project? Of course the odds of success were not good and there wouldn't be any remuneration initially. On the plus side he already had backers, which I had to admit was a lot further than I'd got with my own proposal. I said I'd think about it.

It didn't actually take me long to think about it because Peter's project was already a reality. He had assembled a group of the hippest architectural writers and photographers and top-notch graphic designers to launch the groundbreaking architecture and design magazine *Blueprint*. The editorial team included Deyan Sudjic, who had been at the AP a little before my time, and Jonathan Glancey, Dan Cruickshank, Lloyd Grossman and the art editor was Simon Esterson, most with previous at the AP. The group was top-heavy with creative talent and Peter was just about the only one shouldering the business side of things. He clearly needed some support in this function which was where I came in. I might not have had much standing with architectural critics and graphic designers but I was known to the gatekeepers at W H Smith Wholesale and John Menzies and I had connections with most of the avant garde and design publication outlets like the Institute of Contemporary Arts Bookshop and the Triangle Bookshop at the Architectural Association. Although this meant putting my own project on hold, I was flattered to be invited to join such a trendy group.

Before I was formally on board Peter had organised some advance publicity. A photo of the core members of the group had appeared in a Sunday colour supplement captioned 'The Style Gang by Moonlight'. This was an oblique reference to the fact that the majority of the contributors were moonlighting, ie working for *Blueprint* in their own time whilst holding down full-time jobs elsewhere. In my case not only did I not have a full-time employer but I was emphatically going to have to conduct my functions for *Blueprint* in the daylight hours. I was unlikely to get an evening appointment with a W H Smith account executive. But I convinced myself that I could make it work. I was soon included in the *Blueprint* share distribution and I set about trying to get good availability at key outlets.

Naturally enough my efforts were not entirely successful. *Blueprint* was a design-led publication. One of the key ideas to which I had not been party because it was decided before I came on board was that it would be produced in a non-standard large format paper size. It was also not produced on the coated paper that was usual for high specification publications. What this meant was that W H Smith didn't really know how to handle it. It was too large to go on shelves for upright display.

It would have fitted nicely on the face-up display shelf at the bottom of many newsagents display racks but this was a hotly contested space. Few newsagents were going to relegate proven sellers on the off-chance that there was a large untapped readership for a trendy design magazine.

Like any start-up we had little in the way of a promotional budget. But what we did have was allocated to a launch party to which the great and the good in the worlds of architecture and design were invited. Deyan and Peter were well connected in those worlds and pulled off the amazing feat of persuading enough important people to let us hold the launch party in the half-built Lloyd's building in Lime Street in the City designed by Richard Rogers. It was a glittering occasion and made quite a PR splash. But for the sullen account executives in the wholesale news trade a launch party in a half-finished office building which had most of its insides hanging out was not going to help them persuade Mr Patel to stock extra copies.

In the end we got a reasonable distribution, but *Blueprint* was an expensive publication to produce and as I knew only too well it would be quite some time before we knew the extent of our unsolds and even longer before we would see revenue from copy sales. I wasn't privy to the precise details of the cashflow, but it didn't take a financial genius to work out that at some point we were going to hit the buffers. Peter had done a brilliant job at getting the project off the ground but soon a considerable amount of new capital would have to be raised if the company was not to go bust.

Once again Peter and Deyan worked their contacts and managed to raise more capital, mainly from Terence Conran and Rodney Fitch. This covered the costs of production and the basic expenses of a small staff for the foreseeable future. But this left most of us on the team still moonlighting, or in my case daylighting, which was by now having a serious impact on my ability to pay my mortgage, not a pleasant situation when you have a two-year old child and a second baby on the way. Eventually I told Peter that I would have to step down as circulation director. He understood and pointed out that I was still a shareholder, which was true but we had been heavily diluted by the Conran and Fitch investments. Fortunately I was able to increase the number of days I was working elsewhere but it was going to take a long time to restore the health of my finances.

The last time I looked, *Blueprint* was still being published. I used to go along to AGMs but eventually the founding shareholders were wiped out and I ceased to attend. Peter and Deyan eventually moved on too but not before they had developed *Blueprint* into one of the best magazines in the world.

In the meantime Christina and I had bought a small house in Cambridge, so for much of this period I was commuting into London. I had also become increasingly concerned about the direction that the Thatcher government was taking especially after the Falklands War and I joined the local Labour party. In retrospect the 1983 General Election was clearly a fiasco for the Labour Party. The manifesto has been called the longest suicide note in history. But at the time I found it inspiring. At least the Labour Party stood for something and the manifesto hadn't been assembled by slide-rule wielding psephologists targeted on maximum blandness. So I threw myself into the campaign and more or less gave up my freelance work for the duration. I was initially apprehensive about the door-to-door canvassing fearing that I would be put on the spot about some item in the manifesto. But for the most part any doorstep debate was conducted in the most general terms. Since I had a car I was put on the list of those prepared to chauffeur visiting bigwigs and ferry elderly or infirm voters to the polling station. Actually since my car was a VW Beetle I was pretty much limited to chauffeuring one person at a time. Getting an elderly person into the back seat of a Beetle is not the easiest manoeuvre.

The bigwigs I was appointed to collect from the station and take to public meetings were Denis Healey and Clive Jenkins. Denis Healey is a name that still has considerable resonance enhanced by the great age he lived to. During the first draft of this section he was still alive and it looked like he might make 100. Alas that was not to be, but 98 is not a bad innings. Clive Jenkins on the other hand is a name that has faded from public consciousness confused perhaps with Roy Jenkins, Gang of Four member, SDP founder and a former President of the European Commission. But at that point both Healey and Jenkins were considerable figures in the Labour movement and I was looking forward to rubbing shoulders with them.

Healey had been Chancellor of the Exchequer in the 1970s and Secretary of State for Defence in the 1960s. People still say that he was the best Prime Minister we never had. But he had a blunt manner and did not suffer fools. More crucially he did not seek to build a following and had interests outside politics, a so-called hinterland. When Jim Callaghan stepped down as leader in 1980 it was assumed, not least by Healey himself, that he would become leader. But discontent was already brewing in the party and Michael Foot was elected leader. Healey had to content himself with being elected unopposed as Foot's deputy. At that time the leader was still elected by the Parliamentary Labour Party and a number of those who voted for Foot almost immediately left the party to form the SDP. They reasoned that a Labour Party with Foot as its leader would be unelectable and so would enhance the prospects of the fledgling SDP. In the subsequent turmoil the party decided to change the way it elected its leadership by introducing an electoral college with votes from the constituency parties and trade union affiliates counted alongside the votes of MPs.

Clive Jenkins's CV is not quite as illustrious but in his day he was a big beast. He had become the general secretary of the forerunner to the ASTMS union at the early age of 35 and through the 1970s built it into one of the biggest unions of its time with nearly 500,000 members. He was somewhat shunned by more traditional trade union leaders but his ready wit and quick turn of phrase meant that he was a frequent guest on current affairs television programmes and eventually became a prominent member of the TUC general council. In 1983 both men had an extremely high public profile and were what you might call larger than life. But as is so often the case with larger than life individuals or those only previously encountered via the broadcast media both men were in fact quite small.

The only thing that was troubling me as I drove to the station to pick up Healey was that I was far from being an enthusiastic supporter of either man. Healy was the deputy leader at that point and I certainly was loyal enough to respect his position. But like many of my generation I had a sneaking admiration for Tony Benn who once the electoral college system for electing the leadership had been set up challenged Healy for the post of deputy in 1981. But on the other hand Benn and Foot (and Clive Jenkins too for that matter) had been opposed to Britain joining the European Community. Healy had hardly been an enthusiast. The best that might be said of his position during the years leading up to accession was that he was equivocal. He felt the arguments were finely balanced and he respected Wilson's manoeuvring on the subject. In his autobiography referring to this period he wrote 'I had more sympathy for Harold Wilson's conduct on this issue than on some others. As Attlee had demonstrated during the Bevanite challenge in the fifties, in Opposition the overriding duty of the Leader is to keep the Party together.'

As a former modern languages student and someone who had had first-hand experience of working in Europe before accession and the concomitant hassles of work and residence permits I was firmly in favour of Europe and had voted as such in the referendum in 1975. The campaign leading up to the referendum had thrown up some strange alliances. Benn, Foot and Enoch Powell against; Heath, Roy Jenkins and Thatcher for. But I also favoured loyalty and discipline. No group endeavour can be successful without most of the members of the group suspending some proportion of their beliefs. So I was far from impressed by those former members who had broken away to form the SDP and I was prepared to work very hard for Foot and Healey despite my admiration for Benn.

Whatever the policy differences between these politicians they all had immense abilities as public speakers. As I drove Healey from the station in my yellow Beetle he asked me how it was going on the doorstep. A few minutes later my callow observations about the local situation were incorporated into a speech of power and wit which seemed to show that Healey had an intimate understanding of the general election battle in Cambridge. No doubt this was a trick that he was able to pull off day after day as he toured the election frontlines. He then moved on to excoriating the economic record of Tories since 1979 and wound up with some scathing comments about the SDP. Nor was he able to resist some withering asides about the activist tendency in the party which had been campaigning for Benn. Unless Labour closed the gap between the party activists and the average voter it would never get power and all the aspirational baggage of the manifesto was so much empty verbiage. One does not tend to think of Healy as a proponent of the union block vote, but he referred approvingly to Sidney Webb's description of constituency parties being dominated by fanatics, cranks and extremists.

But by 1981 that system of checks and balances had been amended by the creation of the electoral college in which for the first time individual members had had a direct vote for the election of the leader and deputy leader. It was this change that had nearly swept Healey from his position and which threatened to destabilise the internal workings of the party for some time to come.

If there is a criticism to be made of Healey it is that he used his undoubted rhetorical skills to rough up his opponents rather than to inspire his followers. Towards the end of *The Time Of My Life* in ostensibly praising Nigel Lawson's intellectual exuberance as a backbencher he remarks, 'He had a raffish insolence which reminded me sometimes of Steerforth in David Copperfield, sometimes of a rather tubby Alcibiades.' A considerbaly thinner, though somewhat dottier, Nigel Lawson might well cherish such a dithyramb.

Benn on the other hand rarely engaged in ad hominem attacks partly one supposes because he was so often the target of them himself. And he had a marvellous way of relating whatever the contemporary debate was about to deep trends in English history. So once he got into his New Jerusalem and other Eden mode it was easy to believe that arrangements for electing the leader of the Labour Party were part of a continuum linking the English Civil War, the Chartists and the Suffragette movement. Thrilling oratory, but dangerous simplifications. In the same way his inclusiveness provided a rallying point for a

169

considerable number of those who had been and in some cases remained members of groups outside the Labour Party and who did not really have the party's best interests at heart.

Of course both Healey and Clive Jenkins had been members of the Communist Party, though in Healey's case this had been during the 30s and in Jenkins's case when he was very young. If prior membership of a leftist party had ever constituted grounds for being rejected as a member of the party then many subsequently prominent rightwing figures in the party including such scourges of the left as Peter Mandelson would have been affected. But then the terms left and right when applied to politics have always been seriously misleading.

In my own case whilst never a communist or trotskyite or indeed a member of any organisation further left than the mainstream Labour Party, I had read a fair amount of Marx mainly in the context of German 19th century thought and appreciated that international solidarity between workers and oppressed groups was necessary. If capital operated on an international basis, then it was vital for the representatives of labour to be just as international. We are now at the high noon of global capitalism and it feels like this lesson still has not been learned.

Neither Healey nor Jenkins could hit the rhapsodic notes that seemed to come so naturally to Benn but they were certainly gifted speakers. Healey was like your favourite uncle full of nudge nudge jokes with serious punchlines. Jenkins by contrast loved the play of words and seemed to get carried away by his own fluency. At the end it wasn't at all clear what he had said about the Labour programme, but you were left with a powerful impression of a man who was a master at promoting the brand, though you had a sneaking suspicion that the brand was in fact Jenkins himself. The days driving Jenkins and Healey to their meetings were a welcome relief from the leafletting and door-knocking. Their attitude to me as their driver and temporary minder was decent and friendly and Jenkins even offered me a nip from his hip-flask, an offer I declined because I could tell it wasn't orange squash or tea which it would have been if I'd been Benn's driver.

In Cambridge according to the canvass returns things were

not looking too bad. But the personal attacks on Michael Foot were unrelenting. Foot was a decent man, a proper intellectual and nowhere near as shambolic as the gutter press made him out to be. The Conservatives had swept to power in 1979 with the infamous Labour Isn't Working poster pointing to the fact that 1.2 million people were unemployed. Whatever your affiliations you have to admit this was a brilliant piece of political copywriting. But in fact by the end of 1981 the total had risen to 2.9 million and during 1982 it went through the symbolically significant 3 million mark and did not get substantially less than that until 1987. Nor were the inflation figures much better. The Conservatives had excoriated Labour on its inflation record which had peaked at 24% in 1975 but by mid-1980 inflation was once again over 20%. As in 1973, the immediate cause was political turbulence in the Middle East and its effect on the price of oil which almost quadrupled.

So the economy was not in any sense on the mend. Reports had emerged of serious differences of opinion within the cabinet with regard to the implementation of monetarist policies. If even the politicians found it difficult to distinguish the different money supply measures, what were the electorate to make of M1, M0 and M3. And as George Schultz, Ronald Reagan's secretary of state had said in a different context 'The economist's lag is the politician's nightmare.'

And this was exacerbated by the cuts that the Conservatives had initiated on taking office. One target of these cuts was the defence budget. In 1981 the Defence Minister was John Nott and he was determined to try and bring defence spending under control. Amongst the proposals was the idea of selling one of the Royal Navy's aircraft carriers to Argentina. This was resisted by the Foreign Office though not definitively rejected. But one cut that was carried out was the withdrawal of HMS *Endurance* from the Southern Atlantic. In itself the *Endurance* was not a particularly formidable warship but the message its removal sent to the Argentinian junta was unmistakeable not least because there had already been a number of bilateral discussions with the Argentinians about the future of the islands including a clandestine meeting in Switzerland in 1980 between Nicholas Ridley, then a Foreign Office minister, and his opposite number in the Argentinian administration to discuss the transfer of sovereignty. So when the Argentinians finally invaded it was hardly a surprise. Indeed both Callaghan and Healey had expressed concern several times in the House of Commons about Argentina's intentions.

It is probably true to say that the majority of Britains had only the vaguest idea of where the Falklands were. This vagueness was shared by Thatcher herself. When she was discussing with Admiral Leach the plans to retake the islands her assumption was that it would only take three days sailing for the task force to get there rather than three weeks. The events leading up to the invasion constituted a serious misjudgement by the Thatcher administration but once the decision had been made to retake the islands by military force Thatcher was in her element. A task force was quickly scrambled and much against the odds the Argentinian force was defeated. It could have turned out quite differently however. The Argentinian air force was equipped with Exocet missiles which sank the *Sheffield*, the *Atlantic Conveyor* and damaged the *Glamorgan*. The Royal Navy also lost the *Coventry*, *Ardent*, *Antelope* and *Sir Galahad* in other actions. Had the Argentinians performed better at fusing their bombs or been able to acquire more Exocets or had the British not had a number of vessels that had effective anti-missile equipment fitted the losses might have been much more considerable. Losing the *Atlantic Conveyor* with its supplies and helicopters was bad enough but the loss of even one of the aircraft carriers probably would have doomed the mission. In the event a difficult and bloody land campaign decided the matter.

Almost immediately Mrs Thatcher was promoted to the pantheon of great British war leaders. Her administration's record on economic and social matters was poor but her own approval rating soared. Never one to miss an opportunity she decided to bring forward the date of the General Election. She was conscious of how leaving the election to the last moment had undone Jim Callaghan.

One of the problems with human psychology is that we all

suffer from confirmation bias. In other words we find the evidence to support our intuitive beliefs or views. So knocking on doors in 1983 to canvass people's views about the forthcoming election was a curious experience. Our pitch was to point out that Labour was the party of fairness and justice and that Conservative policies over the previous four years had led to things getting worse for working people and disadvantaged groups with the rise in unemployment to levels last seen in the Depression, the increase in prescription charges, the freezing of the untaxed element in income at a time when inflation was ripping and swingeing increases in the excise on petrol, tobacco and alcohol. But that seemed of little concern to the majority of people or if they did acknowledge it what they really wanted to talk about was the break down in law and order, the decline of deference and the patriotic pride in the British armed forces in the Falklands conflict. It was of no avail to point out that the invasion had been partly caused by the penny-pinching and dithering of Mrs Thatcher's administration.

To anyone who had dabbled in Marxist ideas it was no surprise to encounter people who voted against their own best interests. But false consciousness seemed a rather pallid explanation for the phenomenon. No doubt we all consider ourselves rational agents but even a cursory reading of Freud will show that our behaviour is substantially influenced by unconscious impulses. In addition there is a considerable difference between logical reasoning and what might be called moral reasoning. Moral reasoning is how we feel about things. It seems to be a post-hoc rationalisation for judgements we have already made based on intuition or gut-feeling. It turns out that this is by no means a new idea. David Hume in *A Treatise of Human Nature* (1739) wrote that 'reason is, and ought only to be the slave of the passions, and can never pretend to any other office than to serve and obey them.'

More recent neurological thought tends to support this view. Antonio Damasio in *Descartes' Error* (1994) shows the extent to which the faculty of reason is dependent on the emotions. More than 30 years later this was all brought into focus for me by Jonathan Haidt's marvellous book *The Righteous Mind*

173

(2012). But back in 1983 it just seemed to me that I was a poor advocate for a patently superior system.

If I'd had access to the thinking behind Haidt's book I would have realised that implicit in the left-liberal's attitude to conservative views is a heavy dose of condescension. Those on the left see the world clearly and just want to help people, whilst those on the right merely act out of self-interest. Haidt identifies left-liberals as caring people motivated by issues of fairness, justice and liberty. But they are also very often blind to, or dismissive of, issues of deference, respect for traditions, loyalty and, in particular, patriotism. If they consider these matters at all it is to dismiss them as not fundamental. But by doing so they are failing to engage effectively with the people they most need to persuade. As Haidt points out, 'You can't make a dog happy, by forcibly wagging its tail. And you can't change people's minds by utterly refuting their arguments'. The wider the range of values to which you can appeal, the more likely your advocacy is to succeed. And it would appear that conservative (with a small c) advocates are better at this than progressives. And that is perhaps why we had to wait for Clinton, Blair and Obama to break the right's hegemony.

In fact under the conditions that had prevailed for the post-war period the result ought not to have been quite so bad for Labour. But in 1983 the electoral arithmetic was complicated by the existence of the SDP. The Conservatives share of the vote actually declined despite the Falklands effect but because the opposition vote was split by the presence of the SDP-Liberal alliance and thanks to the quirks of the British first past the post system the Conservatives increased their majority from 44 to 141 seats. In our little activist bubble we had somehow convinced ourselves that we had done quite well and we had planned a party for election night. We weren't as naive as to suppose that we would be celebrating a handsome victory in the constituency or indeed in the country but we did in the apocryphal words of the Iron Duke think that it was a damn close run thing. But in the event it wasn't and the party never happened. It was not to be the last time that I experienced an election night party fizzling out.

My first impulse in the aftermath of the defeat was to give up on politics completely not least because I had seriously damaged my freelance earnings as a consequence of my political and entrepreneurial games. But as I digested the various post-mortems I came to realise what was obvious to many others that the Labour operation needed more than just renewal, it needed serious updating too. I wondered if there might be a role for me in a professional capacity rather than as a foot-soldier in a constituency. During the campaign I had found the best analysis in *Tribune* and decided to contact the publication to see if they could do with some help in marketing and circulation.

I wrote to the editor, Chris Mullin, offering my services on a part-time basis and received a reply a few days later inviting me to visit the *Tribune* offices near King's Cross to explore the idea further. Chris was interested in my offer and he thought that in the wake of a second election defeat it was a good moment to try and increase the paper's circulation. The paper was broadly Bennite and it seemed that there was a considerable thirst on the left for solutions that might draw on Tony Benn's ideas. He said that he would need to put the proposal to other colleagues and then he would get back to me. But first he wanted to introduce me to Sheila Noble.

Sheila was nominally the editorial secretary but in the way of these things she was so much more than that. Production manager and keeper of the *Tribune* flame might have been a better title. She had previously been Dick Clements' secretary and before that Michael Foot's assistant. So she was well-connected politically. She looked me briskly up and down and asked me about my name. I explained that my grandmothers were Irish. Did that mean I was a Catholic? I was a little taken aback at being quizzed about my religious affiliation. I confirmed that I had had a Catholic upbringing but that I had been a practising atheist since the age of 16. She said something to the effect that Catholics who lost their faith always ended up being lefties and that I would be joining her and Chris in the apostate's branch.

Once again I realised that I was a candidate in an unconventional interview process and that by a quirk of my cultural formation

175

I had been successful in my application. Clearly Sheila's support was enough to convince other colleagues. It was only later that I discovered that there was also a certain amount of opposition to the idea. And it has to be said that my record of labour activism was rather limited, whereas the marks of social and educational privilege were all too evident. But in that regard I was in good company. Blissfully ignorant of this dissenting opinion I started work on a two day a week basis at the appropriate SOGAT rate. Many a mickle makes a muckle, but the *Tribune* mickle scarcely covered the cost of commuting into London. But then that wasn't really the reason for taking the job.

If the subscription system at The Architectural Press had been Dickensian, it was positively Heath-Robinsonesque at *Tribune*. One thing they had in common was reliance on the infernal Addressograph system. Shrugging off the unsettling feeling that history was about to repeat itself and possibly as farce, following the model in Marx's quip in the '18th Brumaire of Louis Napoleon', I decided that the Addressograph system would have to go and I would transfer the subscriptions to a computer. I persuaded myself that I would learn from the AP experience and not attempt to get the computer to do too much. It would simply keep a record of subscriptions and produce the weekly mailing labels. There would be no interfacing with accounting systems or advertisement sales systems. And most importantly I would buy a personal computer and program it myself.

Under the circumstances this was about as hubristic as you could get. But it wasn't completely without merit. My time at the AP had shown me the kind of pitfalls to avoid and I had also learned some useful lessons while fettling the RIBA's subscription system. More particularly the advent of the personal computer meant that I could at last apply the skills I had acquired in evening classes at the City University when I had been at Kiver-Patterson.

When I talked my plans over with Chris and Sheila they were reasonably positive but warned me that I might encounter opposition from other quarters. I wasn't quite sure what they meant by this but set about the project with a certain sense of trepidation. Soon my concerns about opposition from other quarters were submerged in the more pressing anxiety that my programming skills might not be quite as serviceable as I had been saying they were. What's more I hadn't anticipated that my choice of computer would be controversial.

This was in late 1983 or early 1984 and the first flush of personal computer enthusiasm. In the UK the great success story had been the BBC Micro designed and built by Acorn which had won the contract for a microcomputer to accompany the BBC's Computer Literacy Project. The immediate effect of this was that the machine was designated as one of two machines (the other being Research Machines 380Z) which the government agreed to subsidise to the tune of 50% for educational sales. At its peak the BBC Micro had around 80% of the schools market. On the back of this endorsement the company grew rapidly but the subsidy from the government bred a certain amount of complacency which resulted in a slowing of the pace of technological innovation. Consequently by the end of 1983 the BBC Micro was underpowered and overpriced. You could get a Commodore 64 with 64K of memory, twice the amount of the BBC Micro B, for about 80 quid cheaper. So that's what I bought. Bear in mind that *Tribune* ran on a shoestring and that the money for the computer had had to be raised by a special reader appeal. So £80 really mattered. In fact the BBC machine had many innovative features but in practice these were not relevant to the majority of use cases. And indeed in due course Acorn ran into cashflow problems and had to be rescued by Olivetti, eventually losing its independence.

The great problem that computerisation projects run into is the gulf of misunderstanding between the client and the programmer. In this case I was both. More problematic was dusting off my rusty BASIC. The evening classes I had taken at the City University had been run on the mainframe via a teletype terminal, essentially a keyboard controller with no screen. Results were printed out on dot matrix printers. Storage was no doubt on large tapes in the basement but in practice one never needed to bother about that aspect. However with micros external data storage was on a cassette. Floppy disks did exist but were not yet standard at the hobbyist or home office level.

Thankfully I had no one looking over my shoulder and I started to make some progress. Before I had got to the stage where I could demonstrate a prototype Chris called me into his office and said that he'd had a call from Tony Benn who although he approved of the project wanted to know why we were using an American machine rather than a British one. Would I mind going around to see him to talk about it? Of course I'd be happy to. What else could I say?

When I had heard Tony Benn speak during the election campaign little did I think that within a few months I would be meeting the man himself. And so a few days later I found myself making my way to his house in Holland Park. I was invited into his basement office which was an Aladdin's cave of filing cabinets, papers and books. Tony was welcoming and invited me to sit down. We had a few moments of chit-chat. Despite his attempts to put me at my ease I found it difficult to relax. This was after all the man who in 1968 as minister of technology in Harold Wilson's first administration had overseen the creation of ICL in an attempt to create a British computer industry that could compete with companies like IBM. He was also noted as a enthusiastic adopter of gadgetry. Eventually he brought the conversation around to the issue of the *Tribune* computer. I explained that the decision was based entirely on cost benefit analysis. I also outlined to him my theory about Acorn's complacency. The subsidy paid to Acorn by the government for computers sold into the education service meant that there was no need for the company to compete on price for the ordinary user and consequently they were not reacting to developments in the market. I was afraid that he might be angry about my smuggling into the conversation a tribute to the free market. But he just said that it was sad that such a technologically innovative country so often seemed unable to exploit commercially the fruits of our research and development. I nodded and then we got on to talking about where information technology was heading, a subject on which he seemed genuinely well-informed. Eventually it became clear that he had other things to get on with. As I took my leave he wished me well with the project.

I do not think that I am alone in having been affected by Benn's undoubted charisma. One of my uncles was the chairman of a Conservative Association in Chesterfield where Benn became MP after he lost his Bristol seat. My uncle was no enthusiast for Benn's brand of politics but in the course of the inevitable constituency argy-bargy came into contact with him on more than one occasion. He found him to be a perfect gentleman. Of course he may have been influenced by the fact that Benn was a genuine toff, whereas his own background was rather humbler.

The other topic that Benn had wanted to talk to me about was how to increase *Tribune's* circulation. He suspected that the newstrade was using specious commercial arguments to hinder the spread of a political view to which they took exception. I was not convinced by this as I had had exactly the same problem with architectural magazines. But I did think that the duopoly of W H Smith and Menzies meant that publications from independent publishers or those that addressed a specialist audience were not well served. Of course when you raised this with executives they pointed to the numerous model railway and hobby magazines and the magazines like Smash Hits and The Face which had gone from tiny beginnings to mass circulations without the backing of giant corporations. They also pointed out that many lavishly supported magazines failed shortly after launch and that any magazine that had a loyal readership after 50 years was a considerable achievement. Tony asked me to draft a letter in his name to be sent to the chairmen of W H Smith and Menzies. In due course he got sympathetic replies, but newstrade sales remained static at best.

For the next few weeks I beavered away at my BASIC programming and eventually had a working prototype. I thought that this would be a good moment to let everyone see what I had been working on. One afternoon I gathered everyone in the administration office and ran through the application. Given the creaky financial state of *Tribune* I thought that the advantages in respect of efficiency and cost savings would be obvious. I hadn't bargained, however, for the strong luddite tendency that emanated from certain quarters of the room. Some people seemed to think that the new system would transgress unspecified union demarcations. Others that it was the thin end of a wedge which would result in job cuts.

You would have thought that people involved in the struggle for worker representation would have realised that capitalism is endlessly innovating and will simply outflank the opposition unless it too innovates. Technology after all is neutral. Fundamentalists who want to return us to a set of mediaeval social relations nevertheless wield Kalashnikovs, mobile phones and make extensive use of the internet. But for some of the *Tribune* old guard a Commodore 64 was most certainly the work of the devil.

Chris and Sheila were not surprised by the reaction and said that people would eventually come around to the idea. In any case what was uppermost in people's minds was the miners' strike which was approaching its critical phase. *Tribune* rented office space in the Agricultural Workers Union office block in Gray's Inn Road. The NUAW had been absorbed into the TGWU a couple of years previously and now most of the office space was surplus to requirement and was let out to deserving causes like Tribune. At the back of the building there was a boardroom, now seldom used and an apartment previously for the use of the General Secretary. The building was probably less than 20 years old but somehow in its redundant shabbiness seemed much older, although it was challenged in this dubious distinction by Tribune's office furniture. The most rickety chair in the office was wryly referred to as Orwell's chair. So the empty floors of the building became temporary dormitories for miners down to London to lobby their MPs and to attend demonstrations in support of their cause.

There was only one rather unreliable lift in the building and with the passage of time and the increased traffic it started to break down more and more frequently. I had yet to personally experience the lift jamming and remained unconcerned. One Friday evening Sheila and I found ourselves the last people in the office. As we stepped into the lift Sheila mentioned that Chris never but never used the lift if he was the last one in the building. I think we might have smiled at one another in silent acknowledgement of Chris's timidity as the doors slid shut. Chris had a reputation for carefulness, but his caution *vis-à-vis* the lift proved to be justified.

The lift started its descent and then juddered to a halt. We looked at each other in disbelief. As lapsed Catholics we knew that the Devil kept a close eye on us and must have laughed as we entered the lift so smugly ignoring Chris's good advice. He clearly had a more realistic appreciation of the extent to which the demonic inheres in the inanimate world. I sprang to the control panel and punched the floor numbers one after another but to no avail. The lift stayed decidedly jammed. These days we would simply pull out a mobile phone and before long salvation would be at hand. But the ubiquitous mobile phone was still some years off. So we were going to have to find some other way of alerting others to our plight.

Even though we were the last people to leave the *Tribune* office, Sheila thought it just possible that Jack Dromey, then General Secretary of the Agricultural Workers Union might still be somewhere in the building. He was fond of a drink in the Lucas Arms over the road on a Friday evening and might not have made his way over there yet. So she suggested pressing the alarm bell. Disconcertingly a faint buzz came from what sounded like a long way away. On the principle that alarms are nearly always ignored we decide to shout. In such circumstances you can't beat the word *help*. It is short and apposite and conducive to getting a lungful of air behind it. By contrast sentences shouted at the top of one's voice tend to disintegrate into meaningless syllables. Even with a single vowel there is an element of self-consciousness involved in shouting in a confined space with another person present. Our first attempts were a little sedate and lacking in conviction. It was as if getting to the point of shouting for help in front of another person actually confirmed that we were trapped. Until that moment it might have been some stupid mistake or a temporary fault.

Once we had got over this initial hesitancy we developed a more confident approach and duetted for a few minutes, initially in unison but increasingly introducing more complex rhythms. Eventually we had exhausted our improvisatory repertoire and subsided into a breathless silence. It was pretty evident that whilst we had established that there was no one else in the building, we had at the same time broken through a barrier of reserve that might be thought peculiar to the British. Which was just as well because it looked like we were going to be in close proximity to each other for quite a lot longer.

Normally our loved ones would have been expecting us home, it being a Friday evening. But on this particular occasion I was planning to stay in a room I rented in Deptford because I had a meeting the next day so Christina would not be expecting to see me. She wouldn't necessarily be expecting a phone call either since the flat was not equipped with what we would now call a landline. She would certainly be irritated that I hadn't attempted to call her from a call-box but she knew me of old and in any case she had two small children to feed and put to bed. Nor would Sheila be immediately missed as her husband would probably assume that she was at some tiresome meeting. Eventually, of course, he would realise that there was some more sinister reason for her continuing absence. So it was starting to look as if it might not be some hours before John would decide to travel across London to Gray's Inn Road, spot Sheila's Renault 5 in the car park and then summon one or other of the emergency services. In the meantime to complicate matters our families had no idea that we were together, nor were they aware of each other. So we were in for a long wait in a confined space. It even seemed as went through the logic of the situation that we might be there until the following morning.

The thought was not a comfortable one. Twelve hours or more together in a space less than six feet by six feet was going to be a challenge. And then there was the problem of bodily functions. Perhaps the same thing had occurred to Sheila because she started examining some black plastic bin bags that had been left in the lift by the janitor. I wasn't sure if this was the right moment to share my concerns, but managed to ask her in a far from nonchalant way how she was able to remain so calm. She said that if I'd ever been in the middle of the North Sea in a force eight gale in a small boat as she had been I'd know what an uncomfortable situation was. And at least it was dry and warm.

Anyway Sheila was not the type to let a male of the species go to pieces in a tight corner. Her husband was an electrical engineer, the sort of person who had actually built his own computer and written his own disk operating system, which is the really difficult bit. Because I had just programmed a subscription system on a Commodore 64 Sheila seemed to assume that my technical abilities might be of the same order as John's. She felt sure that if we could remove the cover plate of the control panel we might find a reset button or we might be able to do something by swapping fuses around or there might be some obviously defective part which we could replace though it was not entirely clear with what. A hairclip? I was dubious about the logic, though she had undoubtedly seen John magically coax all sorts of mechanical and electrical objects back to life. My own skills in this respect were little short of woeful and had given rise to much mirth on occasion in the past. Reluctant to come across as a complete wimp I said that she was undoubtedly right but we had no tools not even a screwdriver. At which she triumphantly produced a large Swiss Army penknife from her handbag. It looked large enough to be the kind that has a tool for taking stones out of horses's hooves. She handed it over to me and invited me to start dismantling the interior of the lift. I was far from sure that this was a good idea. But Sheila as I might have already suggested was not a woman to brook dissent.

I unscrewed the cover plate on the control panel to reveal— virtually nothing. Cables snaked away somewhere else seemingly to the roof of the lift car. I looked up and realised that there was a trapdoor in the roof. I was just tall enough to reach up and push it to one side. I then gripped each side of the hatch and pulled myself up. It had been quite some while since I had been in a gym and my arms were trembling with the effort, but Sheila gave me a shove which providing me with enough of an upward impetus to get my head through the hatch and hook my elbows on either side of the trapdoor opening. I looked around me but it was dark and I could see little. Cables disappeared

183

above my head into the lift shaft and there were metal fixtures on top of the car. I let myself back into the cabin. As I recovered my breath I told Sheila that at this stage I was reluctant to do anything that might make our situation worse. Actually I was reluctant to do anything that might get me caught up in the machinery or that might short out the power so that not only would we remain trapped if I managed not to electrocute myself but that we would do so in pitch darkness. She was kind enough to take my pathetic excuses seriously but I imagine that she was privately thinking that John would have much more resourceful under similar circumstances.

Having exhausted the most obvious routes of escape or rescue we sat down on the floor together and became more philosophical. We started to focus on the chances of the janitor coming into the building the next morning and decided to try and conserve our energy and try and sleep. We were chatting fitfully still a couple of hours later when Sheila dug me in the ribs and asked me if I could hear anything. I listened intently. At first there was only the distant rumble of traffic but after a bit I thought I could hear a door being shut somewhere in the building. Immediately we resumed our cries of help. We paused for a moment and listened again. Nothing. And then somewhere the sound of footsteps, someone singing. We intensified our cries and also thumped on the sides of the lift. Eventually we heard a man's voice quizzically calling 'Hello?' Sheila said she thought it must be Jack. We shouted back that we were stuck in the lift. Eventually the person who now seemed to be above our heads shouted out that he would get help. The silence then resumed and for a while I had the odd feeling that the encounter had been a wish fulfilment hallucination.

It was about eight o'clock. We had jumped to our feet when we had been shouting and remained standing now waiting for our rescuer to return and set us free. I wasn't quite sure how he intended to do this. Was he going to get the janitor who would know a way of resetting the lift control apparatus? Or call the lift manufacturers? It was a Friday evening and it might take a while to locate a qualified operative. Ten or fifteen minutes passed when suddenly we heard quite a lot of footsteps and a confused antiphony of shouts then the sound of metallic bang-ing. Eventually the outer door of the lift was forced open and we heard a cheery male voice announcing that the Fire Brigade had arrived and that they'd have us out of there in a jiffy. We then heard noises above our head and the lift began to slowly move upwards as if being manually winched from the top of the building. When the bottom of the lift got level with the floor which had been above us the doors were forced open once again and we were pulled out by a couple of burly firemen.

They were solicitous and friendly and took a few notes. But you could see that they were chuckling quietly at our plight. It was after all one of the more minor rescues they would ever have to make. Perhaps it ranked a little above a cat stuck up a tree. But that was about it. You couldn't help feeling that what they were going to be smirking about in the tender as they made their way back to the station was how we might have passed our hours in such close proximity. Fortunately Jack was hovering in the background and suggested that what we both needed was a stiff drink and we did not demur. As we sipped our drinks in the Lucas Arms we asked Jack what had prompted him to re-enter the building. Apparently he had been heading off when he noticed Sheila's car in the car park, thought it un-usual and decided to check if she was still in the building. So we owed our rescue to a Renault 5. And Jack Dromey, of course.

Sheila and I had got on from the start of my association with *Tribune*, but after the lift episode we became firm friends. Another friendship begun at Tribune and forged in curious cir-cumstances was with Nigel Williamson. Nigel had been a con-tributor to Tribune for some time and was part of the group of young movers and shakers around Tony Benn that included Tony Banks, Chris Mullin and Jon Lansman. Nigel had not gone to university after school but had hit the hippie trail with his girlfriend Magali. In the way of the times they made it to Nepal or somewhere similar and got married there. On their return with a child on the way Nigel had to curtail the hippie life-style and got a civil service job. Shortly afterwards he joined the union and pretty soon became a union rep. Through his union activities he became more involved in the turmoil in the Labour party in the aftermath of Margaret Thatcher's 1979 election victory. At the same both he and Magali realised that they should take up the university places they had missed out on when they were younger. Magali was a talented biochemist and in due course got her PhD and became a cancer scientist. Nigel in turn got a place to read English at University College London. It sounds like he was a first class student and his tutor A. S. Byatt had high expectations for him. But at the end of his second year the post of literary editor became vacant at *Tribune*. Chris offered the job to Nigel. It did not take him long to accept it and that was the role he was in when I fetched up at Tribune. A. S. Byatt apparently was not amused.

Nigel and I hit it off immediately. For one thing we had a shared interest in West Coast psychedelic music even if our political views weren't completely aligned. I also hoped that Nigel would be prepared to put some book-reviewing work in Christina's direction, which he duly did and which was the start of a writing career that is now in its fourth decade. Nigel was one of those people who seemed able to pack a huge amount into his life. For most people editing a weekly political magazine would have taken up all their energies. Apart from his job on the magazine and the political networking that went with it he also managed to review opera, keep a boat on the Medway and play cricket which is not one of those games you can play for an hour or two a week. Occasionally *Tribune* itself fielded a team, which Nigel captained. Most of the players were not staff members but associates and supporters of the magazine and it's main *raison d'être* was to play the *New Statesman* team.

For years this match had been played at the estate of J. P. W. Mallalieu, the author of *A Very Ordinary Seaman*, a book which I had read as a teenager and admired immensely. Mallalieu had been a Labour MP and a minister in Harold Wilson's administration. Alan Watkins recounts in his book *Brief Lives* that Michael Foot used to turn out for *Tribune* in the annual match against the *Statesman* well into his sixties and that he was a promising batsman but negligent in the field, (rather the opposite of my own cricketing skills in fact). But following Mallalieu's death in

1980 the venue had moved slightly closer to London.

Anyway, I think I might have regaled Nigel with my boyhood love of cricket. I had been lucky enough to see a number of test matches in the early 1960s. My father who drove into London every day would drop me off at a tube station and I would head for the Oval or Lords. This was the era of 'Fiery Fred' Truman and Brian Statham, Ted Dexter and Colin Cowdrey. Inevitably my involvement had been more bookish than practical. I had borrowed numerous books from the public library on how to bowl and how to bat. In particular I had studied a book by the Bedser twins in considerable detail and would practice my grip on a cricket ball for various spin techniques. Spin bowling is what particularly intrigued me and I would avidly read accounts of classic cricket matches and imagine myself playing for England and winning the game against the Aussies with a devastating spell of spin bowling. I even joined the local cricket club under the influence of my friend Kieron Heath who was himself a fine cricketer.

But the practicalities of cricket were another matter entirely particularly for someone with rather poor eyesight. I had been born with amblyopia and had had the lazy eye corrected when I was five but the condition had left me with a depth perception deficit so judging the speed of a fast moving ball coming towards me was not my forte. Consequently my favourite shots were off the back foot which gave me a little more time to sight the ball. Unfortunately this also meant that I was susceptible to being bowled by a good length ball. Nor was health and safety much of a concern in those days. Protection was minimal and it was considered acceptable for 16 year olds to bowl at 11 year olds. So I found batting in the nets a very scary business indeed. For the same reason I was also a reluctant fielder especially if directed to field close in to the batsman. The lack of protection was disconcerting to say the least. On the other hand I did consider myself a reasonable bowler and the endless hours spent poring over the Bedsers' book had fed into my bowling technique. As in so many sports the emphasis is increasingly on strength and speed but what fascinated me was guile. My model was much more Fred Titmuss than Fred Truman.

187

But I could still talk cricket and I remember sharing with Nigel over a pint or two one particular anecdote relating to my rather brief school cricket career. I had been drafted into the school Colts team. Unusually we had the honour of playing on the First XI pitch. We were facing quite a handy batsmen who was hitting us all over the place and I had been directed to field deep on the on side i.e. to the right of the bowler as one looked at the batsman and some way behind the stumps. As our bowlers toiled ineffectually this mighty hitter decided to go for a six. He opened his shoulders and skied a ball somewhat in my direction. For a moment my thoughts were frozen whilst I calculated whether I could reach the line of the ball or not without looking like a total incompetent. But then I decided that if I didn't at least make some kind of attempt I would receive intense opprobrium from my teammates. I set off at a half-hearted jog to intersect the flight of the ball and then realised that my lacklustre pace meant that I wasn't even going to get close to the ball. Despairingly I launched myself in a rather theatrical dive with my right hand outstretched. In my mind's eye I could see myself arcing over the perfect sward. The momentary reverie must have been enough to suppress the analytical brain and allow my reflexes to take over because the next second the ball had lodged in my hand and stayed there. A ripple of applause ran around the ground and my teammates ran over and patted me on the back in amazement. But no one was more amazed than me. I don't think I'd ever held a catch before. We still lost the match but I felt elated. Perhaps that dream of playing for England was not so ridiculous after all.

I was still basking in the glow of my teammates' incredulity later in the pavilion when Mr D'Arcy, the first team coach, came over and congratulated me. I was pleased at the recognition especially since D'Arcy had never previously seemed to be aware of my existence, but the bubble of pleasure was almost immediately punctured by his request that I report to the nets for the First XI squad the next day. I pointed out that the catch was a fluke because I actually had bad eyesight and that what I was really interested in was athletics. But in the kind of school I went to cricket was the preeminent activity exceeding even

Ancient Greek and Quantum Mechanics in prestige and my protestations cut no ice with Mr D'Arcy. I spent the rest of that term providing copious proof of my cricketing inadequacy before I was allowed to transfer to the unfancied athletics squad. I don't think D'Arcy ever spoke to me again after that.

Nigel no doubt had not retained the fine detail of this anecdote. In his mind I had achieved some minor distinction as a cricketer and so I came to be drafted into the *Tribune* side as eleventh man for the annual match against the *New Statesman*. I arrived at the ground in Cheshunt blissfully unaware of what lay in store for me. It was a hot day and Christina and I had brought the children. As we settled down near the pavilion, Christina pointed out that one of the *New Statesman* players was Julian Barnes, at that time starting to make serious waves in the literary world. *Tribune* had won the toss and had elected to bat first. The wickets were going down rather quickly. Nigel came over to me and said that one of the *Tribune* team had still not turned up so would I get ready to bat just in case. I protested that I hadn't wielded a cricket bat for 15 years. Nigel was having none of it and pointed me in the direction of the equipment. Suddenly my lazy Sunday was in tatters. I cursed myself for ever having mentioned my schoolboy cricketing exploits and tried to work out whether the Staggers were still using fast bowlers or had changed down to spinners. By way of compromise Nigel had put me as last man on the basis that there was a good chance that the errant member of the team would turn up in the meantime. But soon *Tribune* was in such a parlous state that Nigel indicated to me that I should go and pad up. I trudged over to the bench where the equipment was and buckled on the pads, found a spare box that I slipped down my trousers and picked up a bat that didn't look as if you needed to be Hercules to swing it.

At that moment a half-hearted ripple of applause indicated that the penultimate *Tribune* wicket had fallen. With a sick feeling I tucked the bat under my arm and walked out to meet the retiring batsman. He muttered a few words of encouragement and as I walked towards the wicket the other batsmen came towards me and pointed out that it was the last ball of the over

189

coming up. All I had to do was block the ball and on no account were we to try for a single. That way he would take the strike on the new over. I took a centre stance and then as the bowler started his run-up I realised in horror that I had forgotten to put on any gloves. What to do? Should I hold up play whilst a pair of gloves were fetched or should I just carry on as if I were cast in the W. G. Grace mould? Fortunately my stupefied reaction prevented me from attempting any kind of attacking stroke and I managed to kill the ball. As the fielders took up their new positions for the change of bowlers, I waved over to the pavilion to indicate I needed a pair of gloves and a pair were brought over to me. The first ball of the over sat up nicely for my partner and he caught it in the middle of the bat. He indicated that we should go for two runs and no more, so that he would be back on strike, which we managed without mishap. My mood changed. I was beginning to enjoy the experience. Thoughts of some kind of last wicket stand in the annual Staggers and *Tribune* cricket match flashed through my mind.

As my partner took his stance to face the next delivery I could see from the flush of elation on his face and the way he was opening his stance that he had decided on the strength of the previous ball that he had got the measure of the bowler. But although the bowler's run-up looked identical, from my vantage point it was obvious that the ball this time was fizzing much more dangerously. Instead of sitting up invitingly it shot under his bat and dislodged his bails. A wiser batsman would have forced himself to remain in a zen-like state of indifference which is much more conducive to instinctive behaviour. But as in golf, one good shot starts to make you think you have mastered the art and promptly leads to disaster. Nevertheless, for a tailender he had added a decent number of runs to the *Tribune* team's paltry total. As we trudged back to the pavilion I commiserated magnanimously with my partner and although I had contributed exactly zero runs to that total I felt that the fact that I was not out was something of a minor triumph.

It was decided that now would be a good time for tea. This is another reason why cricket in its essential nature is the most civilized of sports. In what other sport do the participants stop for cups of tea and cucumber sandwiches? As I munched on my triumphant sandwich the missing player turned up and so my thoughts of taking a few *New Statesman* wickets in a devastating spell of spin bowling, perhaps even the wicket of Julian Barnes, evaporated.

# Peer to Peer Networking

A WEEK OR SO LATER as Nigel and I were chuckling about my cricketing exploits over a pint I mentioned that I was probably going to have to get a full-time job which unfortunately would mean giving up the days I spent at *Tribune*. He asked me what I had in mind and I had to admit that I didn't really have any good leads at that precise moment. A few days later he told me that he had put out feelers and that he had found out that the GLC were looking for someone who was politically reliable to be based in the Programme Office at County Hall. He'd mentioned my name to Reg Race, who ran the Programme Office and if I was interested I should phone Reg to arrange an interview. The Programme Office was the unit at County Hall that monitored delivery and implementation of the council's policies. Whilst not being an elected member Reg was one of the most powerful officials in County Hall and close to Ken Livingstone. I didn't actually know him but I knew about him as he had been my MP when I lived in Bounds Green. He had lost his seat when the Wood Green constituency had been abolished in 1983. A substantial proportion of the constituency was incorporated into the neighbouring Tottenham constituency and following moves by the hard left to deselect Norman Atkinson, the incumbent MP, Reg had had hopes of being selected for the constituency but when the dust settled it was Bernie Grant, the leader of Haringey Council who received the nomination.

Reg had a reputation as being an organised member of the hard left and a good administrator and strategist. That sounded fine to me, but my knowledge of local government was woefully inadequate and I felt that I wouldn't have enough time to improve my basic understanding of how local government worked before an interview. Nigel told me not to worry because he'd been told that the job was only loosely connected with the Programme Office's central function but he was not able to tell me what the job might actually entail.

A few days later I presented myself at County Hall and asked for Reg. It is a measure of the extent to which my *sang froid* had been dented that I presented myself in Austin Reed blazer and silk tie and shiny shoes. And of course I realised as soon as Reg appeared that I had made the wrong choice. He was in an open-necked shirt and jeans. He took me down to the staff canteen and as I looked around it was evident that most of the other diners in the canteen were in casual gear too. I started to give a quick summary of the key points of my career but Reg seemed completely uninterested. He was more interested in whether I had any problem working unconventional hours. I explained that I rented a room in Deptford and only rejoined the family on a Friday evening. After a few more minutes of chit-chat he said that he had to get back and that he'd be in touch. As I left County Hall I reflected that it seemed that I had singularly failed to impress Reg. Or at least that was how I interpreted his apparent indifference to the account I gave of myself. Sadly it looked as if my ability to talk my way into a job had forsaken me just when I needed it most. As I sat on the bus I cursed the blazer and its shiny buttons.

In fact a conservative-looking geek was exactly what was required since the job would involve liaison between County Hall and Parliament. What I should have realised is that in the normal run of events I wouldn't have been interviewed by someone as senior as Reg or as informally. The briefness of the interview reflected the huge workload he had and the fact that having decided I was suitable for the job there was no point in prolonging the meeting. A few days later I got a letter asking me to start as soon as possible. I would be part of a small team briefing MPs and in particular members of the House of Lords on issues arising out of the Government's plans to abolish the GLC and the metropolitan county councils. Before the interview I had been conscious of my ignorance of local government, but suddenly my ignorance of parliamentary procedure looked like an even greater failing. On the way back to Saffron Walden that Friday I bought books on both subjects and speed-read them over the weekend. The more I read, the more apprehensive I became. Once again I was going into something about which I knew very little. When I had been slogging around the doorsteps during the 1983 election I had longed to be more at centre of political events. A little more than a year later it looked as if my wishes were coming true. As they say, be careful what you wish for.

Getting your bearings in a new job is always tricky. Working out the official hierarchy is not so difficult, but understanding the actual vectors of power is crucial. And these are the ones you really need to know about. In political jobs this is doubly difficult, because there are two parallel structures—the bureaucratic and the political. Though notionally a member of the Programme Office I was actually attached to the Parliamentary Affairs Briefing Group (PABG) which was chaired by Tony Banks, an elected member. No doubt as in the Whitehall Civil Service there was meant to be a gap between the two structures, so that as a local government officer there was a chain of command reaching up to heads of department and directors who received their policy directives from the appropriate committee of elected and co-opted members. But in the radicalising generation that had come to power in 1981 the distinction had become blurred.

Many of the newer councillors in the ruling Labour group were deeply suspicious of the career bureaucrats and were convinced that they were intent on thwarting the aims of the elected ruling party. At the same time a number of key official posts had been filled by individuals who were certainly not politically agnostic. If this now applied to me in a minor way, it was much more the case for Reg, who had added to his portfolio control of the GLC's multi-million pound press advertising and parliamentary lobbying campaign. Apparently in a small way this is where I came in. To begin with, however, my role was extremely vague.

For the first week or so I didn't have a permanent desk, nor in fact did I have any specific tasks. The Programme Office was based in a large open-plan office and in the modern style Reg sat in with the team. No separate office for him. Egalitarian it might be, but it did mean that he had a tendency to micro-manage. Documents submitted to him would come back full of crossings out and pencilled emendations, not primarily because of infelicities of language, though he was severe on those too, but because of failure to express the current nuances of policy accurately. On the plus side this meant that he could nip unauthorised initiatives and bureaucratic pussy-footing in the bud. On the negative side it meant that he had a huge workload. This technique even extended to elected members, indeed was primarily a device to stop elected members improvising policy.

One morning Reg was glancing over the elected members' appointments for the day when he saw something that met with his disapproval. He looked around and his gaze unfortunately fell on me. He called me over and told me to go up to Illtyd Harrington's office and tell him he should cancel a particular meeting for later that day, a press conference I seem to recall. I gulped. Illtyd was the chairman of the council. Furthermore Illtyd didn't have the foggiest idea who I was. Reg must have seen the doubt and perplexity on my face and at least had the grace to add 'Tell him, I don't think it's a good idea'. To my mind this fell some way short of a cogent rationalisation but I realised it was all I was going to get and that it probably reflected the balance of power so I set off with a heavy heart for the elected members' floor.

I reached the chairman's outer office where his receptionist sat and told her who I was and asked to see Illtyd. I felt certain that she would send me packing. As I quavered on the threshold it seemed that the whole scenario was not so much an issue of policy control or of keeping Illtyd in his box but of testing me. If Reg had wanted the press conference pulled why didn't he simply pick up the phone or go and see him in person? To send the most recent recruit to the team seemed an odd way of going about things. But to my surprise I was ushered into Illtyd's presence forthwith. He asked me with what appeared unfeigned courtesy what I wanted to see him about. I rather hesitatingly paraphrased what Reg had said. I waited for the explosion of outrage but instead he just shrugged and nodded his assent. I wanted to check that that was a 'yes', but I thought that might be pushing my luck a bit, so I muttered my thanks and headed back to the office. I was more than a little dazed that a neophyte apparatchik could derail the plans of a senior elected member at such short notice. But I reflected that the titular head of an organisation was seldom the fount of power.

For the next few days I flitted from desk to desk and carried out a range of menial tasks until the administration found me a permanent desk which turned out to be in the basement. The Programme Office itself was based on one of the principal floors of the building, close to the political leadership. By contrast my new accommodation was opposite a large office which housed what was know as the outreach team. If the Programme Office had its gaze fixed on the council's own programmes, the outreach team was the council's eyes and ears in the community. To some they were Ken's shock troops; to others they were a sensible way of staying in touch with what the electors and the council's client groups actually thought. In fact the member who took most responsibility for the team was John McDonnell, at this stage still the deputy leader.

To the extent that my task was to liaise with members of Parliament I probably had more in common with the outreach team than with the cerebral analysts in the Programme Office. And certainly once located in the basement I was pulled into more meetings run by McDonnell himself. These couldn't have been more different from Programme Office meetings which were on the whole dourly functional. McDonnell had a large wood-panelled office as befitted his status. We would cram into his office to get our orders and he would conclude with a rousing peroration of a vaguely ideological nature. The effect was rather like being harangued by an overenthusiastic public school housemaster before the commencement of some inter-house sporting rivalry.

Superficially this change of focus should have been welcome but I was deeply suspicious of the mood of ideological revivalism generated in McDonnell's meetings. It felt cultish, as no doubt it was. I seemed to have been cut loose from the sterner solidarity of the Programme Office. And I still didn't really know what I was meant to be doing. To make matters worse the room I had been moved into was huge and unfurnished. I had also been told that I would be sharing the room with a young woman called Angi Driver, who had previously worked for Jeremy Corbyn so she already had considerably more political experience than me. She also had organisational abilities I could only marvel at, which meant that before long we acquired desks, chairs, filing cabinets and a conference table. We eventually became good friends and a competent team.

We were joined by an amiable bearded gent called Rex Osborn. I was never quite sure what Rex's job was. He seemed to be there to keep an eye on the activities of the outreach team for John Carr the chair of the staff committee whose politics were more grown-up than the utopian initiatives emanating from McDonnell. Rex had been on the executive of the National Union of Students in the early 1970s and so was well-connected to that rising political generation that included Jack Straw, Charles Clarke, Trevor Phillips and Peter Mandelson. Rex was undoubtedly from the pragmatic wing of the party. That's really what I considered myself to be. But from the outside it must have looked as though I was from the Bennite wing. Fortunately I didn't give much thought to the contradictions inherent in this position until much later. Despite these differences we all got on pretty well and Rex's connections to John Carr meant that I got a lot more protection at member level than I might have otherwise expected in the early days, especially once John McDonnell had been deposed as deputy leader.

Eventually the bill to abolish the GLC and the Metropolitan Counties was published and we could get on with some real work. The phoney war had ended. The plan was to provide a series of briefing notes for each stage of the legislative process so that opponents of the bill and agnostics could be better informed about the services that the GLC provided and the likely impact of their loss or transfer to other bodies. We were also going to provide comparative studies of European local government structures. My ignorance in all these areas was almost fathomless, but to an extent this turned out to be an advantage. For any given subject of local government competence, housing, say, or waste transfer, Angi and I had access to the appropriate in-house experts. We were given the authority to convene a series of mini-seminars in our room which the appropriate officers were required to attend and by this means we were able to build up a dossier of expert papers and executive summaries on all the GLC's services and activities. Our room soon started to fill with filing cabinets.

We also started to draw up a chart of MPs and peers whom we thought might be prepared to attend briefing events or would be prepared to receive briefing material. We acquired copies of Dod's *Parliamentary Companion* and Roth's *Parliamentary Profiles* and started to construct a grid of supporters and waverers. It was also thought, given the size of Thatcher's majority in the Commons, that our best hope of amending or defeating the bill would be in the Lords. Accordingly a series of lunches and receptions was planned so as to keep the issue in focus for our supporters in the Lords whilst the bill wound its way slowly through the committee stage in the Commons.

This sounds as though Angi and I had suddenly transformed into high-level parliamentary strategists. But this was not the case. The GLC had run a similar operation during the Local Government (Interim Provisions) Bill, colloquially known as the Paving Bill, to considerable effect. Our activities were directed by a body known as the Parliamentary Affairs Briefing Group (PABG) chaired by Tony Banks. Tony was the chair of the GLC's Arts and Recreation Committee. He had also been elected as the MP for Stratford in East London at the 1983 General Election. The charismatic, flamboyant persona he affected concealed a serious, hard-working politician. His deputy was Stephen Benn, Tony Benn's eldest son. Stephen was a much more academic figure. He covered endless sheets of paper in his neat handwriting. If the discussion veered off at a tangent as it often did, his meticulous note-taking and standing as deputy chair enabled him to bring it back to the subject in hand.

The conduct of politics is essentially about information and consequently generates huge numbers of documents. There was a constant flow of briefings, reports, position papers, agendas and minutes. These all had to be typed or photocopied and then distributed to the members of the committee. The reprographic department in County Hall pretty much worked around the clock. Once we understood a little of what we had to do we too started to contribute to this deluge of paper. We acquired our own secretary and started to produce analyses of parliamentarians' attendance and voting records and synopses of the arguments for retaining a strategic authority for a city the size of London. We also started to contact members of the House of Lords to check that we had their contact details up to date and to establish a communication channel before we actually needed it in earnest. For the Labour peers we were able to work through the chief whip's office.

The Labour chief whip in the Lords at that time was Lord (Tom) Ponsonby one of the relatively few Labour hereditary peers and a delightful man. He had also been an elected member of the GLC in the 70s and chairman of the council from 1976 to 1977 and so had an informed appreciation of the GLC's functions. As a consequence he and the members of the Parliamentary Labour Party who worked for him were extremely helpful when dealing with GLC requests. It might have been supposed that the PLP would be 100% behind the GLC, but of course things are seldom that simple in Labour politics. Many in the PLP had a profound distaste for Livingstone and all his works. They saw the GLC shenanigans as a massive distraction from the proper business of politics and they shared the government's horror of women's committees and the high profile that the GLC gave to feminist, gay and lesbian, and racial minority issues. So it was a relief not to be faced with the same obstructionist attitudes in Tom Ponsonby's office. Even so cold-calling a peer of the realm on behalf of the GLC felt on occasion like an arcane version of panhandling PPI mis-selling compensation. The lordly distaste transmitted down the telephone line was at times almost palpable.

In the meantime the bill began its progress through the Commons. The second reading debate took place on on 3rd and 4th of December with the debate on Clause 1 of the bill conducted in a committee of the whole house on 12th and 13th December. The debate then passed to Standing Committee G for clause by clause debate commencing on 18th December. The sessions were held in one of the committee rooms over-looking the river which was where I spent most afternoons and evenings, Fridays and periods when Parliament was in recess excepted, for the next ten or so weeks.

The Labour side was led by Dr John (Jack) Cunningham with Jack Straw as his deputy. Cunningham was not a physician but held a doctorate in chemistry and was an experienced parlia-mentarian having been first elected in 1970. He had dark hair and was rather dashing but he exuded a slight air of menace especially if you happened to be the hapless GLC apparatchik tasked with briefing him on the GLC's views of how to manage the debate. The first time I presented myself at his office he was chatting with Straw. I wasn't exactly sent away with a flea in my ear but it was made clear that such visits were not necessary and not to be repeated in the future. I put my sheaf of papers on the table and exited quickly. I wasn't sure what I was going to say at PABG next day but was relieved to hear Straw incor-porate enough phrases in one of his speeches to claim that the material had been used.

Straw was considerably less urbane than Cunningham. His intense manner was accentuated by the black framed glasses he wore at that period. His voice was adenoidal and he had a jittery delivery unlike the languid periods affected by Cunningham, which admittedly sounded at times as if he could scarcely be-lieve that he was having to address such a trivial issue. But Straw proved to have an eye for detail. By contrast it often seemed that mastery of the details was beneath Cunningham's dignity. He specialised in a high-level view of the subject and undoubt-edly had considerably rhetorical gifts. Unfortunately over the coming weeks and months countless hours would be devoted to very low-level debate indeed; waste transfer, parks, traffic lights. The tedium of these subjects did nothing to improve his mood and truth to tell I was not much delighted by the arrangements for waste transfer myself.

Cunningham's opposite number on the government benches was Kenneth Baker. He was an owlish individual, bespectacled, with brilliantined hair and a bland, fleshy face. His vocal manner was as smoothly oiled as his hair. He was courteous even to the irregulars and never seemed to lose his temper or get flustered. He was an occasional poet and anthologist of poetry. This meant he had to endure choice extracts from his oeuvre being quoted at him at opportune moments during the debate, a penance that on the whole he bore with good humour. His deputy was Tim Sainsbury, a scion of the supermarket family. He seemed ruthlessly efficient and, one felt, frustrated to be condemned to the grubby business of chewing the fat about the various functions of the GLC.

The committee room was a microcosm of the main chamber. At one end was a table on a dais where a deputy speaker and his clerks sat to chair the debate. The principal chairman was Sir Michael Shaw, a Conservative with the Labour MP, Ted Leadbitter as his deputy. At right angles to the dais along the body of the room were two rows of pews facing each other very much as in the choir of a chapel, which is of course how the chamber of the House of Commons had in fact evolved. The horseshoe shaped chambers favoured by foreign and municipal legislatures, such as the GLC were far too new-fangled for the Palace of Westminster. At the foot of the room were several rows of chairs for members of the press and public, in effect the congregation. It is well known that members of the public can queue to hear debates in the main chamber, with Prime Minister's Question Time being the weekly highlight. But it is also possible to attend the committee stage of debates which are often much more informative.

For the next few months either Angi or I and sometimes both of us would head over to Westminster after lunch in the GLC canteen and settle down for a long session in committee room 14. These would often go on deep into the evening. Fortunately,

202

from our point of view, our PABG boss, Tony Banks, was also a member of the committee. He would often take pity on us and when the session had wound up for the day take us to one of the cafés or bars. Tony was a resolute vegetarian but he was not any kind of faddist when it came to alcohol, so as often as not we would end up in one of the bars. Occasionally debates would go on very late indeed. If we were still at work at 10pm we were allowed to call a taxi and charge it to the GLC account. Even though I affected a veneer of cynicism I still enjoyed being picked up by a cab in Palace Yard. But compared to a cabdriver I was a mere novice when it came to cynicism. If any of them ever mistook me for a MP, they would have soon revised that supposition when they had dropped me off at my dingy flat in Deptford. The Crossfield Estate might have been ok for Dire Straits, but it was not the kind of place haunted by thrusting young MPs.

Parliamentary debates are just a formal kind of business meeting and as we all know, the more people involved in a meeting, the longer it takes to come to a conclusion. Not counting the chairman and the officials Standing Committee G had nearly 50 members so the potential for inertia was quite high. When a bill is not too contentious the opposition may elect not to contest non-substantive clauses and reserve their firepower for a particular feature of the bill. Since committees reflect the government's majority and the Thatcher 1983-87 administration had a substantial majority, the chances of the Labour side making any kind of serious dent in the bill were extremely small. But when the measure is contentious or when relations between the rival whip's offices have broken down, then an opposition might contest every clause as a way of slowing down the government's legislative programme in general. Indeed it is not unknown for particular bills to fail to make it onto the statute book because of the log jam at the end of a parliamentary session. No doubt fixed term parliaments have changed this feature of the legislative process somewhat.

The government's response to this tooth and nail opposition is to introduce a so-called guillotine or timetable bill which fixes the maximum amount of time that debate on certain clauses can take. Governments used to be wary of using this power because it can suggest some kind of democratic deficit if it is perceived that debate is being truncated. At the same time an opposition has to be careful not to thwart the plans of the elected government just for the hell of it.

In the case of the Abolition Bill it had been decided that this was one of those times when it made sense to table as many amendments during the committee stage as possible. It was felt that it was not generally understood how wide the range of the services was that the GLC provided and that the gay and lesbian stuff that occupied the newspapers was only a tiny part of the GLC's output. It was also important to remind voters that the GLC was actually a Conservative creation. And as had been shown by the defeat of the Fares Fair policy British local authorities did not have a power of general competence. Unlike their homologues in other jurisdictions British local authorities could only do what they were empowered to do by statute. They could not invent a function which was not specifically allowed by the enabling legislation. So it remained possible for the government of the day to amend the legislation to restrict certain activities as well of course to give an authority responsibilities in areas that it had not hitherto covered. To abolish the GLC and the metropolitan authorities looked like a case of throwing out the baby with the bathwater. Or that was what we were hoping to show.

Our main weapon in this trench warfare was my PABG boss, Tony Banks. He had an ability to absorb huge amounts of technical detail and to reproduce that material in speech after speech with considerable humorous brio. As the saturnine Cunningham glowered at the oleaginous Baker, Banks entertained and informed the committee in equal parts. But he couldn't do it all on his own. And tempers were beginning to fray. Tony desperately needed some back up. Enter Harry Cowans MP for Tyne Bridge. Harry had been a miner, had risen through the trade union movement and had consequently become an MP quite late in life. He had a forthright manner and a well-developed sense of humour and referred to all and sundry as 'Bonny Lad' in his beautiful Geordie accent. Unlike Tony he was not great on the detail of the legislation but he had an inexhaustible fund of funny stories. In the campaign these skills were invaluable. He would have both sides in stitches even though the Tories knew full well that he was just wasting time.

The etiquette in the House of Commons is not to refer to members by name but by constituency, thus the honourable member for Chew Magna, say, or right honourable member if the said member is a Privy Councillor. As a sign of affection the Conservative members of the committee referred to Harry as the honourable member for Bonny Lad. In effect a parliamentary version of the Stockholm Syndrome was starting to take effect. After so many weeks confined to the same committee room day after day an element of cross-party solidarity developed. The arm-wrestling over clauses in the bill became an opportunity to polish one's parliamentary persona which was measured by the volume of guffaws a particular contribution elicited.

This fraternisation and the consequent slow progress of debate was not pleasing to the government's business managers and a guillotine debate was scheduled. After a series of ritual objections from the Labour side the bill was carried and debate in the standing committee resumed but now on a much accelerated basis. By the end of the committee stage despite the heroic efforts of Tony Banks and the honourable member for Bonny Lad the opposition had failed to so much as dent the legislation. This was not unanticipated because of the majority that the government had in the Commons but greater things were expected from the Lords.

Notoriously the House of Lords was and remains essentially an unelected chamber. For the defenders of this aspect of our legislature the fact that it is unelected is presented as a virtue. Because peers are not elected and therefore do not represent constituents they are supposedly more independent. In the case of Life Peers they are also often people of great experience having had senior roles in the church, judiciary, civil service and city, which is reflected by the fact that many such peers expressed no party allegiance but sat on the cross-benches. On the other hand in 1985 the majority of members of the House of Lords were hereditary peers. Only a relatively small proportion of the hereditaries would show up for debates on a regular basis, but it might be inferred that on the whole these so-called backwoodsmen supported the Conservative party and they could be called out whenever the government was worried that it might lose a vote. From the GLC's point of view while we were wary of the inbuilt Tory majority, we were hopeful that cross-benchers would be more open to the GLC's case. It was a little ironic that we were relying on an unelected chamber to defend the structures of municipal democracy.

The transition from the elected chamber of the Palace of Westminster to the unelected chamber is disconcerting. The Commons is relatively austere, all green leather and plain oak studded here and there with brass portcullises, the symbol of the Commons. By contrast the Lords is a riot of crimson leather, gold leaf and gothic curlicues. But my delight at being immersed in this gothic fantasy was soon displaced by the serious job of convincing enough peers to support the GLC. We had been running a series of lunches and receptions, in County Hall and in the House of Lords itself. Some of these gatherings had a surreal way of collapsing the normal historical perspective. One such event was held in a room in the House of Lords and hosted on our behalf by Lord Longford, who was a far from insignificant figure though much derided for his moralising views and bleeding-heart campaigns.

Even though it was early in the day there was plenty of alcohol on offer. I got into conversation with Lord Leatherland who at that time was a little short of his 93rd birthday and still active in the Lords and not only that but he downed a couple of large whiskies before lunch time. I suppose I shouldn't have been surprised by a man who had signed up in 1914 by pretending to be 18 and served for five years rising to the rank of Company Sergeant Major. It was in fact still possible to encounter more venerable sages in the gilded chamber. Manny Shinwell who was 100 at that point in 1985 still came in fairly regularly to debates. And on one occasion I sat at the same table at lunch as Lord Fenner Brockway, the great anti-war campaigner who was an extremely lively lunch companion at the age of 97. By this time Shinwell was sitting as an Independent but Brockway still took the Labour whip.

Almost as venerable at a mere 91 was the former Conservative prime minister, Harold Macmillan, who, as the Earl of Stockton, had been one of the last non-royal recipients of a hereditary peerage in 1984. This paradoxically meant that by the standards of the Lords he was a new boy. Also on the roll-call of former prime ministers in the Lords was Lord Home (pronounced Hume) of the Hirsel, Sir Alec Douglas-Home. Not only was Lord Home one of that select group of 18 individuals who have disclaimed a hereditary peerage so as to be able to sit in the Commons, albeit only four days after he had become prime minister, but he was also one of an even more select group who, on retiring from the Commons, have been ennobled once again. Another such was Quintin Hogg who disclaimed the title of Viscount Hailsham in 1963 and was then ennobled as Baron Hailsham in 1970. Naturally enough the second title was a life peerage as indeed were most new peerages after the Life Peerages Act 1958. One might imagine that there were days when these men might wake up and think 'Well, who the hell am I today?'.

One of the leading campaigners for the Life Peerages Act had been Tony Benn. He had inherited the title Viscount Stansgate in 1960 whilst he was the sitting MP for Bristol South East which had required him to stand down and had precipitated a by-election. Benn stood in the by-election and received the majority of the votes but he was disqualified by an election court which declared the Conservative runner-up, Malcolm St Clair, to be the new MP. Ironically St Clair was also the heir presumptive to a title. When, three years later, Benn was able to disclaim his title, St Clair honourably applied for the Stewardship of the Manor of Northstead, which is the legal fiction by which a sitting MP resigns his or her seat. In the ensuing by-election Benn won the majority of votes and re-entered the Commons.

Although an individual might disclaim his title, he could not do so for his descendants so that his heir would inherit in due course. A person who is next in line to inherit the title but whose claim might be displaced by the birth of another is an heir presumptive. By contrast an heir apparent is a person, essentially the eldest son, whose right to inherit cannot be displaced by the birth of another person. Heirs apparent therefore had special rights in the Lords and were permitted access to sittings of the house as of right. It so happened that Stephen Benn, one of my political bosses, was the heir apparent of the Viscountcy of Stansgate.

On one occasion at a particularly sensitive moment in proceedings Stephen decided to come across with me to the Lords and we both acquired passes from Tom Ponsonby to sit in one of the side galleries rather than the public gallery. It was a warm afternoon and the debate dragged on. Lulled by the monotonous voices of the aged peers below us we both nodded off only to be jolted awake by one of the doorkeepers who virtually dragged us into the corridor and announced that our passes had been rescinded because nodding off was a breach of respect due to the chamber. I was hoping that Stephen would throw off his modest bourgeois disguise and reveal himself as the heir apparent of a viscount. Of course he was far too sensible to do any such thing and we both trooped a little shame-facedly out to the lobby and hung around until we judged that there had been a change of shifts and we could creep back in to monitor the debate somewhat more attentively.

At that point in 1985 there were five former prime ministers still alive. Any edition of the I-Spy Book of former prime ministers is by definition going to be a slim volume. I had already ticked off Macmillan and Douglas-Home. But Ted Heath and Jim Callaghan were still in the Commons. Fortunately they were both frequent attenders, Heath in particular taking every opportunity to glower at the back of Mrs Thatcher's bouffant hairdo, and I was eventually able to tick them off too. This left only Harold Wilson, but he proved to be a much more difficult spot He had entered the Lords as Lord Wilson of Rievaulx in 1983 but was reputed to be unwell and by this stage did not attend quite so often. It was starting to look like I wouldn't be getting my feather and order of merit from Big Chief I-Spy.

The House of Lords is considered a revising chamber. For the harmless drudges from County Hall like me this meant following a clause by clause discussion of the bill for a second time. Once again the strategy was to table a multitude of amendments. But this time any amendments were supposed not to breach the Salisbury convention which stipulates that the Lords should not reject any bill at second or third reading which has been explicitly contained in the government's general election manifesto. (In the obscure ways of parliamentary procedure, second and third readings are debates and a first reading is just the formal introduction of a bill.)

Opposition to the Interim Provisions Bill the previous year had garnered cross-party support because it seemed undemocratic to abolish elections before the act to abolish the authorities was on the statute book. So it was hoped that we might be able to draft something similar that would have the support of cross-bench peers and even some Tories. And though the Conservatives had an in-built majority in the Lords, in practical terms that voting strength was not a precise figure and for the right amendment the size of the potential opposition was considerable. But Lord Denham, the government chief whip in the Lords was a canny operator and was bound to be scanning the lists of tabled amendments to sniff out trouble.

The second reading, which is a debate on the general principle of a bill, had been a fractious affair. The opposition had tabled an amendment which whilst stopping short of attempting to wreck the bill regretted 'the failure to provide a democratic and local framework for the strategic services essential to the capital city and the metropolitan areas'. The debate had lasted 11 hours and not ended until 2am which was quite unusual for the Lords. The government had whipped hard in order to avoid an embarrassing defeat and won handsomely by 235 votes to 109.

The first two days of the committee stage were scheduled for 29th and 30th of April. Somehow we needed to table a 'stinger', a committee stage amendment which would command cross-party support while being in effect a wrecking amendment without looking like one and without Denham smelling a rat and having his backwoodsmen on hand. It is in the nature of legislation that the general aims of a proposed law are set out at the top of the bill. Early clauses address various high-level issues, while later clauses are more likely to address particular matters of detail.

So if we wanted to damage the bill at a structural level we were probably going to have to amend one of the early clauses. Denham would therefore expect us to come out with all guns blazing on 29th and we would encourage him in that belief. But the plan was to table a stinger for 30th at the last moment. Even though the last moment tabling of amendments is deprecated it was not actually against the rules of procedure. Accordingly we made a made a big hoo-hah about the amendments we were tabling for 29th; a proposal to set up an Independent Committee of Inquiry to look into the best means of securing the future provision of services of the GLC and the metropolitan authorities before the abolition date, a proposal to hold referenda on the abolition of the authorities, and a proposal to delay the actual abolition date by one year.

Our real amendment, however, was to accept the abolition of the GLC and the Metropolitan Counties but to create in the London area an elected body to be called the London Metropolitan Authority which would be the strategic authority for Greater London with similar bodies in the areas of the metropolitan counties, in other words the resurrection of the abolished authorities in all but name. Despite the parliamentary chicanery the amendment had the support of a number of prominent peers who did not take the Labour whip including Lord Plummer, a Conservative and former leader of the GLC. Even so we were going to need the attendance of every Labour peer who was not at death's door and require them to stay for a vote.

Part of our problem was that there were quite a few Labour peers who rarely attended the house. Some of these peers had legitimate commitments elsewhere, either professionally or in regional politics and some were known to be in poor health. The sight of several of these well-known absentees all present on the same day would be bound to set alarm bells ringing. But we hoped that we might also be able to turn this reflex to our advantage by triggering it on 29th April. So we set about trying to persuade our infrequent attenders that being present for the vote on 30th April was of the utmost importance but that we also needed a substantial number of them to come in on 29th April to reinforce the illusion that we were serious about the decoy amendments. In the end we managed to get an encouraging number of commitments, including, via Lady Falkender, from Lord Wilson.

Notoriously Wilson's resignation honours list had included his private secretary, Marcia Williams, who had received the title Baroness Falkender. In retrospect the fuss this created seems overdone. Whatever the merits of the particular case, during the Abolition Bill it was decidedly to our advantage because Wilson still valued Falkender's judgement. The key to getting Wilson to come in and stay for the vote was to persuade Falkender which also meant we got two votes. The word was that Lady Falkender could be a rather difficult person so I was glad that I was not detailed to make that contact.

Of course despite our best efforts we were unable to convince every peer who took the Labour whip. And sadly there were also a number of refuseniks who came in most days but never stayed to vote. Surprisingly, or maybe not, several of these were former trades union leaders, most notoriously Lord Gormley, the former president of the National Union of Mineworkers. The cynics said that he stayed long enough to qualify for his daily allowance and then went home. It is hard to imagine that the pension of a former president of the NUM was meagre enough to justify such behaviour.

But I was given an assignment that turned out to be challenging in a rather different way. Wilson's predecessor as leader of the Labour party had been Hugh Gaitskell. Rather as John Smith's untimely death in 1994 had opened the way for Tony Blair, Gaitskell's death in 1963 had provided Wilson's opportunity to lead the party and subsequently become Prime Minister. Notoriously there were hints of skullduggery in Peter Wright's book *Spycatcher*, but never anything that has been substantiated. And whatever else might be said about Wilson, he turned out to be an electoral genius.

A year after his death, Gaitskell's widow, Dora, was made a peer. This was not as tokenistic as it might seem. Lady Gaitskell had been active in Labour politics since she was a teenager. Unfortunately by 1985 her health was not so good and her attendance in the Lords declined. She was also finding it harder to follow the debates but she was still willing to be available for important votes. In view of her frailty it was decided that we should offer to collect her in a GLC limousine and someone should go along to help her. That honour fell to me. And even though I had given up wearing my Austin Reed blazer I still felt unable to embrace the open-necked *déshabillé* affected by most of my colleagues and still wore a suit and tie. So perhaps it was just a tribute to my inveterate sartorial conservatism.

On the day of the decoy amendments I climbed into the back of the big black limousine which was waiting for me in the turning circle at the Members' Entrance on Westminster Bridge Road. The myth that had been put about in the early days of the Livingstone incumbency was that the members' limousine service had been abolished. It may have been considerably reduced in scale but it certainly hadn't been abolished. And no doubt this was a breach of members' privileges, but with the enemy at the gates no one paid such niceties much attention any more. We headed up to the Gaitskell residence in Frognal, Hampstead. I got out of the limousine and walked up the drive of an imposing house. Lady Gaitskell was already waiting for me in the porch of the big front door. She greeted me like I was a prodigal grandson, friendly but a little chiding. I took her arm and helped her into the car. We settled in the back and set off for Westminster.

As we stopped at traffic lights I was aware of people peering into the limousine trying to work out who the personages in the back were, some dowager duchess and her shabby genteel equerry, no doubt. By way of chitchat I started to sketch in how important this vote was and that we had a plan to wrongfoot the government whips. She brushed this explanation aside to tell me that she didn't think my tie was suitable and she promised to buy me a nicer one. I thanked her for her generosity but wondered what was wrong with the rather nice Paul Smith tie I was wearing. At the Palace of Westminster I accompanied her into the lobby and then went up into the public gallery to follow the debate. I looked down and saw Lady Gaitskell take her seat and chat amiably to another Labour peer. I also noticed that Lord Wilson and Lady Falkender were present.

The government whips had also spotted our infrequent attenders and no doubt the phones had started ringing because before long the government benches started to fill up. They were determined to make sure that they had a comfortable majority. In the course of the debate on the decoy amendments the government ministers were melodramatically scathing. They claimed at considerable length that the amendments were in breach of the Salisbury Convention. So when it came to the vote all three were decisively defeated, which was pretty much what we had expected and planned for. As we trooped out after the division we tried not to look too pleased with ourselves.

The following day I was once again driven up to Frognal in a GLC limousine. Once again Lady Gaitskell was ready and waiting. We drove to Westminster, I accompanied her to the Peers Lobby and went upstairs to take my seat. This time when I looked down I was dismayed to see that she had rather drawn attention to herself by trying to sit on the Government benches. As I watched anxiously a couple of kindly Conservative peers pushed her gently to the other side. I just prayed that she hadn't had time to tell them why she was there. With luck she was still on the subject of suitable neckties.

The debate began with a tetchy set of exchanges about whether the two amendments on the order paper should be taken together or consecutively. The interruptions prompted Lord Hayter who had moved both amendments to say that he was beginning to feel that he was speaking in another place. In the parlance of the Lords another place was the Commons and Hayter was suggesting that this sitting was descending to the level of debate typical of the Commons whereas the Lords prided itself on the civility of its proceedings. But this was only the beginning of the lordly incivility because of course the government whips had realised what was going on. They were furious and they were determined to spin out the debate, another practice normally alien to the higher standards of conduct in the Lords, until their urgent summonses had brought enough Tory peers to the house to swell the division lobby.

The debate continued in like manner for the next couple of hours. The Government handed the baton of debate to Lord Boyd-Carpenter, a former barrister and an experienced parliamentarian or in other words an old bruiser, to run down the clock. One of Labour's eminent lawyers Lord Mischon attempted to puncture Boyd-Carpenter's flow by pointing out that whilst a great debater, he knew little about London government. Boyd-Carpenter's response was typical of the level to which the proceedings had now descended. 'The noble Lord was polite about my capacities as a debater but his intervention was a singularly adroit, but largely irrelevant, piece of debating.' It takes one to know one, I suppose.

Lulled by this Monty Pythonesque sketch of a debate conducted in terms of chivalrous insults, I suddenly realised that I'd lost track of Lady Gaitskell. I scanned the Labour benches once again to no avail. I'd been given strict instructions to keep her in the Lords until the vote on the amendment. In view of the tedium of the debate, she'd probably toddled off to the tearoom for a cuppa. But I thought it best to check.

When I got down to the lobby she had her coat on and she was heading for the exit. I touched her on the arm and told her the car wouldn't be ready until a little later. She looked a little puzzled and I realised she didn't recognise me out of context. So then I told her that I worked for Tom Ponsonby and that the vote hadn't taken place yet and would she mind staying a bit longer. She looked a little doubtful. I started to steer her back towards the chamber when one of the doorkeepers came over and told me that I was not allowed to lobby a peer. Not being elected, they had no constituents. If I persisted he would ask me to leave the building. I replied that I wasn't lobbying, I was acting on behalf of Lord Ponsonby. Fortunately at this moment Lady Gaitskell seemed to remember why she was there and headed back into the chamber. I smiled weakly at the doorkeeper and went back up to the public gallery.

No doubt by now Lord Denham had realised that not only

were Wilson, Falkender and intermittent attenders like Lady Gaitskell present, but so too were very infrequent attenders like Lords, Crowther-Hunt, Glenamara, Hirshfield, McCarthy, Parry and Wedderburn, none of whom had been present the previous day, the supposed day of the concerted attack on the bill. Even the notorious Lord Kagan of Gannex raincoat fame, who had served a ten month prison sentence for theft in 1980 and been stripped of his knighthood but not his peerage was in the house. No doubt the Whip's office was frantically phoning around. This was not strictly in the days before mobile phones. Vodafone and Cellnet had both launched services on 1st January that year, but the phones were the size of a small suitcase, weighed 5kg and stayed charged for only 30 minutes. Even though 12,000 of these monstrosities had been sold by the end of the year it is hard to imagine that many members of the House of Lords were among the early adopters of this new technology. Even answering machines were not that widespread. So that meant getting hold of the errant peers must have been quite difficult even if a few of them had pagers.

In the meantime the Government peers in the chamber were trying to extend the debate without filibustering, which, as has been mentioned, was against the rules of procedure in the Lords. Even Lord Elton who was leading for the government was having qualms about how they were conducting matters. Just before 5.30pm sensing that the mood of the house was to proceed to a division but that there were not yet enough government peers in the Lords, Lord Elton re-entered the debate by claiming that since this was not a Second Reading debate he was allowed to speak 'umpteen' times. This was not quite the view of the opposition to judge from the disapproving murmurs rising from their benches.

And Lord Gowrie, Elton's seconder, was getting visibly redder in the face. At one stage he got into a tetchy exchange with Lord Stewart who said he understood why the noble Lord might be annoyed. To which Gowrie replied, when Stewart had given way, 'I am not annoyed. I am furious.' Once again this was rather contrary to the spirit of decorum that was supposed to prevail in the proceedings of the House of Lords and showed how rattled the Conservatives were. Both Elton and Gowrie must have found it hard not to think about the hot water they would be in with Mrs Thatcher if they allowed the amendment to be carried.

Shortly before 6pm Viscount Colville rose to his feet to be met by cries from the opposition benches demanding that the minister speak. Coville swatted these demands aside and settled into a tedious speech about planning and waste disposal. When he had wrung as much as he could out of a series of generalisations and handed on to Lord Bellwin the cries were now for Gowrie to wind up the debate prompting Bellwin to say that he thought it rather unfair that people on his side of the debate who were against the amendment were being denied the opportunity to speak. Bellwin managed to spin things out for a few minutes and eventually handed over to Gowrie who thanked him for his efforts with the words 'The looks coming from the Government Front Bench towards my noble friend Lord Bellwin are of universal love and approbation. He has nothing whatsoever to worry about,' which in the arcane language of the Lords shows how heated things had got.

He then recalled that many years before he had been in favour of the abolition of the hereditary peerage but that had that policy been implemented he would have missed 'a debate of great interest and occasional high drama about an important and controversial subject.' This was too much for many members of the opposition. A hereditary peer was expressing a considerable degree of satisfaction in being part of the process of abolition of a number of democratically elected bodies. What was more the government had only managed to prolong the debate and defer the vote by bending the rules of procedure.

Eventually after 15 minutes the house divided. When the votes had been counted the government had won by 4 votes. Given their inbuilt majority this was a narrow squeak and it was probably the case that at the moment of division the government whips couldn't have been certain that they had a majority. I was glad to see that despite the tedium of the debate Lady Gaitskell had stayed the course and made her vote count. I wasn't sure if Lord Wilson and Lady Falkender had managed the same and was wondering how soon I would be able to get the voting record. As I sat in the lobby one of the Labour peers, Lord Monkswell came over and commiserated with me. Despite the fact that in professional life he was an engineer and was based in Manchester he had been present at all the crucial votes on the bill. We had been working for this debate for months and it seemed unlikely that we would get another chance as good. Monkswell could see how glum I was and suggested I join him for some dinner.

We walked along to the peers's dining room but the attendant shook his head sadly. The dining room was full, no doubt with landed earls and marquesses quaffing a glass of something delectable supplied by a grateful chief whip. We were about to beat a retreat when a lady diner attracted Monkswell's attention and indicated that she and her companion had finished their meal and that we were welcome to have their table. I then realised with a start that her companion was Harold Wilson and that Falkender and Wilson had indeed stayed for the vote. Sadly the same could not be said of Lord Gormley who had in fact put in an appearance in the chamber after lunch but had not stayed to vote. And when I checked the next day nor had Lords Greene, Cooper or Scanlon bothered to attend the debate. Nor for that matter had Lord Soper who had served as a member of the GLC and its forerunner the LCC. If we had had those votes we would have carried the amendment. Still, I was now in a position to send off my I-Spy book of former prime ministers still living to the Big Chief.

This was not entirely the end of the matter. A few weeks later on the first day of the Report stage we were able to give the government an even bigger scare. We tabled a set of amendments to do with strategic planning issues. This time we ran a lower profile whipping operation but when the house divided on the first of the amendments the government only defeated the motion by 146 votes to 145. Once again Lady Gaitskell, Lady Falkender and Lord Wilson turned up to vote and once again Lords Cooper, Gormley, Green and Scanlon failed to vote although Gormley was almost certainly in the house at the start of the debate. Naturally enough when a vote is so narrowly defeated it is tempting to focus on those within one's own ranks who let the side down. But on this occasion Godfrey Barker the diarist for the House magazine decided that the extra vote on the government side was probably provided by Lord Zouche of Haryngworth, (a title to conjure with), who had only attended five times in the 1983-4 session but who happened to be on a visit from his home in Australia for several weeks. Alternatively the dubious distinction must go to Lord Thurlow who voted with the government on this occasion despite not having attended the house once during the 1983-4 session.

In due course the bill made its way through the Lords attracting few substantive amendments, most of which were overturned in the Commons and passed into law on 16th July. All that now remained was the task of dividing up the functions of the GLC between the various successor bodies, which were for the most part the boroughs, who in many cases were expected to form joint committees to coordinate the transferred functions. Those functions which did not have an immediate successor to which they could be transferred were retained in an organisation called the Residuary Body, one of whose main tasks was the winding down and the disposal of County Hall itself. And indeed scarcely had the Act made it onto the statute book than County Hall started to hollow out.

Some of the old style senior officers who could scarcely be considered apparatchiks took up appointments in other organisations. Lower down the scale specialists found their skills in demand in the boroughs or working for the new joint committees. And many of the more political appointees transferred to voluntary bodies that had received substantial transfusions of cash during the death throes of the GLC. But some of us considered ourselves part of the rearguard and were determined to wind down the GLC in an orderly fashion.

As the corridors became more depopulated it was decided that it would be more convenient for those of us working on the transition to be on the principal floor, so we moved to the Members' Library, a beautiful panelled room with river views. Tony Banks, who was now the chairman of the council, had suggested the move so that we would be closer to his office. The library had been emptied of most of its collection by the time we arrived, as part of the process of transferring the council's archive to the Greater London Record Office which itself was passing to the City of London Corporation. But the library had been used temporarily to store a much more remarkable collection.

When the library was still operational Derek Holdaway, one of the council's legal officers, had been given permission to use the library to consult a volume on its shelves. Whilst searching for the particular book in a storeroom at the back of the library he came across a large number of paintings which had been stacked against each other covered in dust and cobwebs. On closer inspection Holdaway realised that these paintings were in fact portraits of the council chairmen dating back to Lord Rosebery in 1889, many by eminent artists. Fortunately Holdaway, although a legal officer, was also knowledgeable about art and had been involved in the acquisition of the Suffolk collection in 1974 which had been subsequently displayed in the Ranger's House on Blackheath. He had also been involved in the arrangements for removing the artworks from the Middlesex Guildhall in Parliament Square which had passed to the GLC when the county of Middlesex had been abolished and when the building was subsequently acquired by the government for use as a court. Amongst those pictures was a Reynolds and a Gainsborough. So he was by no means ignorant of the importance of the GLC's collections.

Holdaway asked to see the chairman and brought to his attention the plight of the portraits. He felt that without some kind of catalogue of the works it would be difficult to keep the collection together. He also pointed out that the council's treasures extended well beyond portraits of former chairmen. Banks immediately commissioned Holdaway to prepare a catalogue of the paintings and the council's works of art in general and gave him the authority to extend his researches beyond the canvases he had found in the library and to employ the services of one of the GLC's official photographers. Eventually Holdaway identified and catalogued 89 portraits of former chairmen, the paintings that had originally been housed in Middlesex Guildhall, a

219

number of busts and many commemorative pieces of silver. By the time he finished the project just a few weeks before the demise of the GLC he had itemised more than a thousand pieces. The portrait collection alone contained works by Alma-Tadema, Clausen, Collier, Herkomer, Llewellyn, McEvoy, Nicholson, Orchardson, Orpen, Philpot, Poynter and Strang. The collection of bronzes was also outstanding containing work by Wheeler, Epstein and Frink among others. Whilst Banks and Holdaway were both concerned to preserve this wonderful collection as a record of London's strategic authority and worried that the collection might be broken up and the items sold off piecemeal, their motives were not completely aligned.

This misalignment came into focus when Banks was informed that Holdaway had been summoned to a meeting with Sir Godfrey Taylor, the chairman of the LRB. Holdaway was an old school bureaucrat, conscientious in the extreme but not any kind of rebel. His intention in creating the catalogue was to force the Residuary Body to acknowledge the existence of the collection and make proper arrangements for its housing and care. And his fears were perhaps not misplaced. In the account on his website he relates that Sir Godfrey Taylor's described the portraits as 'rubbish' and thought that they should be given to the sitters' relatives or sold off. This was not a course of action that appealed to Holdaway, a man who had spent most of his career as a legal officer for the GLC and its forerunner the LCC and had a great loyalty to the respective organisations and their heritage.

Tony Banks on the other hand was a rebel to his fingertips. He took the view that the Tories were vandals who had always hated municipal socialism and simply wanted to rub out all trace of the GLC and he was prepared to use all the powers that remained to him in his position as last chairman of the council to thwart that intention. So far as he was concerned Taylor was simply Thatcher's hatchet man and his brief was to get the job done as quickly as possible. It was extremely doubtful if he or anyone on his team had given any thought whatsoever to the council's artistic treasures. It seemed to Banks that there might be a way of transferring the collection *en masse* to the Museum of London or another appropriate body before 31 March 1986 and present the LRB with a *fait accompli*.

For that reason he considered Holdaway's dialogue with the LRB chairman unfortunate to say the least. He feared that Taylor would now be alerted to both the monetary and propaganda value of the collection and he knew that under the terms of the Local Government Act 1985 council officers would be required to comply with any request from Taylor in relation to the collection. Banks immediately fired off a note to the director-general's department requiring the catalogue to be placed in his room forthwith. In his own account Holdaway says that he anticipated this and had produced two copies of the catalogue so he was able to comply with Banks's request.

A few days later Banks called me into his office and asked me to go up to Holdaway's office and bring down to his own office the trolley of council treasures I would find there. I was aware of some of the salvoes that had been discharged between Banks and the director-general's office so I was aghast at what he was asking me to do. He brushed aside my qualms by saying that he had agreed the matter with the LRB. I wasn't at all sure that this was the case but I located the trolley and brought it down to the chairman's office. At least no one tried to stop me. I helped Tony unload the trolley. It was packed with all sorts of beautiful things including several portraits amongst which were a portrait of Lord Rosebery, the first Chairman of the LCC and Sir John Williams Benn, great-grandfather of Stephen Benn, together with many silver *objets* and diamond-encrusted badges of office. The selection of pictures and objects remained on display in Tony's office until the last day of the GLC. Apparently at midnight when LRB staff entered the chairman's office to return the items to storage the room was empty. Under cover of the biggest fireworks display London had ever seen up to that point and to the strains of Elgar's 'Nimrod', Banks had removed them to a place of greater safety.

Over the next few months there was an increasingly intemperate correspondence between the LRB and Banks demanding the return of the items that he had removed from County Hall. Banks's aim was to give the existence of the collection as high a

221

profile as possible and to publicise the fact that he had a copy of the Holdaway catalogue to discourage the LRB from breaking up the collection. Eventually court action was threatened to retrieve the items. Reluctantly Banks handed them over to the LRB. But he had one last trick up his sleeve.

In the adjournment debate in the Commons before Christmas on 19 December 1986 he was able to ask Christopher Chope, the Under-Secretary of State for the Environment a number of questions about the performance of the LRB during which he once again raised the issue of the sequestrated items. He also stated that whilst the LRB had two copies of the catalogue, presumably the two that Holdaway had made, there also existed a third copy which he had in his possession and which he asked for permission to place in the House of Commons Library 'for the benefit of students of London local government and to preserve an independent record of the GLC's collection'. Chope did not jump at the opportunity and it is unlikely that this request was acceded to.

For some time the collection was stored in County Hall during which time certain items were disposed of or otherwise disappeared. But eventually the bulk of the collection was passed to the Guildhall Art Gallery where they are still stored. This was not quite what Banks had wanted. His preferred destination was the Museum of London, but it was better than the entire collection being sold off. As he said in his 19 December 1986 speech 'I want that collection to stay in one piece. It represents an important account of London's local government history, and it would be monstrous if the Government allowed the LRB to sell it off.' At the time of writing about 50 or so of the portraits are viewable on the Guildhall Gallery's website, though not any of the more modern portraits and certainly not the portrait of the last chairman of the council which is apparently in storage. And whether a copy of Holdaway's catalogue is also there is another matter too.

And so on Easter Monday 1986 I was once more unemployed. It was as if I was being pursued by some angry god who had taken a personal interest in thwarting my haphazard attempts to build a career. But it was a little worrying that a god might bring down the largest metropolitan authority in Europe just to spite me. Even so I made a mental note not to apply for a job with the United Nations. Of course when I had accepted the GLC job I had realised that in all probability it had a limited life-span. This was after all the high-water mark of Thatcherism. She had a huge majority and and in all honesty no amount of procedural jiggery-pokery in the House of Lords was going to save the GLC.

As the final months ticked away I received a number of approaches about life post-GLC. I was considered to be one of the people who knew quite a lot about the new structures, particularly the joint committees to run various London-wide services. The fact is I did not really see myself as a bureaucrat, even though I was probably rather better in that role than as a politician or policy instigator. Having felt at the centre of events during the Abolition Bill I baulked at moving to a borough-level backwater. As the GLC started to subside beneath the muddy waves of the Thames I failed to take any decisive action to find new employment even though the end point was clearly marked on the calendar and the final weeks were punctuated with numerous farewell events like a series of rumble strips at the end of a fast road.

# Hesitations before Socialism

AT THE LAST MOMENT my procrastination was rewarded. I was approached by Stuart Weir, the editor of *New Socialist*, the Labour party's journal of debate, to become the magazine's business manager. Once again Nigel Williamson had been the conduit for this approach. Stuart came to County Hall and over lunch he told me a little of what the job involved. He also told me that the magazine had parted company with the previous business manager under acrimonious circumstances, that the situation was still being appealed and that the individual involved had his supporters both amongst the staff and on the NEC. It wasn't quite clear what the issue was that had led to this rupture but Stuart assured me that Larry Whitty, the general secretary, was adamant about the decision. It hardly needs saying that I should have looked into the situation in much more detail. But I felt absurdly confident that having survived the internecine warfare of County Hall for over two years that I would be able to cope with the dysfunctionality of Walworth Road. The Walworth Road snake pit was, however, a viperous knot of a completely different order.

Stuart Weir had been the deputy editor of *New Society* in its heyday when it had been the house journal of the sociology profession. Before that he had done time on the *Times*, notably on PHS, the diary column, which was actually an upmarket gossip column. The first editor of *New Socialist* had been James Curran, a media studies academic and an expert on the history of the press. *New Socialist* had been launched as a bi-monthly on the tide of enthusiasm surrounding Tony Benn's deputy leadership campaign. Initially the magazine flourished and there was an understandable desire to move to monthly publication. However James had not wanted to give up his academic career and his position at Goldsmith's College. Eventually he decided that overseeing a monthly publication was incompatible with his academic responsibilities. He handed over the reins to Stuart Weir but remained on the editorial board, which was indeed a roll-call of the intellectual left, including Ben Pimlott, Steven and Hilary Rose, and Raymond Williams.

Weir was seen as a professional journalist rather than a moonlighting academic. Although he had been influential in the Benn campaign he recognised that the momentum had gone out of the movement. Early on in his editorship he commissioned an article from Patrick Seyd called 'Bennism without Benn'. Not surprisingly this attracted the disapproval of Tony Benn who considered it a personal attack. In his diaries he noted that the article claimed that he had been deserted by many of his erstwhile supporters and he identified Stuart as being of the Hobsbawm school. And it was certainly true that under Stuarts's editorship *New Socialist* was starting to explore alternative sites from which to oppose Thatcherism, areas that previously might not have been considered, from a Labour party point of view, as political. During this period the magazine broadened its focus to include sexual, feminist, green and cultural politics. Whilst relieved to see a less Bennite tone to the magazine's editorial line the greater focus on identity politics was not entirely pleasing to the more reactionary sections of the NEC and the party establishment.

Nor was it particularly welcomed by the modernisers headed by Peter Mandelson. Despite the fact that privately he might well have agreed with a number of these perspectives, as the newly appointed director of communications he saw it as his role to tightly control all aspects of the party's public image so as not to give the Conservatives a stick with which to beat Labour in the capitalist press. Unfortunately because of a quirk of the byzantine structure of the administration in Walworth Road the editor of the party's publications reported directly to the general secretary and not to the director of communications.

An additional complexity at the time was the party's battle with the Militant Tendency. It was feared that certain sections of the party had been infiltrated and not just in high profile areas like Merseyside epitomised by the bumptious figure of Derek Hatton. There were thought to be several Militant sympathisers in head office. The mood of paranoia was such that a number of people who were not then nor ever had been members of Militant were tarred with the same brush. Ignoring ideological niceties, former membership of organisations like the International Marxist Group was enough to put you in the firing line. This was certainly the case with my predecessor as business manager, Geoff Sheridan, and Anne Cesek, the person with whom I now shared an office. Actually it would have been difficult to find someone more loyal to the Labour party than Anne.

Nor was it exactly unusual for political activists and officials to have had youthful associations with anathematised organisations. Mandelson himself had been a member of the Young Communist League in his teens and had been a British Youth Council delegate to the World Festival of Youth in Cuba in 1978, an event that was largely funded by the Soviet Union. Current members of the Communist party were well represented in the trade union movement and *Marxism Today* was required reading for political movers and shakers of many different hues much to the chagrin of those of us trying to increase *New Socialist*'s circulation and influence. Weirdly it seemed acceptable to declare a youthful affiliation with Marxism while inviting strong criticism if one declared oneself to be a socialist. No doubt this was a reflection of the fact that Marxism in the version peddled in *Marxism Today* had been sucked dry of all ideological relevance, whereas socialism still had the potential to change people's lives.

I personally was free of all such associations, more a quondam member of the big drinks tendency or the international dreamers group. And possibly not so quondam. To the Militant sympathisers or those who objected to ideological witch hunts I was seen as part of the modernising tendency represented by Larry Whitty and Peter Mandelson. This would have been news to Peter who probably saw me as just another irritating ex-GLC hack. In any case for the most part he studiously ignored me. Whitty was a more conciliatory figure and seems to have accepted the view of his assistant, Tony Manwaring, and Nigel Williamson that whatever the precise nature of my politics I had the professional skills to take *New Socialist* forward on the new monthly publication schedule. But it was not professional publishing skills that I was really going to need.

After the first flush of enthusiasm generated by the Benn deputy leadership campaign *New Socialist*'s circulation had begun to drift down. This trend had been reinforced by the move to monthly publication and so instead of being largely self-financing or at least in a break-even position the magazine now needed a considerable subvention from party funds. Larry wanted the financial situation sorted as soon as possible, Stuart wanted the decline in circulation reversed, which amounted to the same thing and Peter Mandelson wanted the magazine subsumed into his department or better still closed down. So I found myself once again wrestling with the same kinds of problems that had faced me at the Architectural Press, *Blueprint* and *Tribune*. I realised belatedly that my first few months in the job were going to be distinctly uncomfortable. Actually that realisation was almost as wrong as it could be. The discomfort lasted for the next two years, until I finally resigned.

Although I thought I had a pretty good idea about how to manage newstrade distribution, getting on top of the party's arcane financial reporting system was a different matter. The magazine did not have its own accounts. Its operations were seen as a small department within the overall organisation with credits, debits and transfers hard to identify in the party's consolidated accounts. Until I had built my own model of the magazine's financial position I did not feel that I could make any recommendations. In time honoured fashion therefore I started work on an interim report. I should by now have realised that there are in fact only interim reports. In management, finality is a myth, although powerfully constitutive. But the biggest shock was that when I eventually got hold of my predecessor's report, I found it hard to fault.

An important channel of distribution for the magazine had been sales through volunteer sellers at branch meetings. To begin with this had worked reasonably well. On the bi-monthly publication cycle a volunteer could be sure to get to at least one meeting during the time the issue was current. Even so at best we had sellers in only 400 of the 5,000 party branches. Since there was still no central register of party members it was actually quite difficult to increase this level of penetration. Ironically it was easier to reach party members through the newstrade than through the party's own distribution channels. There were already plans afoot to build a central database of members but in April 1986 this was still not on stream. However, once the magazine moved to monthly publication the level of unsolds from volunteer sellers increased. On sale dates and branch meeting dates did not always coincide neatly. Nor was the more diverse editorial coverage necessarily to the taste of the traditionalists amongst the membership who were probably the majority.

Monthly publication had also increased the workload in the office requiring the employment of more freelance staff on both the editorial and business sides of the publication which had not been budgeted for. At the same time advertising revenue had collapsed with the demise of the GLC and its funding for voluntary sector organisations, and the government's assault on the trade union movement. There was little likelihood that we would find alternative sources of advertising revenue in the foreseeable future particularly at the circulation levels we were now registering. In addition the party's financial reporting structures were decidedly rickety. The £7,000 profit for the previous year as reported to an earlier meeting of the NEC's communications committee had become a loss of £11,000 and the loss for the current year was now projected at £23,000 and almost certain to go higher on current sales and advertising revenue trends.

My rather unimaginative stop-gap solution was to put up the cover price slightly, claw back all the credits knocking around in the Labour party's consolidated accounts and budget for a promotional campaign focussed around a planned redesign to encourage the newstrade to take more copies of the magazine and to give it greater prominence.

The one ray of sunshine in this otherwise gloomy prospect was the redesign. It was to be undertaken by Neville Brody, the Wunderkind of contemporary British graphic design. Brody had come to popular attention through his work for *The Face* magazine. In the normal run of things we would never have been able to afford a designer who was this hot. But Brody was sympathetic to the Labour party and only charged us a token fee. He set about a radical transformation of the appearance of the magazine particularly its typography, by creating his own typefaces or using fonts that had been out of fashion for some time but with unconventional letter spacing. The first issue to receive the Brody treatment was the May 1986 edition with a typographic cover featuring the new *New Socialist* logo. The next issue extended the radical treatment to the imagery. The cover featured an image of New York printed as a colour negative to suggest the city in the wake of a nuclear catastrophe. The final issue of the sequence personally supervised by Brody used an image of Parker, Lady Penelope's chauffeur from The Thunderbirds TV series. He then handed over to Phil Bicker, one of his associates to handle subsequent issues and evolve the new style.

Critical reaction, especially from the design community and media commentators was predominantly favourable. But reaction from loyal readers was at best muted and from certain quarters distinctly hostile. This was only partly to do with the redesign. It was as much to do with the greater prominence given to the new politics in the shape of articles devoted to Aids, green politics and feminism, despite the fact that there were still heavyweight articles on traditional political subjects like recent developments in the trade union movement and arguments for and against nuclear power. One article that attracted particular criticism was on the politics of breastfeeding trailed prominently on that issue's cover.

It would be wrong to suppose that this refocussing of the editorial line was a mere whim of the editorial staff. The approach

230

was strongly supported by the magazine's editorial advisory panel and summed up in an article by Raymond Williams in the September 1986 edition entitled 'Hesitations Before Socialism'. The article examined the challenges posed to socialism by interest groups centred around ecological issues, peace issues, sexuality, gender and race. Williams concluded,

> Yet those of us who are socialists have still to argue our whole case, since we know that it is the only general and long-term alternative to capitalism. And to do this properly we must continually respond to reasonable and understandable hesitations among those whom we might expect to be our comrades and allies: not in some routine cry to join us, but in a necessary remaking of ourselves and our movements which would make them, for these serious people, worth joining.

One may quibble with the certainty that socialism is the only general and long-term alternative to capitalism or indeed that the quest for an alternative makes much sense. There were plenty of people in the party who felt that Clause IV of the party's constitution as drafted by Sidney Webb in 1917 was no longer appropriate nearly 70 years later. In fact debates about the meaning of the word socialism were meat and drink to the left activist community whereas single issue politics was seen as the preserve of cranks.

Of course there is a lot to be said for the big tent view of politics. But despite the fact that Michael Foot had persuaded the party to adopt unilateralism in 1982 and despite the fact that CND could bring 300,000 people onto the streets of London to protest against the deployment of Cruise missiles, the Labour party's vote actually fell by over 3 million at the 1983 General Election. It is true that this was the zenith of SDP-Liberal Alliance fortunes but to ignore that fact that a majority of the electorate had consistently been against unilateral nuclear disarmament was to condemn the Labour party to a permanent state of unelectability. Or at least this was the view that Neil Kinnock came to after the 1987 election defeat resulting in the party resuming its support for the pre-existing multilateral policy.

And we were certainly not immune to drinking that kind of Kool-Aid on *New Socialist*. Part of our promotional strategy was a series of events to boost the public profile of the magazine. The GLC had used this tactic to good effect and of course had had the resources to do it properly. I had been present at one of the GLC gigs at the Royal Festival Hall starring Ben Elton and had got to know Addison Cresswell, who was rapidly becoming a major impresario on the burgeoning alternative comedy circuit. Addison at the time was a supporter of Red Wedge, the umbrella group of Labour luvvie sympathisers, and persuaded Ben and Skint Video to perform at a *New Socialist* event at the 1986 Labour party conference in Blackpool. The meeting was attended by more than 700 people. We almost certainly could have sold more tickets, if the hotel's management had allowed us to. But they started to become concerned that they were in breach of fire regulations and turned away a considerable number of latecomers.

We encountered a similar situation the following year when we organised a benefit at the 100 Club in Oxford Street for the Czechoslovak Jazz Section members, who were at that time in prison awaiting trial on charges of unauthorised commercial activity. Actually this was just a proxy for the more serious crime in the Stalinist rule book of the unauthorised communication of ideas. The irony of this situation was that although perestroika and glasnost were already in top gear in the Soviet Union, its satellites still felt unable to embrace the new openness and continued to maintain control of cultural engagement through artists' unions. The benefit was headlined by Courtney Pine, whose debut album, *Journey to the Urge Within* had broken into the Top 40 albums chart, a rare occurrence for a jazz album. Consequently the queue of hopeful punters outside the club stretched a considerable distance down Oxford Street. Once again the management eventually stopped us admitting any more people at which point there were some ugly scenes at the entrance to the club.

As I stood with the bouncers and tried to explain to those at the front of the queue that it would be dangerous to let any more people in, a smartly dressed young black man made his way with some difficulty through the crowd. I started to explain to him as patiently as I could the reason why we couldn't let any more people in. He replied that Courtney had asked him to drop by. Nice one, I thought. I glanced at the bouncers just to make sure they were in touch with me and started to harden my rhetoric when I realised that he was carrying an instrument case and had an American accent. Briefly I wondered if this might be an elaborate hustle but then dismissed the idea as unworthy and asked him his name without being able to entirely mask the note of scepticism in my voice. 'Wynton Marsalis', he replied modestly. I was no great jazz buff but I had certainly heard of the Marsalis family. Covered in confusion I nodded to the bouncers to let him through. I didn't want to be responsible for turning away the greatest jazz trumpeter since Miles Davis. There was a murmur of excitement from the people at the front of the queue and a couple begged to be let in claiming to be absolutely huge Wynton Marsalis fans. I was implacable again. But I moved away from the door just in case Miles decided to turn up too.

The gig was everything we could have hoped for. Courtney's band numbered several of the hottest young jazz musicians including Julian Joseph and the amazing vocalist Cleveland Watkiss. But the high point was when Marsalis got on stage and joined in. For those few hours it felt like we were part of an inspiring, inclusive movement. Of course this euphoric view did not take into account the disconsolate and pissed-off punters who had been unable to get in. And then when the music had finally finished there was the rather sordid matter of sorting out the money in the office at the back of the club.

Credit cards were not yet in widespread use, especially not by young music fans. The majority of people had paid in cash and the table was piled high with notes and coins. None of the performers was taking a fee but there were expenses to be covered, travel and refreshment for the musicians, the club's costs, not least the extra security they had had to put on and so on. As ever sorting out the money was the least edifying part of the event and inevitably there were a few disputes as to what had been agreed. But the buzz that the music had created took the edge off any rancour and eventually an amicable settlement was reached.

In due course we were able to bank a considerable amount to help fund the defence of the imprisoned musicians. Despite these efforts there was not much hope that the court would dismiss the charges and the two leaders of the Section were sentenced to 16 months and 10 months respectively. Ironically less than three years later amid the disintegration of the Soviet Union Stalinist rule in Czechoslovakia came to an end in what was called the Velvet Revolution.

Exhilarating though it was to organise packed-out events this enthusiasm failed to translate into increased sales or electoral advantage. The Labour party was going to have to do a lot more than scoop up into its tucker bag a pot-pourri of trendy issues if it hoped to garner enough votes to form a government. The truth of the matter was that the Bennite moment had passed. Even though Benn subsequently mounted a challenge to Kinnock in 1988, this certainly did not have the momentum of the earlier deputy leadership challenge and was seen off rather easily. But despite the huge organisational advances under Kinnock public opinion remained unconvinced by the Labour party and the birth pangs of New Labour were still some way off.

Grappling with such weighty matters, however, was way beyond my collectively not-bargained-for pay grade. The main thing that the party wanted from me was to stop New Socialist being a drain on the party's limited resources. The idea that had been cooked up by Whitty and Weir and no doubt one or two others even before I joined was to remove the magazine from the party's balance sheet by hiving it off into a company structure so that it could, on its own account, pitch for investment and raise loans from party members and sympathisers. With the worsening financial situation identified by my report this now became a matter of urgency.

But it was recognised that even assuming all the technical and legal issues could be worked out that there would be considerable opposition on the NEC. It was my unenviable task to pilot the proposal through the NEC's committee structure. What it also meant was that if the project failed I would carry the can. That possibility did cross my mind briefly but I thought that the idea had much to merit it and was in line with my own ideas about modernising the party. The structures of capitalism could be managed and deployed to advantage; it was simplistic to object to commercial activity tout court.

The snag was that to many on the NEC the whole project smacked of privatisation. Not surprisingly Denis Skinner who sat on the communications committee was one of those. Early on in the process when I was outlining how the party's interests in the magazine would be protected in the corporate structure by a golden share he made it clear that he rejected the whole idea. He let me have both barrels. He had seen upwardly mobile types like me and he didn't like our upwardly mobile ways. I wasn't quite sure what was wrong with upward mobility *per se*. Of course it was undesirable if it was at the expense of others. But stasis could hardly be a worthwhile goal for a socialist, let alone downward mobility. Ignoring the *ad hominem* rhetoric I managed to waffle on about pragmatism, although I was pretty sure that was another dirty word in the Skinner lexicon. At that moment I got a glimpse of what it must have been like for some hapless junior minister speaking to a piece of legislation, in which he had had no say, getting the full Beast of Bolsover treatment.

Fortunately I had a least one supporter on the committee in the shape of Gwyneth Dunwoody. I suspect that it was not because she thought the case I was putting was particularly cogent, she just seemed to enjoy putting a spoke in Skinner's wheels. But Larry had got enough of his people on side and the committee agreed that a fully worked-out proposal should be produced with input from the party's legal advisors and auditors. Two members of the committee were delegated to oversee the process, Tom Sawyer, the NUPE deputy general secretary and Gwyneth herself. So began in what was otherwise a couple of years of unrelenting tribulation a decidedly pleasant developmental process.

For the next few months Stuart and I would report back to

Gwyneth and Tom over lunch in the Pizzeria Castello at the Elephant and Castle. The Castello was the main lunch venue for Labour party staff who worked in the Walworth Road offices. On any given day several of the tables would be occupied by politicians and party officers. The main item on the menu was almost certainly some form of skullduggery. Despite her fearsome reputation Gwyneth was in fact a pleasure to work with and an amusing lunch companion. Tom was more delphic in his utterances but that probably reflected the discretion of a person who was destined to be the next Labour general secretary. When we had completed the document Gwyneth spoke strongly in favour of it at a meeting of the communications committee. Larry and Tom had already convinced most of the waverers and the item was forwarded to the full NEC.

NEC meetings were held in a large conference room on the top floor, which was the same floor on which the New Socialist offices were located. As a consequence it was not unusual for Kinnock or other members of the NEC to ask to use our phones during breaks in long meetings. This was after all the edenic period before mobile phones. So I did not have far to go to be on hand to answer questions about my report. I was a little nervous and had worked out answers to what I considered were likely to be the trickiest questions. I sat down at the back of the room on the opposite side of the table from Tom and waited for him to introduce the report. Larry was moving briskly through the items on the agenda. But when it came to the *New Socialist* company proposal Larry said that that item would be held over to another day. Having keyed myself up for this moment for the best part of a year I was too stunned to take in what had just happened. Or more precisely not happened.

It is standard operating procedure in politics to have lined up one's supporters before any meeting actually takes place. So my first assumption was that Larry, Tom and Gwyneth had been unable to muster enough support for the proposal and rather than risk having it shot down had decided to hold it over so they would have more time to twist arms. Then I decided that a cock-up solution was more likely. It was simply that the meeting was overrunning. In fact neither theory was correct. Mrs

Thatcher, emboldened by the by-election result in Greenwich, had decided to call a General Election a year earlier than she needed to. Whatever the Conservatives's public pronouncements about Kinnock they knew that he was a much more formidable opponent than Michael Foot and it was obvious that the modernisation programme under Whitty and Mandelson had only just got going. A year further down the line it would be a much better oiled machine. Say what you like about Mrs Thatcher, you could never accuse her of lacking courage. It was battle stations and a little earlier than we had expected.

In the 1983 election the Alliance had received just 675,985 fewer votes than the Labour party but because of the quirks of the first past the post system this had translated into only 23 seats compared to Labour's 209 seats. This meant that it took 338,302 votes to return one Alliance MP as against a mere 40,463 votes to return a Labour MP. This state of affairs seemed to many to be inequitable. But from a Labour perspective even more worrying was the fact that it would only take an extra 300,000 votes or so in the right constituencies to swing the balance of seats won in the Alliance's favour. Rosie Barnes' victory for the Alliance in Greenwich seemed to suggest that the tide was still flowing in the Alliance's favour.

In a first past the post system a divided opposition not only prolongs the ruling party's grip on power, but generally results in the decline of the least electorally credible components of that opposition. After the first world war that had certainly been the fate of the Liberals to the ultimate benefit of the Labour party. The fear now was that it might be the Labour party's turn to be replaced as the official opposition by the SDP Liberal Alliance.

At such moments voices are raised in favour of proportional representation but the mechanics of agreeing on such a major constitutional change are difficult to arrange. Inevitably therefore thoughts turn to more informal kinds of coalition. In 1986 this found expression in the tactical voting movement. Following Raymond Williams' 'Hesitations before Socialism' article Stuart had commissioned a series of articles on electoral reform culminating in an article under his own by-line appearing to advocate tactical voting. Actually the article was much more nuanced than that. It recognised that the Labour party could not point blank advocate tactical voting but argued that a commitment to proportional representation should be a central plank of the Labour party's manifesto.

Just before the issue was about to go to press Stuart took me to one side and told me about the article. He also said that he knew that he was risking his position. I said that it was probably inadvisable to publish such a piece in the party's own magazine just weeks before a general election. I accepted that the thrust of the piece was implicit in the direction that the magazine had been taking editorially but that I would be unable publicly to support that line myself even though I had some sympathy with it. Nevertheless I assured him that I would keep the information to myself. I wasn't sure how my failure to intervene would be seen in any post mortem but by now I had given up thinking that there was any simple way to plot a course through this minefield.

When the issue appeared the editorial advisory panel made it clear that it had not been consulted about the article, so Stuart had no option but to stand down, although the statement that was issued by the party concluded that this was by mutual consent. The last thing that the party wanted a few weeks before a general election was an unfair dismissal fight with the editor of its journal of debate. It probably suited Stuart too. He had recently become a father again and it meant that he could do more of the hands-on fathering that the magazine had been advocating. In fact the period of belated paternity leave only lasted to the autumn when against the odds he became the editor of the *New Statesman*. I had to admit that whilst we both seemed to be specialists in the frying-pan and fire event he was performing at a much more advanced level.

In the meantime the party had encumbered itself with yet another publication. The modernising tendency had put a huge effort into building a central database of party members. Now that it was completed the party was able for the first time ever to communicate directly with the membership. One of the first projects to exploit this resource was *Labour Party News*, a glossy monthly magazine that was to be sent in the post to every Labour party member as part of their subscription package rather than relying on volunteer sellers or the vagaries of the newstrade. So far as the sceptics were concerned the last thing that Labour needed was another loss-making publication. But from the point of view of its proponents with a guaranteed circulation of 300,000 the magazine would be able to generate serious amounts of advertising revenue. On the downside the production and distribution costs were going to be substantial. Editorially the magazine was not going to be a journal of debate. It would be informative about the party's policies but would steer clear of controversy. Essentially it was seen as a campaigning tool.

Given the tribulations that the party was facing with *New Socialist* and *Labour Weekly* the role of editor would be crucial. When Nigel Williamson had taken over the editorship of *Tribune* he had dropped the Bennite stance of Chris Mullin, his predecessor and had swung the paper behind Neil Kinnock. This was a far from popular move among Nigel's former comrades but was welcomed by the beleaguered Kinnock camp and they had now returned the favour and offered Nigel the editorship of *Labour Party News* which he duly accepted.

With Stuart's departure I now found myself running a magazine that had no editor with a plan to turn it into a company which so far as I was aware was still awaiting approval from the NEC and to spice the mix a general election was looming. I appreciated that Larry had many other fish to fry but it took me some time to get a meeting with him to find out what he expected me to do.

When I eventually got to see him, he told me that Nigel Williamson would not only be editing *Labour Party News* but would also be taking over as Editor of *New Socialist* on a temporary basis until the NEC had decided on its future. For the moment though the *status quo ante* applied and that once the election was out of the way we would be proceeding with the flotation of *New Socialist*. That was a considerable relief to me given the amount of work I had done on the project and I began

239

to think that I might be able to enjoy the election campaign. Nigel and I were good friends and I knew we would have no trouble working together. More worryingly Larry also made it clear that I would have an important role in *Labour Party News* too.

When I had started work on *New Socialist* I had persuaded Larry to let me have an IBM personal computer and I had turned myself into a competent user of Supercalc, a forerunner of the Excel spreadsheet program. Having seen the spreadsheets I had built for *New Socialist* Larry asked me if I could build a series of detailed projections for *Labour Party News* and present them to a meeting of the directors. The meeting got off to a bad start. Peter Mandelson did not seem to be happy about my presence at the meeting, but more I suspect because he considered the whole project a distraction from getting on with planning for the coming election and so showed little interest in my presentation.

This might have been a little dispiriting but in fact he had accorded the reports from the research and organisation directors the same lack of interest. His own report was a model of concision and since his own department was within budget there was not much more to be said. By contrast my own projections made it clear that on the proposed publishing schedule *LPN* would make a loss and require a substantial loan to tide it over until advertising revenues had grown. I pointed out that one way of mitigating the funding shortfall was to reduce the number of issues per year, but Larry said this was politically unacceptable at this stage. He felt sure that the Co-operative Bank would provide the necessary loan.

Meanwhile Nigel and I set to work on producing a plan for the next few issues of *New Socialist*. We parted company with Phil Bicker and reverted to a simpler layout which enabled us to do a lot of the page make-up ourselves with the help of freelance sub-editors. I also started going to the typesetters myself. Not much had changed in that context since the *Radio & Record News* days although the Desktop Publishing revolution was just around the corner. And the atmosphere in the office was a bit lacklustre. Despite Larry's positivity about the future of the magazine there was a strong sense that our days were numbered. But I consoled myself with the thought that we were now into a general election campaign and at least I would be able to throw myself into that. This time around I was going to be close to the centre of events rather than slogging around door to door in a constituency. I couldn't have been more wrong of course.

Larry called me into his office and said that for the duration of the campaign a number of departments including *New Socialist* would have to vacate their offices. These departments would instead transfer to a former SOGAT building in Borough High Street and he wanted me to manage this outpost. I am sure I was unable to hide the dismay on my face but of course it made complete sense. So I spent the next few weeks almost completely detached from the cut and thrust of the campaign.

As in 1983 the public pronouncements in the run-up to polling day were upbeat and a party was arranged in the NEC meeting room at Walworth Road for the evening of polling day itself. Once I had finished the day's work in Borough I went over to Walworth Road in the evening. But it was already becoming evident that that result was going to be very far from a victory. The exit polls were not encouraging and Kinnock, once he had realised the way the wind was blowing, had decided to remain in Wales. The few panjandrums who were in Walworth Road disappeared and the party fizzled out when the DJ who had been hired for the evening started to pack up his kit after having played only a handful of discs. As I trudged home I calculated that the next election didn't need to be held until 1992, by which time I was unlikely still to be a Labour functionary.

The next few months were a period of trying to keep the magazine going while the NEC decided whether to close it completely or not. The solution favoured by the editorial advisory panel was to return to bi-monthly publication. Even so the NEC was reluctant to shoulder the ongoing losses. There was a view that the financial problems of the party were to a great extent the result of problems in the party's publications and sales and marketing department. Certainly no one could pretend that the deficit wasn't considerable. But despite the valiant efforts to modernise driven by Whitty and Mandelson the party organisation was still plagued by terrible inefficiencies and those areas exposed to a market forces already subject to the impact of new technology and changing patterns of consumer behaviour were particularly vulnerable.

Eventually the Russell Press came to the rescue. They would take responsibility for the production, distribution and business aspects of the magazine and the Labour party would provide the editorial input under Nigel Williamson. This rather reduced my role, but I was to manage the transfer of the publishing functions to the Russell Press and then handle liaison between them and the party. At the same time my informal role on *Labour Party News* would be formalised. This is not quite what I had envisaged when I had joined *New Socialist* 18 months previously, but at least it still meant I had a job. Nevertheless I was beginning to think that it was time for me to move on once again. Anne Cesek was also dismayed by the turn of events and we discussed ideas for setting up our own business.

The party conference that year was in Brighton. Because of the magazine's precarious position and the proximity of Brighton to London I was not able to justify a hotel room and commuted on a daily basis. This meant less late night boozing, which was probably better for my liver, but meant less convivial interaction too. But I did meet Bill McLellan, whom I'd first encountered at *Tribune* four years earlier. I told him about what was planned for *New Socialist* and that I would probably be moving on in the new year. He said that he had been thinking about launching a magazine the following year. It was to be a what's-on guide for parents, providing information on the best things to do with children in London and the South East. Why didn't I come on board as publisher? I was pretty sceptical about the idea, but said I'd think about it.

On the way back to London I bumped into Chris Mullin on the platform at Brighton railway station. Having stood unsuccessfully in a number of elections Chris had eventually been selected to stand in Sunderland South and had been elected in the recent general election. I congratulated him and we climbed into a compartment. He asked me about how things were at *New Socialist* and as I started to bring him up to date a portly figure boarded the train just as it was pulling out and joined us in our compartment. It was John Smith, the shadow chancellor of the exchequer. Pleasantries were exchanged. He had no idea who I was but Chris introduced me and then we settled down to rattle back to London.

Smith's public persona was rather sensible, verging on the dour, which was no bad thing for a future chancellor, but I saw a different side of him on that journey back to London. He was a great raconteur with an inexhaustible fund of anecdotes about a wide range of people in the Labour movement. Chris's probing journalistic mind and his modest demeanour were the perfect foil to Smith's raconteurship. They would have made a great double act. Smith was particularly amusing about Mick McGahey, the great Scottish miner's leader and his ability to operate even with a monumental hangover. One got the impression that this was a skill that Smith himself admired and indeed shared. But on a more serious note it was clear that neither Smith nor Mullin was particularly optimistic about Labour's immediate prospects. By the time we arrived in London I'd decided to take my chances with Bill McLellan's project. But that really is another story.

# Ackowledgments

WRITING IS SUPPOSEDLY A solitary business, but I have been lucky enough in the composition of this work to have been accompanied by a whole group of supporters, whom I should like to thank.

In the front rank of this select group of readers are Christina Koning and Adam Mars-Jones. They are both expert writers, critics and teachers and offered me their thoughts at considerable length. If the book is not better for their input, it is because I failed to heed what they were saying.

They are closely followed by Henry Murphy, Ralph Jones and Patrick Coyne. Much of the book was written in the beautiful village of Canillas de Albaida in Andalucia. Henry, a distinguished Irish barrister and a published writer, was sojourning in that delightful place at the same time and was also engaged on a work of literary composition. As the senior literary man he was extremely encouraging. We consoled each other in Gustavo's or Cerezo's over a bottle of wine or two on numerous occasions when the writing was not going too well. And even when it was.

Both Ralph and Pat are friends of many years. In the penumbra of retirement we have met every three months or so in the Boot and Flogger in Borough to put the world to rights and encourage each other in late-flowering literary endeavour. The need to make a quarterly report on progress with the writing has been made more bearable by the knowledge that the other chaps are under the same pressure. One hears a lot about how competitive authors are, but in the case of the Boot and Flogger chapel I can only report solidarity. On the other hand if Pat's cross-dressing, piratical, space opera trilogy starts to sell well, I might start to feel a little different. More like a real writer, in fact.

It would be remiss of me not to mention the encouragement I have received from my children, Anna, James and Molly. If there is ever an expanded edition, that will be down to Anna, who is a proponent of what she calls the director's cut. Though half my age James already puts me to shame in his command of language and his literary productivity. Molly is a stern critic of my quips and verbal tics and as a consequence I have honed them to such an extent that they now account for much of the tone of the book.

The book's cast of characters is extensive. Where possible I have tried to give those substantially mentioned in the text the chance to read the relevant section and correct any errors of fact. In this context I would like to thank Sheila Noble, John Keay, Tom Golzen, Jill Golzen, Peter Murray, Adrian Hodges, Angi Driver and Sally Banks. In particular I would like to thank Derek Holdaway, a former GLC legal officer, for his help in telling the story of the fate of the GLC's heritage collection. I feel particularly honoured that he was prepared to send me two large albums containing a full colour print out of his material relating to the Council's treasures. I will certainly treasure both albums.

I would also like to thank those friends and family members who were brave enough to read the text at various stages of its composition and offer their thoughts. They include Ruth Watson, Moray Coulter, Mike Sheppard, James McCulloch, Irene Grant, Jane Garner, Lorenzo Bacelle, Juan Christián Gutiérrez-Maupomé, John Guerrasio, Simon Dale, Bill Reed, Henry Jones, George Cannell, Kathleen Locke, Jo Cameron, Nick Vincent and my parents Alfred and Sheila Vincent.

But the person to whom I owe most is Jill Evans despite the fact that she took a dim view of my way with connectives. It wasn't so much the 'ands' and 'ors' as the 'buts'. When I countered that my style was antithetical and therefore 'buts' were inevitable, her barristerial mind was having none of it. I duly tracked through the text and culled a few of the offending conjunctions, often by simply transforming them into the equivalent adverb. And if at times she felt like clapping her hands over her ears on hearing for the twentieth time the latest formulation of a particular anecdote, she didn't show it. Instead she just encouraged me to take the project seriously and get on with it.

www.ingramcontent.com/pod-product-compliance
Lightning Source LLC
LaVergne TN
LVHW091214080426
835509LV00009B/996